THE CINEMA OF GERMANY

·

A Wallflower Book
Published by
Columbia University Press
Publishers Since 1893
New York • Chichester, West Sussex
cup.columbia.edu

A complete CIP record is available from the Library of Congress

ISBN 978-1-905674-91-6 (cloth : alk. paper)
ISBN 978-1-905674-90-9 (pbk. : alk. paper)
ISBN 978-0-231-50152-1 (e-book)

Design by Elsa Mathern

∞

Columbia University Press books are printed on permanent
and durable acid-free paper.
This book is printed on paper with recycled content.
Printed in the United States of America

c 10 9 8 7 6 5 4 3 2 1
p 10 9 8 7 6 5 4 3 2 1

THE CINEMA OF
GERMANY

EDITED BY

JOSEPH GARNCARZ & ANNEMONE LIGENSA

WALLFLOWER PRESS london & new york

24 FRAMES is a major series focusing on national and regional cinemas from around the world. Rather than offering a 'best of' selection, the feature films and documentaries selected in each volume serve to highlight the specific elements of that territory's cinema, elucidating the historical and industrial context of production, the key genres and modes of representation, and foregrounding the work of the most important directors and their exemplary films. In taking an explicitly text-centred approach, the titles in this list offer 24 diverse entry-points into each national and regional cinema, and thus contribute to the appreciation of the rich traditions of global cinema.

Series Editors: Yoram Allon & Ian Haydn Smith

OTHER TITLES IN THE **24 FRAMES** SERIES:

THE CINEMA OF LATIN AMERICA *edited by Alberto Elena and Marina Díaz López*

THE CINEMA OF THE LOW COUNTRIES *edited by Ernest Mathijs*

THE CINEMA OF ITALY *edited by Giorgio Bertellini*

THE CINEMA OF JAPAN & KOREA *edited by Justin Bowyer*

THE CINEMA OF CENTRAL EUROPE *edited by Peter Hames*

THE CINEMA OF SPAIN & PORTUGAL *edited by Alberto Mira*

THE CINEMA OF SCANDINAVIA *edited by Tytti Soila*

THE CINEMA OF BRITAIN & IRELAND *edited by Brian McFarlane*

THE CINEMA OF FRANCE *edited by Phil Powrie*

THE CINEMA OF CANADA *edited by Jerry White*

THE CINEMA OF THE BALKANS *edited by Dina Iordanova*

THE CINEMA OF AUSTRALIA & NEW ZEALAND *edited by Geoff Mayer and Keith Beattie*

THE CINEMA OF RUSSIA & THE FORMER SOVIET UNION *edited by Birgit Beumers*

THE CINEMA OF NORTH AFRICA & THE MIDDLE EAST *edited by Gönül Dönmez-Colin*

THE CINEMA OF INDIA *edited by Lalitha Gopalan*

FORTHCOMING TITLES:

THE CINEMA OF CHINA & SOUTH-EAST ASIA *edited by Ian Haydn Smith*

THE CINEMA OF SOUTHERN AFRICA *edited by Jacqueline Maingard*

CONTENTS

Notes on Contributors vii
Acknowledgements xii

INTRODUCTION Joseph Garncarz 1

01   DES PFARRERS TÖCHTERLEIN Martin Loiperdinger 9
02   DAS CABINET DES DR. CALIGARI / THE CABINET OF DR. CALIGARI Uli Jung 19
03   DER LETZTE MANN / THE LAST LAUGH Sidney Gottlieb 29
04   METROPOLIS Tom Gunning 39
05   BERLIN – DIE SINFONIE DER GROSSTADT / BERLIN – SYMPHONY OF A BIG CITY
      Daniel Kothenschulte 51
06   DIE WEISSE HÖLLE VOM PIZ PALÜ / THE WHITE HELL OF PITZ PALU Annette Deeken 61
07   DIE DREI VON DER TANKSTELLE / THREE FROM THE FILLING STATION
      Christian Junklewitz 69
08   OLYMPIA Joseph Garncarz 79
09   DIE GROSSE LIEBE / THE GREAT LOVE Stephen Lowry 89
10   DER WEISSE TRAUM / THE WHITE DREAM Anna Sarah Vielhaber 99
11   DIE MÖRDER SIND UNTER UNS / THE MURDERERS ARE AMONG US Erica Carter 109
12   GRÜN IST DIE HEIDE / THE HEATH IS GREEN Harro Segeberg 119
13   DIE BRÜCKE / THE BRIDGE Claudia Liebrand and Gereon Blaseio 129
14   DER SCHATZ IM SILBERSEE / THE TREASURE OF SILVER LAKE and
      DIE SÖHNE DER GROSSEN BÄRIN / THE SONS OF GREAT BEAR Annemone Ligensa 139
15   DER GETEILTE HIMMEL / THE DIVIDED HEAVEN Ursula von Keitz 149
16   ABSCHIED VON GESTERN / YESTERDAY GIRL Thomas Ballhausen and Günter Krenn 159
17   DIE LEGENDE VON PAUL UND PAULA / THE LEGEND OF PAUL AND PAULA
      Wolfgang Mühl-Benninghaus 169
18   JEDER FÜR SICH UND GOTT GEGEN ALLE / THE ENIGMA OF KASPAR HAUSER
      Knut Hickethier 177
19   DEUTSCHLAND IM HERBST / GERMANY IN AUTUMN Dietrich Leder 187
20   DAS BOOT / THE BOAT Peter Krämer 197
21   MÄNNER / MEN Holger Römers 207
22   LOLA RENNT / RUN, LOLA, RUN Sabine Gottgetreu 217
23   GOOD BYE, LENIN! Seán Allan 227
24   DAS WUNDER VON BERN / THE MIRACLE OF BERN Malte Hagener 237

Filmography 246
Bibliography 256
Index 261

NOTES ON CONTRIBUTORS

SEÁN ALLAN is Reader in German Studies at the University of Warwick, UK. He is co-editor (with John Sandford) of *DEFA: East German Cinema, 1946–1992* (Berghahn, 1999) and has written a wide range of articles on representations of East Germany and post-unification German identity in contemporary German cinema.

THOMAS BALLHAUSEN is coordinator of the Department for Studies and Advanced Research at Filmarchiv Austria in Vienna. Recent publications include, as author, *Bewegungsmelder* (Haymon, 2010) and, as co-editor (with Günther Friesinger and Johannes Grenzfurthner), *Mind and Matter: Comparative Approaches Towards Complexity* (transcript, 2011).

GEREON BLASEIO is Lecturer in Film Studies at the University of Cologne, Germany. Together with Hedwig Pompe and Jens Ruchatz he co-edited a book on concepts of popularity, *Popularisierung und Popularität* (DuMont, 2005).

ERICA CARTER is Professor of German and Film at King's College, London, UK. Her publications include, as author, *Dietrich's Ghosts: The Sublime and the Beautiful in Third Reich Film* (British Film Institute, 2004) and *How German is She?: Postwar West German Reconstruction and the Consuming Woman* (University of Michigan Press, 1997), as editor, *Béla Balázs: Early Film Theory* (Berghahn, 2010) and as co-editor (with Tim Bergfelder and Deniz Göktürk) *The German Cinema Book* (British Film Institute, 2002).

ANNETTE DEEKEN is Professor for Media Studies at the University of Trier, Germany. Her publications as author include *Seine Majestät das Ich: Zum Abenteuertourismus Karl Mays* (Bouvier, 1983) and *Reisefilme: Ästhetik und Geschichte* (Gardez, 2004).

JOSEPH GARNCARZ teaches Film and Media Studies at the University of Cologne, Germany, and has regularly been visiting professor at several European universities. His publications include, as author, *Filmfassungen: Eine Theorie signifikanter Filmvariation* (Lang, 1992), *Maßlose Unterhaltung: Zur Etablierung des Films in Deutschland, 1896–1914* (Stroemfeld, 2010) and *Hollywood in Deutschland: Zur Internationalisierung der Kinokultur 1925–1990* (Stroemfeld, 2012).

SABINE GOTTGETREU taught Film Studies at the University of Cologne, Germany. She is author of *Der bewegliche Blick: Zum Paradigmawechsel in der feministischen Filmtheorie* (Lang, 1992) and *Der Arztfilm: Untersuchung eines filmischen Genres* (Aisthesis, 2001).

SIDNEY GOTTLIEB is Professor of Media Studies at Sacred Heart University of Fairfield, USA. He is co-editor (with Richard Allen) of the *Hitchcock Annual* and is currently writing a book on Hitchcock's silent films.

TOM GUNNING is the Edwin A. and Betty L. Bergman Distinguished Service Professor at the University of Chicago, USA. Among his publicatiosn as author are *D. W. Griffith and the Origins of American Narrative Film: The Early Years at Biograph* (University of Illinois Press, 1991) and *The Films of Fritz Lang: Allegories of Vision and Modernity* (British Films Institute, 2000).

MALTE HAGENER is Professor for Media Studies at Philipps-Universität Marburg, Germany. He is author of *Moving Forward, Looking Back: The European Avantgarde and the Invention of Film Culture, 1919–1939* (Amsterdam University Press, 2007) and, with Thomas Elsaesser, of *Filmtheorie zur Einführung* (Junius, 2007), published in English as *Film Theory: An Introduction Through the Senses* (Routledge, 2010).

KNUT HICKETHIER is Professor Emeritus for Media Studies at the University of Hamburg, Germany His numerous books include *Geschichte des deutschen Fernsehens* (Metzler, 1998), *Einführung in die Medienwissenschaft* (Metzler, 2003) and *Film- und Fernsehanalyse* (Metzler, 1993).

ULI JUNG teaches at the Department of English Studies at the University of Trier, Germany. Among his books are as author *Dracula: Filmanalytische Studien zur Funktionalisierung eines Motivs der spät-viktorianischen Populärliteratur* (WVT, 1997), with Walter Schatzberg *Beyond Caligari: The Films of Robert Wiene* (Berghahn, 1999), as editor *Der deutsche Film: Aspekte seiner Geschichte von den Anfängen bis zur Gegenwart* (WVT, 1993) and as co-editor *Geschichte des dokumentarischen Films in Deutschland, Vol. 1: Kaiserreich 1895–1918* (Reclam, 2005).

CHRISTIAN JUNKLEWITZ is a freelance author and PhD student at the University of Cologne, Germany, currently completing a dissertation on popular television series in the US and Germany.

URSULA VON KEITZ is Professor for Film and Media Studies at the Rheinische Friedrich-Wilhelms-Universität Bonn, Germany. She has written numerous articles on film history and aesthetics. Her publications include, as author, *Im Schatten des Gesetzes: Schwangerschaftkonflikt und Reproduktion im deutschsprachigen Film, 1918–1933* (Schüren, 2005), as editor, *Früher Film und späte Folgen* (Schüren, 1998) and as co-editor, *Mehr als Schein: Ästhetik der Oberfläche in Film, Kunst, Literatur und Theater* (diaphanes, 2008), and *Mediale Transformationen des Holocaust* (Avinus, 2012).

DANIEL KOTHENSCHULTE is a staff film critic of *Frankfurter Rundschau*. He is author of *Nachbesserungen am amerikanischen Traum: der Regisseur Robert Redford* (Schüren, 1998) and has written numerous articles on silent film, media art and animation.

PETER KRÄMER is Senior Lecturer in Film Studies at the University of East Anglia, UK. He is the author of *The New Hollywood: From Bonnie and Clyde to Star Wars* (Wallflower Press, 2005), *2001: A Space Odyssey* (BFI, 2010) and *A Clockwork Orange* (Palgrave, 2011), and the co-editor of *Screen Acting* (Routledge, 1999) and *The Silent Cinema Reader* (Routledge, 2004).

GÜNTER KRENN works as a film historian at Filmarchiv Austria in Vienna. Recent publications as author include *Romy Schneider: Die Biographie* (Aufbau, 2008) and as co-editor (with Nikolaus Wostry *et al.*) *Cocl & Seff: Die österreichischen Serienkomiker der Stummfilmzeit* (filmarchiv austria, 2010).

DIETRICH LEDER is Professor for Television Studies at the Kunsthochschule für Medien in Cologne, Germany. He is co-editor of *Am Puls der Zeit: 50 Jahre WDR* (Kiepenheuer & Witsch, 2006) and author of numerous articles on German television.

CLÀUDIA LIEBRAND is Professor of General Literary Studies and Media Theory at the University of Cologne, Germany. She is author, editor and co-editor of a number of books, including *Gender-Topographien: Kulturwissenschaftliche Lektüren von Hollywoodfilmen der Jahrhundertwende* (DuMont, 2003) and *Hollywood hybrid: Genre und Gender im zeitgenössischen Mainstream-Film* (Schüren, 2004).

ANNEMONE LIGENSA is currently employed in the research project 'Visual Communities: Relationships of the Local, National and Global in Early Cinema' at the University of Cologne.

Recent publications include, as author, *Stars und ihr Publikum am Beispiel Clint Eastwood* (Kovac, 2011) and as co-editor (with Klaus Kreimeier) *Film 1900: Technology, Perception, Culture* (Libbey, 2009) and (with Daniel Müller and Peter Gendolla) *Leitmedien: Konzepte, Relevanz, Geschichte* (transcript, 2009).

MARTIN LOIPERDINGER is Professor of Media Studies at the University of Trier, Germany, and co-editor of *KINtop: Jahrbuch zur Erforschung des frühen Films*. His publications include, as author, *Der Parteitagsfilm Triumph des Willens von Leni Riefenstahl: Rituale der Mobilmachung* (Leske + Budrich, 1987) and *Film & Schokolade: Stollwercks Geschäfte mit lebenden Bildern* (Stroemfeld, 1999), as editor, *Celluloid Goes Digital: Historical-Critical Editions of Films on DVD and the Internet* (WVT, 2003), *Travelling Cinema in Europe: Sources and Perspectives* (Stroemfeld, 2008) and *Early Cinema Today: The Art of Programming and Live Performance* (Libbey, 2011), as co-editor (with Rudolf Herz) *Führerbilder: Hitler, Mussolini, Roosevelt, Stalin in Fotografie und Film* (Piper, 1995) and (with Peter Zimmermann *et al.*) *Geschichte des dokumentarischen Films in Deutschland, Vol. 1* (Reclam, 2005).

STEPHEN LOWRY is Professor of Media and Communication Studies at the Hochschule der Medien in Stuttgart, Germany. He has written on social aspects of cinema and German film history. Publications include *Pathos und Politik: Ideologie in Spiefilmen des Nationalsozialismus* (Niemeyer 1991).

WOLFGANG MÜHL-BENNINGHAUS is Professor of Theory and History of Film at the Humboldt-Universität in Berlin, Germany. His publications include *Das Ringen um den Tonfilm: Strategien der Elektro- und der Filmindustrie in den 20er und 30er Jahren* (Droste, 1999) and *Vom Augusterlebnis zur UFA-Gründung: Der deutsche Film im 1. Weltkrieg* (Avinus, 2004).

HOLGER RÖMERS is a freelance writer. He has written on film for various German and Austrian publications as well as for *Cineaste, Film International, Screening the Past* and *Senses of Cinema*.

HARRO SEGEBERG is Professor Emeritus of German Literature and Media Studies at the University of Hamburg and Head of the DFG-Research Training Group Kunst und Technik (University of Hamburg/Hamburg University of Technology/HafenCity University Hamburg). Publications include as author, *Literatur im Medienzeitalter: Literatur, Technik und Medien seit 1914* (Wiss.

Buchges., 2003), as co-editor (with Corinna Müller) *Cinema's Public Sphere: Emergence, Settlement, Differentiation (1895–1920)* (Schüren, 2008) and as editor *Mediengeschichte des Films, Vol. I–VIII* (Fink, 1996–2012).

ANNA SARAH VIELHABER received her PhD at the University of Cologne, Germany, for her thesis on popular German film (*Der populäre deutsche Film 1930–1970*). She has worked for various film industry and film funding institutions and has published essays on German film history.

ACKNOWLEDGEMENTS

This volume is the result of a collective effort. Our thanks go first and foremost to the authors for their expertise, enthusiasm and patience. We also thank the numerous translators (they are given credit individually at the end of the relevant chapters). For their editorial assistance and support, we thank Yoram Allon and Glen Danquah of Wallfower Press. For the pictures, we are especially grateful to the contributors who obtained copies from archives or from directors and their associates, whom we also wish to thank. We gratefully acknowledge the Theaterwissenschaftliche Sammlung of the University of Cologne (chapters 02, 03, 05, 06, 08, 12, 20), the Nederlands Filmmuseum (01) as well as Kairos-Film/Edition Filmmuseum (16, 19), for making pictures available. The rest of the pictures are from Joseph Garncarz's personal collection (07, 09, 13, 14, 17, 21, 22, 23). Finally, due to some unavoidable delays in the preparation of this volume, certain very recent films and publications are not referenced.

Joseph Garncarz & Annemone Ligensa
Cologne, Germany
June 2012

German cinema is often regarded as an antithesis to Hollywood – typically, the art films of the Weimar period and the propaganda films of the Third Reich immediately come to mind. The canon of German art cinema mostly includes films from the 1920s, such as *Das Cabinet des Dr. Caligari* (*The Cabinet of Dr. Caligari*, 1919), *Der letzte Mann* (*The Last Laugh*, 1924), *Metropolis* (1926) and *Berlin – Die Sinfonie der Großstadt* (*Berlin – Symphony of a Big City,* 1927), as well as films of the New German Cinema from the 1960s and 1970s, such as *Abschied von gestern* (*Yesterday Girl,* 1967) or *Jeder für sich und Gott gegen alle* (*The Enigma of Kaspar Hauser*, 1974). The filmmakers' self-definition seems to confirm this view: throughout German film history, famous German directors, screenwriters, cameramen, set-designers, musicians and actors regarded their task as 'making the cinema a true art form'. German films are either analysed for their aesthetics or their politics – and many films for both. Not only explicit propaganda films, such as *Die große Liebe* (*The Great Love*, 1942), but also genre films, such as *Der weiße Traum* (*The White Dream*, 1943), of the Nazi era are examined for their potential political meanings and effects. Conversely, the propaganda films that are aesthetically innovative, particularly Leni Riefenstahl's, receive most attention. German cinema is usually periodised along the lines of changing political systems, such as 'Weimar cinema', 'Nazi cinema' and 'postwar cinema', implying that film production as a whole and/or reception are more or less shaped by the dominant ideology. Furthermore, the argument usually runs, since art and politics are antithetical to popular entertainment, Hollywood films have always dominated the German market, because they provided universally attractive films for audiences at large. The conceptualisation is very similar for East German cinema: it is mainly analysed for its aesthetics and politics, not as popular entertainment. Thus, what remains unacknowledged is the important fact that for a long time German films were most successful with German audiences, including some of the art and propaganda films. The German film industry succeeded in creating popular entertainment with hits such as *The Great Love* and *Grün ist die Heide* (*The Heath Is Green*, 1951), which each attracted a domestic audience of over twenty million. In this sense, German cinema was a national cinema – and thus very similar to Hollywood.

This book tells the story of German cinema in a fresh way. The selected films represent all the trends mentioned above: innovative art cinema, Nazi propaganda, critical New German Cinema, but also popular entertainment. For this purpose, I would like to introduce a new model of German cinema history, which is not based on political developments, but on the popularity of films, defining phases by the respective country (or countries) that supplied the greatest number of successes. By re-framing German cinema in this way, I hope to arrive at a better understanding of the cultural specificity of German popular cinema, what made some of the propaganda films popular, the enabling conditions of German art cinema and the main differences between German art films of the 1920s and the 1960s/1970s.

On this basis, three phases can be identified. Between 1910 and 1963, the overwhelming majority of successful films were German productions. As a consequence of World War II, popular German cinema declined during the 1960s and early 1970s. Films from these decades, such as *Yesterday Girl* and *Deutschland im Herbst* (*Germany in Autumn*, 1978), broke with the conventions of film form as well as with the mode of production that popular narrative cinema had established. In the second phase, between 1964 and 1979, films from neighbouring West European countries became popular with German audiences, along with German films (thus, I call it the 'European phase'). In the third phase, beginning around 1980, US films have become as popular as German films had been in the first phase. However, in parallel, a new generation of German filmmakers re-established a popular German cinema, with films such as *Das Boot* (*The Boat*, 1981) and *Lola rennt* (*Run, Lola, Run*, 1998).

With the establishment of permanent cinemas from 1905 onwards and the introduction of multiple-reel feature films, such as *Des Pfarrers Töchterlein* (1913), from 1910 onwards, German audiences turned to German films. During the first phase, from about 1910 to 1963, the country's popular cinema flourished, which provided entertainment for a mass audience with great commercial success. This system was sustained in spite of two totalitarian political regimes, the Third Reich from 1933 to 1945 and the German Democratic Republic (GDR) between 1949 and 1990. Following the takeover by the National Socialist Party in January 1933, the regime created laws and administrative organisations to bring the film industry under their control. Despite such measures, for example employment policy, censorship and economic control mechanisms, most of the films needed a large audience to be profitable. There were only a few exceptions to this rule: Riefenstahl's *Olympia* (1938) was not dependent on box-office returns, because the film was financed by public funds – nevertheless, it was enormously successful with audiences. After a short phase of decline immediately following World War I, in which the less popular *Trümmerfilme* ('rubble films'), such as *Die Mörder sind unter uns* (*The Murderers Are Among Us*, 1946), were produced, popular cinema was re-established in the 1950s, which featured *Heimat*-films such as *The Heath Is Green*. The GDR also developed a popular cinema: its film company DEFA was subject to state control, but it was financed from box-office returns (it faced a greater challenge than West Germany, because the audience was smaller).

The mainstream German cinema between 1910 and the mid-1960s is the work of a generation of filmmakers for whom the production, distribution and exhibition of popular entertainment was a regular part of their professional practice. Principles such as orienting their work towards audience preferences, technical competence and efficiency of service were commonly shared standards. German cinema from the 1920s to the 1960s was comprised mainly of genre films and star vehicles. It was structurally very similar to Hollywood, but with nationally specific content and style. Hit German genres included the mountain films of the 1920s (e.g. *Die weiße Hölle vom Piz Palü* [*The White Hell of Piz Palu*, 1929]), operettas from the 1920s to the 1950s (e.g. *Die Drei von der Tankstelle* [*Three from the Filling Station*, 1930]), revue films from the 1930s to the 1960s (e.g. *The White Dream*), and *Heimat*-films (e.g. *The Heath Is Green*) as well as war films in the 1950s (e.g. *Die Brücke* [*The Bridge*, 1959]). West and East German cinema sometimes shared common trends, as with the 'kraut western' (e.g. the West German *Der Schatz im Silbersee* [*The Treasure of Silver Lake*, 1962] and the East German *Die Söhne der großen Bärin* [*The Sons of Great Bear*, 1966]). German stars included Henny Porten, Willy Fritsch, Hans Albers, Zarah Leander, Heinz Rühmann, Ruth Leuwerik, Romy Schneider and Til Schweiger.

The success of German genre films and star vehicles with their domestic audience was due to their cultural specificity, not their compliance with any 'universal' standards defined by Hollywood's international productions. German films were popular because they best reflected the values of German audiences. In 1985, sociologist Helmut Klages identified two groups of values: those of duty and acceptance versus those of self-realisation. The two groups differ over the degree in which they regard individuals as being dependent on one another. Values of duty and acceptance place the demands of a group (e.g. school, church, military, state) above those of the individual (e.g. discipline, obedience, loyalty, subordination and self-control). Values of self realisation place the demands of an individual above those of the group to which he or she belongs, such as self-sufficiency, self-realisation, pleasure for its own sake and fulfilment of emotional needs. Many popular German films of the first phase primarily expressed values of duty and acceptance. In contrast to classical Hollywood films, the plot is not driven on by the protagonist. Many German films (e.g. *Des Pfarrers Töchterlein*, *The Cabinet of Dr. Caligari*, *The Last Laugh*, *Das Boot*) show (anti-)heroes that are driven by social conditions or inner compulsions. In one of the most successful films of the 1950s, *The Heath Is Green*, which served as a model for many German postwar films, the protagonists are driven by various external factors (anything from forced emigration to issues of poaching etc.) to which they passively give in.

The degree to which the German film industry's creative personnel were able to realise their individual artistic visions depended on a number of factors, including the professional group to which they belonged and the structure of the company in which they worked. Actors usually had less artistic control than directors. The smaller a production company was, the more it was forced by market conditions to orient its production towards audience demand, as losses could not be compensated. Since most of the German production companies of the 1920s were very small, the margin for artistic innovation was narrow. Thus, the majority of the artistically ambitious films of the 1920s were produced by the few existing larger companies. Consequently, Ufa, being the largest company, developed the greatest artistic potential. Its most famous films were produced in the short span of three years, between 1923 and 1926, when Erich Pommer was head of production. Pommer wanted to produce films that were expensive and innovative, suitable for the international market while being typically German. His thirty productions during this period include *The Last Laugh* and *Metropolis*. Ufa's directors, notably Fritz Lang, Friedrich Wilhelm Murnau, Ewald André Dupont and Ludwig Berger, enjoyed the status of *auteurs*. In 1920s Hollywood, the producer supervised the shooting-script, which served as the blueprint for the finished film, before the director began to work on the picture. Pommer, by contrast, only gave organisational and creative support to his directors, who planned and controlled their own films from beginning to end. With this production system, Ufa adopted the established practices of German theatre, which had made the director the focal point of the creative process and of advertising. Furthermore, Ufa's directors each worked with a permanent staff, akin to the stock companies of German theatre. Ufa's directors not only exercised artistic control over the production process, their artistic vision was also respected in the planning of budgets. As a member of the company's board, Pommer represented the directors' interests in financial matters. Ufa was in a position to provide Pommer and his directors with means as no other German company could during this period. Furthermore, Pommer was also generous in organisational matters, from script development to production plans and the scheduling of premieres.

The special production conditions at Ufa enabled directors to cultivate unique styles. Consequently, historiographers have analysed many films of this period as *oeuvres* of individual artists. Since there were no companies with comparable production conditions in the USA at the time, the degree of stylistic variation was much greater in German cinema than in Hollywood. The Ufa directors made films that adapted and synthesised genres and movements of the established arts, e.g. *Kammerspiel*, Expressionism and New Objectivity. Together with their collaborators, they developed new techniques, e.g. the *entfesselte Kamera* ('unchained camera') and the Schüfftan-process. For example, expressionist films, such as *The Cabinet of Dr. Caligari*, have a striking visual style, which extremely distorts everyday objects, such as houses, furniture and streets, to symbolise the inner conflicts of characters. However, in contrast to the art films of the New German Cinema from the 1960s and 1970s, most art films from the 1920s showed a clear commitment towards narrative integration, generic differentiation, cultivation of stars and providing entertainment for a mass audience. Thus, during the first phase, striving for artistic merit was often characteristic even for big-budget films, such as *Metropolis*, while conversely, art films such as *The Cabinet of Dr. Caligari* were not lacking in entertainment values. *Berlin – Symphony of a Big City* is an exception to this rule – the American company Fox Europa produced this famous 'city symphony' as a quota production.

The German production of popular narrative films collapsed in the 1970s. With the exception of a very small number of films, the remaining production slate consisted almost entirely of films that were cheaply produced, featured no stars, and displayed no technical or creative effort. Many were sex comedies – and usually commercial failures. From the 1970s onwards, the German audience increasingly turned to foreign films that followed the conventions of popular narrative cinema, which was no longer on offer from German filmmakers. Since audiences usually particularly enjoy films that affirm their opinions and feelings, film preferences change along with an audience's values. At the beginning of the 1960s, i.e. before the change in the composition of popular films in Germany, there was a profound change in young people's values. These young people increasingly represented the majority of cinemagoers due to the spread of television. This trend was a shift from duty and acceptance towards self-realisation. As a result, Hollywood films were deemed more attractive, because they expressed individualist values like no others did: the protagonists of most Hollywood films function as motors for the films' plot and they control events, instead of passively succumbing to them.

The majority of German films made during this period belong to the New German Cinema: an art cinema with little success at the box office. The New German Cinema broke with the film form as well as with the mode of production that the popular narrative cinema had established. Instead of being generically organised, star-oriented and entertaining, films such as *Yesterday Girl*, *The Enigma of Kaspar Hauser* and *Germany in Autumn* reflected the personal experiences and opinions of their writer-directors; they were complex and unconventional in style and committed to social criticism. Striving for a profit, the basis of commercial film production was regarded as an 'out-dated fetish'. The new German filmmakers (represented by their spokesman, the lawyer Alexander Kluge) successfully lobbied for production conditions that were independent of market concerns. For this, the German theatre system, with its public subsidies and directors' artistic control, served as a model. Furthermore, the rejection of German popular cinema was connected with a self-definition that based its ideals on literary, rather than cinematic, production. These filmmakers regarded themselves as 'authors', and they strove to cross the boundaries between screenwriter, director and producer by practicing a craft-like mode of production. A similar movement can be observed in East Germany, with films such as *Der geteilte Himmel* (*The Divided Heaven*, 1964). However, the break with the forms of popular narrative cinema as well as with its mode of production was much less radical in the GDR. *Die Legende von Paul und Paula* (*The Legend of Paul and Paula*, 1973) was a very successful film that broke some of the taboos of GDR society (ironically, by presenting love and happiness in an individualistic manner), but it was more conventional aesthetically than New German Cinema.

Compared to other European countries' film movements, e.g. the French New Wave, the break with popular narrative cinema was especially radical in West Germany due to a generational conflict that was also highly political. The filmmakers of the New German Cinema were all born during the Third Reich. The main concern of this conflict was the role the parent-generation had played in National Socialism. The new generation demanded the analysis and acknowledgement of individual action and held their parents morally responsible for their participation, sense of duty and blind support. Thus, they disapproved of almost everything their parents had created. The young filmmakers identified traditional German cinema with National Socialism, because many directors of the 1950s had been active and successful during the Third Reich; they therefore rejected popular cinema without exception. The new generation was able to decide the conflict in their favour quickly and consistently, because the parent generation offered little resistance. The directors of the popular German cinema of the 1950s, who were all born during the *Kaiserreich,* had retired by the early 1970s. There was no generation in between, because following the victory over the National Socialist regime, there were no facilities for training young filmmakers in West Germany before 1966. Since the GDR regarded itself as an 'anti-fascist' state and saw historical continuities as a West German problem, the generational conflict was not as strongly expressed in East Germany.

From the 1980s onwards, a new generation of filmmakers (born after World War II) re-established the production of popular films in West Germany with some success, e.g. *Das Boot, Männer* (*Men*, 1985), *Run, Lola, Run, Good Bye, Lenin!* (2003) and *Das Wunder von Bern*

(*The Miracle of Bern*, 2003). This generation, who favoured Hollywood films, no longer shared the reservations of the 'sceptical generation', as Helmut Schelsky referred to them, towards popular cinema. Their films have a strong generic base, and increasingly focused on stars, such as Til Schweiger, Franka Potente, Ben Becker and Jürgen Vogel. The 1980s and early 1990s saw a flood of *Beziehungskomödien* ('relationship comedies') inspired by the surprise hit *Men*. In addition, films dealing with German history (both West and East) have become popular, once again proving that political themes need not be antithetical to commercial success, e.g. *Das Boot* and *Good Bye, Lenin!*

The current generation of filmmakers is faced with serious difficulties in realising their aims, because the preceding generation not only made different films in a different manner, but completely transformed production conditions to suit their purpose. Thus, the new generation is working towards restructuring the film industry. The system of state subsidies is being transformed from cultural to more marked-oriented principles. However, for the production of popular films, not only capital, but also creative and organisational personnel is necessary. The producer has been re-introduced as a separate function, responsible for development of the concept, controlling financing and supervising shooting, postproduction and distribution. Figures such as Bernd Eichinger and Stefan Arndt have been as central to contemporary German filmmaking as Ilse Kubaschewski and Waldfried Barthel were in the 1950s. Film schools have introduced production into their curriculae. A similar professionalism has also been adopted within the field of screenwriting. Furthermore, in the 1990s, the emergence of casting agencies significantly contributed to the star system.

The current German cinema has not reached the level of popularity and independence it had before the 1960s. In the face of powerful competition from Hollywood, even popular German film is only possible through subsidies. In the 1990s, around 80 per cent of German films were subsidised. Current German cinema is not very successful abroad, nor is it as successful as it used to be, but it is much more popular domestically than the New German Cinema was. The current generation of filmmakers is clearly aiming to re-make filmmaking from a craft back into an industry, with both global as well as culturally specific characteristics.

Joseph Garncarz

Translated by Annemone Ligensa

REFERENCE

Klages, H. (1985) *Wertorientierungen im Wandel: Rückblick, Gegenwartsanalyse, Prognosen.* Frankfurt and New York: Campus.

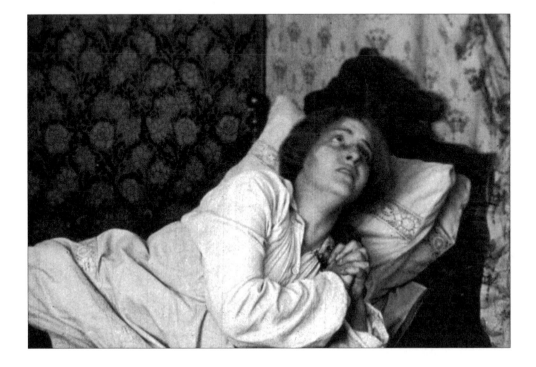

DES PFARRERS TÖCHTERLEIN

ADOLF GÄRTNER, GERMANY, 1913

The 37-minute two-reeler, *Des Pfarrers Töchterlein*, produced by the German film company Messter, premiered in Berlin in late March 1913. Below is a contemporary summary of the film's plot:

> Heinz Langer, a spruce naval officer and son of the old privy councillor, returns to his native village after a long absence. Awaiting him in the garden is a pretty girl who, much to his delight and astonishment, turns out to be Klara, the pastor's daughter with whom he used to play as a child. Revelling in old memories, they exchange a first kiss, then rings, like they used to in the past, when they pretended they were getting married. This time, however, they are both serious. One night, Heinz climbs up a ladder and taps on Klara's window, who lets him in. In order to prevent their son from marrying the poor pastor's daughter, the privy councillor and his wife invite a beautiful rich cousin to their home, and Heinz soon falls victim to her charms. It is the duty of Klara's father to preside over the wedding. In complete despair, Klara falls seriously ill. On the day of the wedding, she drags herself to the church, and the moment her father gives the couple his blessing, her scream shatters the silence. High up in the organ loft, Klara collapses and later dies in her father's arms.

A drama of this kind is typical of the films featuring actress Henny Porten, who plays Klara: a young woman is abandoned by a socially superior lover and preserves her honour by dying of the suffering inflicted on her. One hundred years on, it seems hopelessly old-fashioned. However, in terms of film history, it makes sense to take a closer look at this film, as Henny Porten was in the process of becoming the first German film star.

In the years before World War I, commercial cinema underwent a fundamental change: the transition from the short film programme to the full-length feature film with an accompanying programme – the format that is still current today. In 1908/9, the film industry suffered a classical capitalist crisis of over-production: intent on making the highest profits possible, the suppliers produced and/or distributed considerably more short films than the cinema owners could include in their programmes and afford financially. The film producers and distributors tried to sell or rent out their products by reducing prices. Since they all adopted this strategy, the capital invested in the production and purchase of films was devalued, so that selling prices sank below production costs, and thus the production and distribution of films was no longer a profitable business. To become profitable again, the film industry had to develop a new kind of film format, which would guarantee that selling prices would rise above production costs once more.

But how could higher prices and profits be achieved on the film market? In determining a film's price, the usual criterion abstracted from an individual film's qualities: it was simply calculated according to the film's length. In short film programmes, all films had more or less the same status. Such programmes were attractive, because they satisfied the audience's need for diversity, offering a wide variety of travel, news, comic and tragic films, providing the experience of different moods. As Corinna Müller has shown in detail, three major innovations were implemented. Firstly, the films were extended to at least two acts, with the result that a longer film forced one or more short films out of the programme. Secondly, film stars were promoted as the main focus of longer films, becoming decisive in the viewers' choice of film. Finally, the *Monopolfilm* ('exclusive') distribution system guaranteed cinema owners that the competing cinemas in their district would not be able to show the same film in the same week, so higher admission prices could be charged with reference to this exclusive showing.

In the early 1910s, during the transition from the short film programme to the full-length feature film, the German cinema industry promoted the film stars Asta Nielsen and Henny Porten, whose success endured into the 1920s, and who are ideal examples of different economic, aesthetic and political trends in German cinema. As Frank Kessler and Angela Warth note:

> In films dealing specifically with women's issues, these two actresses represented opposite constructions of femininity. Henny Porten was promoted as a genuinely German counterpart to Asta Nielsen, a Danish actress with international acclaim: while the somewhat plump and dowdy Porten often starred in melodramatic stories of sacrifice and renunciation, the agile and expressive Nielsen portrayed a broad range of strong female characters, specifically in social dramas.

The clearly defined differences between the two most important German film stars of the 1910s are partly connected with their different positions in the film production process. In late 1910, Asta Nielsen's first film, *Afgrunden*, was the first to be released as a *Monopolfilm*, accompanied by an advertising campaign of extraordinary dimensions. In summer 1911, the Internationale Films-Vertrieb Gesellschaft invested the sizeable sum of 1.4 million Marks to engage Nielsen and her husband, scriptwriter and director Urban Gad, under an exclusive contract for four years. The fact that Nielsen herself had a share in the production company and in the profits from the box-office returns of her films gave her an unusually strong position on set.

By contrast, Porten's stardom was very carefully and cautiously built up by producer Oskar Messter, under whose patronage she was to remain. In summer 1910, when she began playing leading roles for Messter in one-reelers, she received a monthly fee. Initially, she remained anonymous: her name was not mentioned in the advertisements for her films. These were so-called *Terminfilme* ('fixed date films'), i.e. the production company made an announcement on which day a certain film would be released. Cinema owners and film distributors could order one or several copies of the film for the given date. In promoting a star, however, exclusivity was advantageous. The Messter company could not guarantee this as long as it sold the films starring Porten as *Terminfilme*.

Nevertheless, the Messter company succeeded in making a famous star of Henny Porten. Throughout May and June 1912, Messter launched a short but lavish advertising campaign in the Berlin trade magazine *Erste Internationale Film-Zeitung*, with double-page advertisements containing film stills of Porten, and a special glossy supplement. Her breakthrough as a star came nine months later, when Messter began premiering her films in prestigious Berlin cinemas. As Müller explains, 'beginning in March 1913 with the premiere of *Des Pfarrers Töchterlein* at two Union cinemas, Porten was honoured by being designated as "the celebrated Berlin artist", her name appearing at the very top of the advertisement in much larger print than the film title'. And, at the beginning of the film, Porten, in close up, was given the opportunity to take a bow and smile at the audience. This opening clearly indicated that she was the star of the film – despite the fact that it was 'only' a *Terminfilm*. *Des Pfarrers Töchterlein* was more than an important milestone in Porten's career, it represented the actress's move from short to long films; it was the last in a long series of two-reelers issued by Messter with Porten in the main role. Only then did Oskar Messter develop his company's star to market maturity: in late May 1913, he issued a three-act film (*Ihr guter Ruf*, 996 metres) and a four-act film (*Eva*, 1408 metres). Two years later than Nielsen, Porten finally became an 'exclusive' star: in late August 1913, the four-act film *Der Feind im Land* played as the first Porten *Monopolfilm*.

In terms of the number of copies and the international distribution of her films, Henny Porten was certainly able to compete with Asta Nielsen. In Germany, Porten may possibly have had the edge on Nielsen with her *Terminfilme*. Judging by information provided by Joseph Garncarz, a sample of programme advertisements by cinemas in nine German cities between 1911 and 1912 indicates that Porten was on the programme twice as often as Nielsen.

Des Pfarrers Töchterlein was ready for distribution in late October 1912. No literary source or script for the film is known to exist. As with most of Porten's previous films, it was directed by Adolf Gärtner, and the cameraman was Carl Froelich. In late February 1913, the Messter company promoted *Des Pfarrers Töchterlein* as a *Terminfilm* with a full-page advertisement in *Der Kinematograph*, stating that 'the next Porten hit', *Des Pfarrers Töchterlein*, will be available on 28 March 1913. The duration given is 37 minutes, the purchase price for a copy was 950 Marks. One week later, 14 March was announced as the last day for orders (*Der Kinematograph*, 322, 26 February 1913 and 323, 5 March 1913). The film's length and its designation as a 'Porten hit' indicate that the Messter company intended it as the main attraction in short film programmes. However, with a film little more than half an hour long, Porten could not yet dominate the usual two-hour short film programmes. Nevertheless, on the day of its release, on 28 March 1913, the Messter company staged the first premiere of a 'Henny Porten film', at the Berlin Union Theater on Moritzplatz. Messter sold 150 copies of *Des Pfarrers Töchterlein* at the high metre price of 1.25 Marks. What surely contributed to this success was the fact that in February and March 1913, the Messter company had published numerous announcements in the trade press denying the 'rumour' that Porten was lured away by the Danish company Nordisk.

Although Porten was the most important German film star alongside Asta Nielsen in the 1910s, about 80 per cent of her films are believed lost. Only sixteen of Messter's 82 feature films starring Henny Porten, made between 1910 and 1918, are extant, more or less in fragments. Hardly any of the copies correspond in length and condition to the versions shown in Germany at the time. Most are significantly shorter than the original versions, many have no intertitles or foreign translations, and/or they are black and white and not, as was customary for projection copies at the time, tinted in different colours. The extant copy of *Des Pfarrers Töchterlein* is from the stock of the Dutch cinema owner and film distributor Jean Desmet, archived at the Filmmuseum Amsterdam. It is a 558 metre-long export version with Dutch intertitles. It tells a complete story, but it is approximately 25 per cent shorter than the 762 metre-long version that passed the Berlin censors, as censorship cards show.

What is surely most difficult for today's audiences to accept is the passivity of the pastor's daughter portrayed by Porten. She keeps house for her widowed father, which explains her social isolation to a certain extent. Consequently, she is naïve, gullible and uncalculatingly smitten when the playmate of her childhood days returns. But the fact that she simply accepts his abandonment for a cousin of his own social class cleverly introduced by his mother, instead of making an attempt to win him back, and succumbs to the triumph of devious class snobbery over love, no longer seems touching today, but rather ridiculous.

At the time, the Messter company intended to appeal to quite different feelings amongst the audience: the film's subtitle *Ein Frauenschicksal* ('a woman's fate') alludes to reception preferences that were satisfied not only by cinemas with their countless *Sozialdramen* ('social dramas'), but also by women's 'dime novels', which had a large readership. The detailed announcement of *Des Pfarrers Töchterlein*, which Messter had printed in trade magazines such as *Der Kinematograph* and attached to film copies, gives the following rationale for Porten's passivity in the role of the pastor's daughter:

> Just as evil spirits in fairytales subdue the characters' spirits, so fate impacts on real life. The pastor observes the lovers kissing and reproaches his daughter. Stroking her blonde hair, he gently but solemnly warns her not to give in to deceptive hopes. The good man, aware of life's seriousness, knows that such hopes are often dashed, and thus he explains to her that it is impossible for the officer and son of a privy councillor to take her, the daughter of a poor pastor, as his wife.

The son of the privy councillor promises the decent pastor's daughter a love marriage, and trustingly she surrenders to him. But 'fate' prevents the memory of their childhood happiness together from developing into a lasting relationship. The pragmatic champion (and, as a protestant pastor, executor) of this 'fate' is Klara's father, who acknowledges the social differences between the two lovers as an insurmountable obstacle to their marriage. Additional human agents of the tragic events are three women: a maid in the councillor's household, who watches through a hedge as Klara and Heinz kiss and immediately tells her mistress; Heinz's calculating mother, who by inviting a cousin of his to their home successfully dissuades her son from entering into a bond with a social inferior; and the cousin who bewitches the handsome naval officer, even pretending to be ill to gain even more attention.

Heinz turns away from Klara and towards his cousin without any sense of inner conflict. He is characterised in the film not as a man with contradictory feelings but as a stereotype of gender and social status. Only the pastor's daughter shows her feelings. In her initial happiness and in her final, fatal suffering, she is the central character around which the whole plot revolves. What she most elaborately displays on screen is her suffering, albeit with a standard repertoire of gestures: statuesque poses of helplessness and despair, in a style that was customary on the contemporary stage.

One evening, as Klara takes an official letter from her father to the privy councillor, she catches sight, through a window, of her beloved Heinz tenderly embracing his cousin – a sight that is clearly heartbreaking for her. She trembles, grasps her bosom and loses consciousness. She is seized by a serious nervous fever and, by the time she recovers, the wedding preparations are complete. The short feature film moves towards its emotional and, for Klara, its fatal climax. The text issued by the Messter company in *Lichtbild-Theater* reads:

> Shivering, she throws a shawl around her and staggers to the church. […] Having climbed up to the organ loft, she stands right next to the organ, and is deeply moved by the chorale. She looks down, shuddering, upon the couple exchanging rings, and has to muster all her strength to prevent herself from screaming. As the couple kneel down before him, the pastor gives his blessing. This act by her father, which for her marks the end of her dream of happiness, is the ultimate test for the weak nerves of the convalescent woman; the unavoidable consequence is a severe recurrence of her pain. No longer can she master her emotions. A shrill scream of grief, reverberating on the walls of the church, testifies to her suffering. Immediately everyone looks around – the scream came from the organ loft – and the pastor catches sight of his child. He falters and can scarcely complete the ceremony. Hans [Heinz] too recognises Klara and guiltily stares at the floor. The ceremony is over and everyone leaves the church. As fast as his feet can carry him, the pastor hurries up to the organ loft and catches the dying Klara, his beloved child, in his arms. He sobs aloud in fierce pain and total despair, then says a silent prayer for this poor creature who came to grief through love.

Before this sequence, the action of the film unfolded in long, static tableaux. For the climax, swift, alternating shots and reverse-shots are employed. The editors even create the impression of the reverberating scream through visual means. The tempo of the shots in this last sequence is significant: the accelerated rhythm in the film's finale clearly contrasts with the rather sedate presentation of the action up to that point, thus heightening the emotional impact of the climax in the church. The shot/reaction-shot structure creates a spatial opposition between altar and organ, which illustrates the moral contrast between the poor decent girl and her rich lover, who marries a woman of his social class. By crosscutting, the gaze of the implied spectator wanders to and fro, from altar to organ, over nine different shots. Guided by the editing, the spectator takes up Klara's viewing position. Thus, the tendency to morally identify with Klara is furthered by cinematographic means.

First, the spectator looks down diagonally on the wedding ceremony at the altar (shot 1); then up from below to the balustrade behind which the organ rises. Klara appears and looks down, full of horror (shot 2). The spectator's gaze at the wedding ceremony now aligns with Klara's – the proceedings at the altar continue without her presence being noticed (shot 3). Again, the shot upwards to the balustrade and the organ is also the spectator's gaze at Klara, who is holding a handkerchief to her mouth to smother her sobs. Klara is now shown in medium close-up, camera and spectator thus moving closer to her (shot 4). Again, the spectator's gaze down to the altar coincides with Klara's (shot 5). The spectator's gaze then wanders back up to Klara, as she collapses behind the balustrade (shot 6). At the altar below, Klara's father blesses the bride and groom and hands them the wedding rings (shot 7). The spectator's gaze returns to Klara, who is literally writhing in pain (shot 8). At the altar, several people involved in the ceremony turn to the camera, look up and turn away. Klara's father covers his eyes. Slowly, the wedding party moves out of the frame, some of them looking up in Klara's direction. The bride looks demonstratively to the side – the groom raises his eyes twice, aware of his guilt (shot 9). The last shot is a view of Klara lying in her father's arms – visible in the background is the now deserted altar. The position of the spectator's gaze spatially aligns with the organ, thus raised above the to-and-fro of the action just witnessed. This last shot provides the 'higher moral viewpoint' of the film's story.

The organ pipes could be interpreted as a visual reference to Klara's inner pain, as Thomas Elsaesser has commented: 'For what gives this moving scene its full melodramatic force is the role played by the organ. Its overwhelming presence visualises the unheard organ tones roaring and raging in the heart of this spurned woman.' Even more important is the positioning of the organ pipes, metaphorically supporting Klara, when interpreted from a moral viewpoint. In Christian cultures, the inwardness of religious feeling is represented by the resonance of a church organ. Thus, organ pipes are particularly suitable for symbolising an invisible, all-prevailing divine authority. Klara has divine justice on her side in the shape of the organ. The last shot, the long gaze directed by both camera and spectator from the organ down onto Klara, marks the unequivocal Christian standpoint of compassion. With it, the conflict between rich and poor, in this case between a socially acceptable marriage and the despair of spurned love, is finally resolved for the spectator in a deep sigh. Only in death can Klara be released from her pain. How consoling for her, and what a nice resolution for a submissive audience. God is on the side of the poor decent girl, supporting the proverb that 'it is easier for a camel to pass through the eye of a needle than for a rich man to enter heaven'.

This 'official' interpretation does not mean that the cinema audience's reception of the film was automatically governed by the dominant, clearly conservative tendency of *Des Pfarrers Töchterlein*. Consideration must also be given to the context in which the film was shown. *Des Pfarrers Töchterlein* is a silent film first shown in spring 1913. Silent films at that time were usually accompanied by live music and the comments of lecturers. Silent films were not yet the all-in-one media products they became as of 1930, when reels carried all the visual and acoustic information required for showing a film. The copies of silent films preserved in film archives are visual relics of an exhibition practice of which the auditory part was transient. Depending on the equipment and location of the cinema, and the composition of the audience, the respective musicians and the individual lecturer, the films projected on the screen were interpreted quite differently.

The catalogue of the exhibition 'Hätte ich das Kino!' at the Deutsches Literaturarchiv in 1976 contains a programme from a cinema in Graz, which includes *Des Pfarrers Töchterlein* and announces that the films would be explained by a lecturer. The catalogue also contains a newspaper article describing the services of such a lecturer in a cheap cinema close to Alexanderplatz in Berlin: 'The lecturer sobbed, the viewers clenched their fists, and a tragedy raced past before their eyes, which was totally different to the one envisaged by the filmmaker.' *Des Pfarrers Töchterlein* provided an adept lecturer with at least as many cues for rousing people against bourgeois snobs who seduce decent girls and then abandon them, as for an appeal to the sublime principles of Christian morality.

Martin Loiperdinger

Translated by Pauline Cumbers

REFERENCES

Deutsches Literaturarchiv (1976) *Hätte ich das Kino! Die Schriftsteller und der Stummfilm.* Munich: Kösel/Klett.

Elsaesser, T. (2002) *Filmgeschichte und frühes Kino: Archäologie eines Medienwandels.* Munich: edition text + kritik.

Kessler, F. and E. Warth (2002) 'Early Cinema and Its Audiences', in T. Bergfelder, E. Carter and D. Göktürk (eds) *The German Cinema Book.* London: British Film Institute, 121–8.

Müller, C. (1986) 'Filmografie', in H. Belach (ed.) *Henny Porten: Der erste deutsche Filmstar 1890–1960.* Berlin: Haude & Spener, 171–232.

DAS CABINET DES DR. CALIGARI
THE CABINET OF DR. CALIGARI

ROBERT WIENE, GERMANY, 1919

Das Cabinet des Dr. Caligari (*The Cabinet of Dr. Caligari*, 1919) appears as a crucial text for the periodisation of German film history. Two eminent accounts carry 'Caligari' in their titles: Siegfried Kracauer's *From Caligari to Hitler*, which analyses the Weimar period, and Paolo Cherchi Usai's and Lorenzo Codelli's edited collection *Prima di Caligari*, which is concerned with Wilhelmine films. For Cherchi Usai and Codelli, *The Cabinet of Dr. Caligari* becomes the end point for the film history of Imperial Germany only because Kracauer had made it the starting point of his history of Weimar film. This indicates the film's significance in the discussions of German film history at large. Moreover, in 1995, when more than 360 German film scholars answered a questionnaire on the hundred most significant German films, the film was elected second (Fritz Lang's *M* from 1931 took first place). What makes it such an important text? When did it acquire this status, which has no parallel in international film historiography? And why has its director, Robert Wiene, not achieved equal significance among directors?

Wiene is mentioned in every history of German cinema because he made *The Cabinet of Dr. Caligari*, but he is maligned for trying, and failing, to repeat his success with *Genuine* (1920) and *Raskolnikow* (*Raskolnikov*, 1923). In fact, Wiene was a veteran filmmaker by the time he made *The Cabinet of Dr. Caligari*. He began his career in 1912 (at the latest) and wrote and directed over forty films prior to his most famous film, often displaying in his work a deep interest in the human psyche and extreme psychological states. Stylistically a rather conventional director, Wiene was a well-respected film personage, and thus a palpable candidate for the producers at Decla to take over the 'Caligari' project from Fritz Lang, when Lang was assigned to *Die Spinnen, 2. Teil: Das Brilliantenschiff* (*The Spiders, Part 2: The Diamond Ship*, 1920). In fact, when comparing *The Spiders* with *The Cabinet of Dr. Caligari* it becomes apparent that, by 1919, it was Wiene who was the more innovative director.

What made *The Cabinet of Dr. Caligari* an original film in its time was not so much its content but rather its visual style, which drew on expressionist art. It tells a rather conventional story of a mysterious mountebank, Dr. Caligari (Werner Krauss), who travels the town fairs of northern Germany. He exhibits a somnambulist, Cesare (Conrad Veidt), who is able to answer every question the audience poses. In Holstenwall, Caligari is treated arrogantly by town officials. Next morning the town clerk is found murdered. In the evening, Francis (Friedrich Féher) and his friend Alan (Hans-Heinrich von Twardowski), both in love with Jane (Lil Dagover), visit Caligari's show. Ecstatically, Alan asks Cesare, 'How long will I live?' Cesare answers, 'Till daybreak.' During that same night Alan is murdered. Francis suspects that Caligari is behind the murders and decides to spy on him. While he is watching Caligari's trailer, Cesare, on Caligari's command, breaks into Jane's bedroom and abducts her. He is followed over the roofs of the town and falls to his death. A search of Caligari's trailer reveals his guilt, but he evades the police and flees to an insane asylum, closely followed by Francis, who learns that Caligari is, in fact, the director of the asylum. Francis leads other doctors of the house in a search of the director's office. They find evidence that Caligari is obsessed with the question whether it is possible to coerce a somnambulist into committing murder. Francis and the doctors confront the director with Cesare's body, at the sight of which Caligari falls into raving madness.

There is a framing story before and after these occurrences. It opens with Francis sitting in a garden, chatting with a man about apparitions. A young woman passes by, whom Francis identifies as his fiancée, and who later turns out to be Jane. Francis begins to narrate the inner story. The closing frame returns to the garden, which now turns out to be part of the insane asylum of the inner story: Francis is a patient, along with Jane and Cesare. When the director appears, Francis experiences a fit of madness and attacks the director, shouting, 'He is Caligari – Caligari – Caligari!' They fight until doctors and nurses force Francis into a straightjacket. The director takes off his glasses (which makes him more recognisable as the Caligari of the inner story), looks into the camera (while an iris is closing in around his face) and says: 'Well, finally, I understand his raving. He believes I am this mysterious Caligari! And now I know a proper way to his healing.' The iris closes completely, and the last title card of the film appears: 'The End'.

This framing story has triggered debate among scholars. Decades later, Hans Janowitz, one of the two scriptwriters, maintained that he and Carl Mayer had conceived of a film meant as a statement against militarism and authority. Caligari was a symbolic character, who had 'gone mad by the misuse of his mental powers'. The stylised sets for the film were to signify 'the "Caligaric world"', the 'crazy world of 1919'. In Janowitz's concept, this criticism was conveyed by the inner story alone, all the more so since the authors envisioned a stylised form that was to signify a world turned upside down. Janowitz maintained that Wiene was opposed to these sets, and criticised him for explaining them away by introducing a frame story that made them appear as a representation of individual madness. Thus, according to Janowitz, it was Wiene who added a frame story where originally there was none. Janowitz regarded this as a felonious transgression against the scriptwriters, since he had a very distinct notion of a screenplay's function: 'To us, a picture-story script had to be a straightjacket for the director, a very tight, precise and balanced straightjacket, with strong belts and fasteners, so that nothing could escape in any way from our instructions.' Thus, Janowitz claimed that Wiene overturned the scriptwriters' authority over the film.

Janowitz showed this manuscript to Kracauer, while the latter was working on *From Caligari to Hitler*, and Kracauer turned Janowitz's somewhat vague ideological intentions into a political reading of *The Cabinet of Dr. Caligari*. He saw a revolutionary film that was turned into a conformist one. Kracauer characterised the film as the 'archetype of all forthcoming postwar films'. For Kracauer, Janowitz's statements came in handy to corroborate his own theoretical perspective, namely that an analysis of German films of the Weimar period would explain why the Germans eventually submitted to a tyrant. Thus, he looked at film history as a version of the 'history of the German collective mentality' – in his view, film as a popular medium offered an access to the inner dispositions of broad strata of the population.

From 1947 on, the reception of *The Cabinet of Dr. Caligari* was overshadowed by Kracauer's verdict. Only after a copy of the original screenplay turned up was the debate over the film pursued through a new perspective. This copy revealed two major surprises. Firstly, it is not written in the specifically 'visual', cinematographic style for which Carl Mayer's screenplays were to become famous in the 1920s. It looks, on the contrary, fairly conventional, and is structurally in no way different from the writing styles of other screenplays of the time. Secondly, the screenplay consists of a story embedded in a frame story, in which Francis and Jane, a happily married couple for twenty years, are entertaining guests on the terrace of their house. A band of gypsies passes by, at the sight of which Francis and Jane become melancholic, so that their guests press them to explain their change of mood. Francis thus begins to narrate the story of Caligari. The inner story varies from the film version only in a few minor details. At the end of the inner story, Francis and Jane are standing in front of a plaque, commemorating the traumatic events: 'Here stood the Cabinet of Dr Caligari / Peace to his victims – Peace to him! / The city of Holstenwall.' Apparently this is the last image of the inner story, which then was to return to the frame story. Unfortunately, the last section of the screenplay is missing. Nonetheless, a reading of this framing story leaves no room for the revolutionary intention Janowitz later claimed. Francis and Jane are conventionally married; they live in comfortable circumstances in a house of their own and invite guests to luxurious summer parties. They seem to have overcome the trauma that Caligari brought about twenty years earlier. This trauma was overcome with Caligari's defeat: the plaque, which belongs to the inner story, indicates that the people of Holstenwall worked through the crisis immediately after the events. In this light, Kracauer's reading of the film must be seriously questioned. His reliance on Janowitz's manuscript alone led him to read the film as a political statement that was marred by the early Weimar film establishment. However, the question remains: what made *The Cabinet of Dr. Caligari* such a pivotal film that it has not lost its appeal in more than ninety years?

The expressionist stylisation of the sets and the title cards still impress audiences. Already in 1926, Rudolf Kurtz praised the film's 'original energy' as well as the connection between the expressionist stylisation and the action, 'which is entirely set against the darkness of the soul'. He linked the film with German cultural traditions, such as romantic author E. T. A. Hoffmann's work. However, Kurtz saw a discrepancy between the expressionist sets and the actors who play their roles naturalistically. Kurtz's conclusion, that the film on the whole was successful in transferring expressionism to film, refers to its worldwide success. Moreover, Kurtz saw a parallel between the film and the revolutionary situation of postwar Berlin where it premiered.

Already by contemporaries the film was regarded as an expression of the troubled social circumstances under which it was produced. On the other hand, the film was produced by a commercial film company, and the producers would only have accepted expressionist stylisation if they saw a commercial potential in it. An eccentric visual style could help to differentiate the film from its competition, foreign as well as domestic. Hermann Warm, one of the set designers, also claimed many years later that it was he who conceived of the film as needing an expressionist form – and Wiene, he maintained, accepted his proposition without reservation. Producer Rudolf Meinert – Erich Pommer was not involved in the pre-production of the film – called it 'mad', but promising.

Since expressionism was on the verge of becoming an accepted art form, the film industry thus ventured into an 'experiment' that might well attract a wide audience. The concept was thus not as innovative as one is tempted to believe. Still, it was innovative enough in a medium that tended to be conservative. The stylised sets did not have any bearing on the way in which the story was narrated. All characters – with the exception of Cesare, Caligari and sometimes Jane – appear in quite 'normal' costumes; the actors play their roles without the extravagant gestures of the contemporary German stage. Thus, the film introduces to cinema stylistic elements that were already established in other cultural fields, but doing so in a moderate manner, so that in terms of commercial risk, this venture must have seemed calculable.

The scriptwriters, it seems, were less concerned with expressionist stylisation than with artistic 'nobilitation' of their film: according to Pommer, they suggested Alfred Kubin as set designer. Lotte Eisner, in 1955, saw clearly that the assignment of Kubin would have changed the course of film history, because Kubin would have avoided an abstract design; the hallucinatory forcefulness would thus have been missing. As a graphic designer and illustrator of numerous books, Kubin was an established artist, and it was especially for that reason that Janowitz and Mayer were interested in him.

The Cabinet of Dr. Caligari was produced before German film censorship was centralised. The period between the abdication of Wilhelm II and the inauguration of the Reich Film Act on 12 May 1920 afforded liberties to tackle subject matter that had formerly been more restrictively censored. A general feeling of opportunity, liberty and independence prevailed; the drive to find new subject matter and new means of cinematic expression was widespread. Thus, all of a sudden, German films reached a new artistic level, and expressionism was only one aspect of this. All the major studies of German expressionist cinema focused on only a small number of films, and Leonardo Quaresima has shown that contemporary critics did not agree over the terminology with which to describe the new style. He found that the term 'expressionistic' was not univocally used in a positive sense, but that it could also pejoratively signify the 'degeneracy' of film, which some saw in the new style. Thus, the identification of Weimar cinema with expressionism came about later, probably after World War II, and especially in the US reception of German film history.

Immediately after World War I, when the Entente-nations were trying to recuperate their expenditures, film became a very interesting commodity. Due to the rapidly increasing inflation of the Reichsmark, German films became inexpensive imports for foreign distributors. With production costs of over 900,000 Reichsmark, *The Cabinet of Dr. Caligari* was not an inexpensive film by German standards, but these costs equalled a mere $18,000, which was downright cheap from a US point of view. Thus, German films promised sensational profits on foreign markets. US distributors acted quickly and bought the distribution rights to numerous German films, before the US government introduced import tariffs. US film companies distributed German films not only in the USA, but also in Great Britain and France. *The Cabinet of Dr. Caligari* was among them, and it was there to stay. Allegedly, it played in a Parisian cinema for seven consecutive years. And it was the French who invented the term *Caligarisme*, with which they denominated films on madness and obsession.

Although *The Cabinet of Dr. Caligari* was immediately successful in Germany, following its premiere on 26 February 1920, it was abroad that the film's reputation survived the Nazi's iconoclasm. Wiene, who had left the country in 1933, was classified as a so-called 'non-Aryan' by the Nazi film administration. Nonetheless, his death on 15 July 1938 was mentioned by the Nazi film press, albeit with the following comment: 'To the last he denied being Jewish, even though there can be no doubt about it.'

The post-World War II reception of *The Cabinet of Dr. Caligari* was heavily influenced by Kracauer's political reading of the film, but this interpretation did not go unchallenged. Barry Salt criticised his reading for the smallness of his film sample, and Thomas Elsaesser questioned the homological relationships of his argument. For Michael Budd *The Cabinet of Dr. Caligari* is a transformation of expressionism from an avant-garde art form to a mass cultural phenomenon. While Siegbert S. Prawer sees the early Weimar period reflected in the film, Michael Minden looks at the original film script as a reflection of nineteenth-century conservatism. John D. Barlow suggests a reading in terms of a modernist personal narrative, which represents Francis's point of view. Jürgen Kasten discusses the film in the context of romantic and neo-romantic horror literature. Dietrich Scheunemann argues in a similar vein that Kracauer's political interpretation obstructed a meaningful discussion of the function of the film's expressionism, and links the film with the *Doppelgänger* of Romanticist literature, who is abundant in German films between 1913 and 1927.

For David Robinson, the framing story remains decisive for the understanding of the film. He dismisses Fritz Lang's claim that he suggested the framing story after seeing the expressionist set designs by Walter Reimann, Walter Roehrig and Hermann Warm, because Warm introduced his sketches after Lang was replaced by Wiene. But it remains a mystery who wrote the framing story. In 1991, Quaresima discovered the contract between Mayer/Janowitz and Decla, dated 19 April 1919, which stipulated that the screenwriters sold their manuscript for 4,000 Reichsmark 'along with all the author and ownership rights'. Decla reserved the right to make 'changes in the manuscript that we might sooner or later find appropriate', and Mayer and Janowitz agreed to 'assist without honorarium' in these changes. Thus, Janowitz's concept of the screenplay as a 'straightjacket' for the director is not corroborated by the contract; it is even likely that Mayer and/or Janowitz 'assisted without honorarium' in the alteration of the frame story. There are handwritten pages in the original typescript of the screenplay, which must be changes of an original; strangely enough, nobody has yet tried to establish if these autographs can be attributed to Mayer and/or Janowitz. When these changes were made, the frame story in its original form was still intact. This indicates that the framing story was changed at a relatively late stage of production. However, since the opening and especially the closing framing sequences necessitated elaborate sets, it is unlikely that it was added while shooting was already under way. Mayer and Janowitz were pleased with the commercial success of *The Cabinet of Dr. Caligari* and were eager to participate financially. On 14 March 1922, they consented to a novelisation of the story as a *ciné-roman*, published the same year. This contract, also discovered by Quaresima, reveals that both screenwriters had not only agreed to the changes of their manuscript prior to the film's production but also sold the rights to a novelisation of the finished film's story. By signing this contract in 1922, they implied acceptance of the finished film with all its changes, including the frame story.

Thus, the academic debate offers a few possible explanations why *The Cabinet of Dr. Caligari* has been regarded as such a pivotal film for such a long time. The film draws on a number of central cultural motifs that inspired German literature and fine arts for at least two centuries: the 'uncanny', the *Doppelgänger*, extreme psychological states, the mind's subjectivity and anxieties. These motifs were carried over from romanticism to expressionism. Thus, not only did the expressionist stylisation of the sets make the film a central contribution to cinematic modernism, but the subject matter (and its narrative presentation) also reflected cultural expectations of post-World War II audiences. Screenings of the film during the last twenty-five years or so have usually been staged as cultural events, often accompanied by elaborate live music of various kinds, from quasi-symphonic to jazz and rock improvisations.

Furthermore, the framing story, regardless of who authored it and what its political meaning is, does play a crucial role for the interpretation of the film as a whole. If the Caligari of the frame story is sane, then Francis's insanity is beyond question. If Francis is insane in the frame story, then he must also be insane in the inner one, but this implies nothing definite about Caligari's sanity in the frame story. Furthermore, in the final shot of the film, when the iris closes in around Caligari's head, it focuses on his intense gaze into the camera. Immediately behind Caligari, clearly visible in deep focus, is the second psychiatrist, whom Caligari had attacked in the inner plot, presumably because he suspected him of usurping his position as director. Thus, it is not a clear-cut reversal according to which only Francis is insane. This last shot of the film stands outside of Francis's narration and could not be part of his fantasy. The suspicion it arouses refers back to the inner story, posing new questions about what is real and what is not. The film's intriguing ambiguity invites multiple interpretations and is highly involving. This even reflects one of the crucial points of the film as medium in general: as an art that manifests itself in shadow images, the question of the real and the imaginary is at its very core.

Wiene, even though he was a prominent filmmaker in his day, went down in film history as a 'one-hit wonder'. This perspective does not acknowledge his career in its entirety, spanning from 1912 until his death in 1938, nor does it recognise that he reached his professional climax not with *The Cabinet of Dr. Caligari*, but rather with his tenure as Austria's senior film director in the mid-1920s. Still, his 'masterpiece' remained a point of reference for Wiene throughout his career. In the 1930s, while living as an exile in Great Britain and France, he planned a sound film remake of *The Cabinet of Dr. Caligari*, which never materialised. A shooting script of this project survived at the Cinémathèque Française; it was probably written by Wiene himself. Interestingly, in the mid-1930s, when surrealism was beginning to be accepted by bourgeois audiences, Wiene envisioned surrealist devices for his remake. There were other surrealist films around at the time, to be sure. But Wiene was apparently planning to popularise surrealism with a commercial film, just as he had done with expressionism in the early Weimar period.

Uli Jung

REFERENCES

Anon. (1938) 'Zum Tode Robert Wienes', *Der Film*, 38.

Barlow, J. D. (1982) *German Expressionist Film*. Boston: Twayne.

Budd, M. (ed.) (1990) *The Cabinet of Dr Caligari: Texts, Contexts, Histories*. Brunswick, NJ: Rutgers University Press.

Cherchi Usai, P. and L. Codelli (eds) (1990) *Prima di Caligari: cinema tedesco, 1895–1920 / Before Caligari: German Cinema, 1895–1920*. Pordenone: Giovanni del Cinema Muto.

Eisner, L. (1969 [1955]) *The Haunted Screen: Expressionism in the German Cinema and the Influence of Max Reinhardt*. Trans. R. Greaves. Berkeley, CA: University of California Press.

Elsaesser, T. (1982) 'Social Mobility and the Fantastic: German Silent Film', *Wide Angle*, 5, 2, 14–25.

Janowitz, H. (1955) 'Caligari – The Story of a Famous Story', unpublished manuscript, New York Public Library, Theatre Collection.

Jung, U. and W. Schatzberg (1999) *Beyond Caligari: The Films of Robert Wiene*. New York and Oxford: Berghahn.

Kasten, J. (1990) *Der expressionistische Film*. Münster: MaKS.

Kracauer, S. (2004 [1947]) *From Caligari to Hitler: A Psychological History of the German Film*. Ed. . Quaresima. Princeton, NJ: Princeton University Press.

Kurtz, R. (1965 [1926]) *Expressionismus und Film*. Zürich: Rohr.

Minden, M. (1988) 'Politics and the Silent Cinema: *The Cabinet of Dr. Caligari* and *Battleship Potemkin*', in E. Timms and P. Collier (eds) *Visions and Blueprints: Avant-Garde Culture and Radical Politics in Early Twentieth-Century Europe*. Manchester: Manchester University Press, 287–306.

Quaresima, L. (1992) 'Expressionismus als Filmgattung', in U. Jung and W. Schatzberg (eds) *Filmkultur zur Zeit der Weimarer Republik*. München: Saur, 174–94.

_____ (1997) 'Wer war Alland?: Die Texte des Caligari', in B. Frankfurter (ed.) *Carl Mayer: Im Spiegelbild des Dr. Caligari – Der Kampf zwischen Licht und Dunkel*. Wien: Promedia, 99–118.

Prawer, S. S. (1995) 'Vom "Filmroman" zum Kinofilm', in H. Belach and H.-M. Bock (eds) *Das Cabinet des Dr. Caligari: Drehbuch von Carl Mayer und Hans Janowitz zu Robert Wienes Film von 1920*. München: edition text + kritik, 11–45.

Robinson, D. (1997) *Das Cabinet des Dr. Caligari*. London: British Film Institute.

Salt, B. (1979) 'From Caligari to Who?', *Sight and Sound*, 48, 2, 119–23.

Scheunemann, D. (2003) 'The Double, the Décor, and the Framing Device: Once More on Robert Wiene's *The Cabinet of Dr. Caligari*', in D. Scheunemann (ed.) (2003) *Expressionist Film: New Perspectives*. Rochester, NY: Camden, 125–56.

DER LETZTE MANN THE LAST LAUGH

F. W. MURNAU, GERMANY, 1924

F. W. Murnau is often thought of primarily as a filmmaker's filmmaker, one who, in the words of Robert Herlth, the set designer on several of his films, is characterised by 'tireless perfectionism, this uncompromising determination to attain a unique visual intensity'. But also central to Murnau's art is a deep interest in character, society, and intricate as well as, in the broad sense of the word, moral storytelling. I emphasise these concerns beyond formalism to suggest that Murnau's films be placed not so much in the realm of art for art's sake as in the realm of art for humanity's sake. This is particularly important when we consider *Der letzte Mann* (*The Last Laugh*, 1924), perhaps his greatest film, because here his formal and technical brilliance is integrated into a thoughtful analysis and deeply moving view of a representative person, family and society; of individual aging and social and economic deficiency and decay; and of our dream of being fully human and happy – unattainable goals through a combination of individual and institutional inadequacies.

The Last Laugh is intimately (but by no means simply) related to the time in which it was made, in the early part of the so-called Weimar period in Germany. The country was, to use the title of one of the films of the time, 'shattered' (*Scherben* [*Shattered*, 1921]). A large part of the male population was killed, maimed or traumatised by the war, and those who survived returned to a society verging on material and psychic collapse. Traditional authorities, in government and business, had become largely discredited. Shortly after the war, scarcity of goods and economic instability were followed by an almost unimaginable hyperinflation and widespread unemployment. Everything and everyone seemed vulnerable, at risk, certainly in transition, often in eclipse.

Somewhat surprisingly, the film industry survived World War I in reasonably good shape, and was determined to regain and expand international markets as well as serve national markets and interests. Eric Pommer, the head of production at Ufa (Universal Film Aktien Gesellschaft) from 1923 to 1926, seemed increasingly attracted to projects that could embody multiple elements of the most successful films of the times: this included stylistically innovative and commercially as well as critically well-received films like *Das Cabinet des*

Dr. Caligari (*The Cabinet of Dr. Caligari*, 1919), and big-budget films with high production values, much visual spectacle and recognisable stars, such as *Madame Dubarry* (1921). One such composite project was *The Last Laugh*, and when Pommer assigned it to Murnau, he had high hopes for it and gave it extraordinary support: a large budget, a long shooting schedule (which ultimately stretched to 180 days), a writing and production team of highly skilled and experienced professionals, and a cast that included one of the most well-known German actors, Emil Jannings. And perhaps equally important, he placed his trust in Murnau, and set him free, urging him and his co-workers, in a now-famous phrase, to 'please invent something new, even if it's crazy!'

Murnau did indeed shape *The Last Laugh* out of unconventional and 'crazy' materials and techniques: repeated use of the '*entfesselte Kamera*', the 'unchained camera' moving freely through space conveying a sense that the world is alternately exhilarating and frighteningly unstable; stylised acting of Jannings as he devolves from a stiffly proud to a nervous and barely upright broken man; and often bizarre and startling images, of such things as horns that blare out powerfully even in a silent film and multiple eyes of women that haunt and humiliate the central character. But before we look closely at some of the key moments of the film and the details of plot and technique, I want to first give a sense of the whole that these parts contribute to, which involves a brief consideration of Murnau's general idea of cinema as well as the overall structure of *The Last Laugh*.

Jo Leslie Collier rightly links Murnau to Wagner as artists who strove to create a *Gesamtkunstwerk*, a 'total' art form drawing from a wide range of resources and unifying them into a new synthesis far more powerful than the sum of the individual parts. Murnau constructed his *Gesamtkunstwerk* in several ways. He envisioned film as an incorporative art, and in *The Last Laugh* drew on not only the resources of cinema but also art history, architecture, engineering and mechanics, theatre, literature and music. Murnau has a reputation as one of the great *auteurs*, whose films reflect a consistent and distinctive personal vision and were shaped by his directorial force, but *The Last Laugh* is to a large extent an ensemble creation, embodying not only the talents of Murnau but also, among others: Carl Mayer, the scriptwriter; Robert Herlth and Walter Röhrig, the set designers; Karl Freund, the cinematographer; and Emil Jannings, the lead actor.

The Last Laugh is a *Gesamtkunstwerk* in another intriguing way: it includes elements from a wide range of cinematic genres and styles. It is perhaps most noticeably a *Kammerspielfilm*, the cinematic equivalent of a chamber play often associated particularly with scripts written by Carl Mayer, focusing primarily on a small group of lower-class characters in a domestic setting undergoing a tremendous amount of stress and normally ending unhappily. But it is also a *Grossfilm*, a large-budget, star vehicle with broad historical, even epic intentions (Jannings' character is both an insignificant door attendant and a nearly mythological image of Old Man, and perhaps Old Germany). While it is in many respects a character-centered film, the main character is not always an individual human: much of *The Last Laugh* is structured like a *Strassenfilm* (for example, *Die Straße* [*The Street*, 1923]), in which the street is not only a recurrent setting but also a metaphoric representation of a life of misery, oppression and strain; and parts of it are also closely akin to the so-called city film (such as *Berlin – Sinfonie der Großstadt* [*Berlin – Symphony of a Big City*, 1927]), a genre that blended sociological analysis with innovative editing and special effects to portray a city as not only a place but an animated life-form.

The style of *The Last Laugh* is often naturalistic, characterised by the kind of precise observation of physical details associated with the artistic and cinematic movement called *Die Neue Sachlichkeit* ('The New Objectivity'). But this is counterpointed by recurrent use of Expressionist elements that lift us out of the 'real' world into one that is nightmarishly unstable and threatening. Further counterpointing the film's realism are many striking elements drawn from the fairy tale, the romance and even the horror film, including magical wish-fulfilment, redemptive love and shocking confrontations with witches and monsters. This multi-generic approach to filmmaking helps Murnau create a richly textured work, one that, it is worth noting, might also appeal to a diversified audience. High art is not always incompatible with high concept.

Murnau blended all these elements into an intricately structured plot based on alternation, incremental repetition, and a final release that bursts out of the carefully established back and forth pattern that starts out promisingly but turns into a relentless downward spiral. There are two key locations for the action of the film: the main character's place of work, a large hotel in a bustling city; and his home. The *Gesellschaft*, the world of business, is shown to be a place of ambition, constant motion, competition and performance; one can thrive here, and it offers numerous enticements and rewards, but it is fundamentally an impersonal and dehumanising place. The *Gemeinschaft*, the realm of community and family, is the proverbial haven in a heartless world, perhaps restricted and provincial, but a place of intimacy, relaxation, mutuality and warmth. Murnau moves his main character between these two real and symbolic spaces, and paired sequences track his decline.

Broadly speaking, these sequences fall into three main acts and a coda. First, the doorman's success at work is matched by his comfort and high regard at home. Next, his extreme disappointment at work when he is demoted is compensated for by his joyous immersion in a family celebration. Finally, the full force of his demotion hits him at work and, in the most deeply ironic and painful section of the film, when he returns home he experiences rejection and an intensification of, rather than respite from, his shame. He returns to his workplace to sink out of sight and, presumably, to die a lonely death. But Murnau does not stop here: the final sequence is unexpectedly – and, according to most critics, unrealistically and illogically – 'happy', lifting the main character completely out of a life spent moving back and forth between work and home, both of which have turned out to be stifling and dehumanising environments. Murnau the sociologist of *Gesellschaft* and *Gemeinschaft* brings us to a climax of pain and bitter desolation; but Murnau the imaginative fabulist envisions a way out of an apparently unresolvable dilemma, and fashions a second ending that is artistically and politically radical, satisfying and instructive.

With the richly composite nature of the film and its dialectical structure in mind, we can now turn to a closer look at some of the details, beginning with its highly allusive title. 'Der letzte Mann' – 'The Last Man' (the title of the American release version was changed to 'The Last Laugh' – because in the same year there was already a film in circulation titled 'The Last Man' – but this too is a remarkably effective choice: it initially conveys a sense of foreboding – the happy times are apparently over – but also foreshadows the surprisingly comic ending, which literalises the popular saying that 'he who laughs last, laughs longest') – sounds somewhat ominous: it perhaps calls to mind the long literary tradition of apocalyptic works focusing on mankind withering away until only one person is left; and more immediately, it concentrates many of the fears of the postwar generation facing not only day-to-day concerns about survival but also crises of authority and masculinity. Man as well as mankind is in danger. From the very beginning we can have no doubt that some kind of fall is imminent, and, in fact, the first image of the film is one of descent, as the camera takes us down an elevator, across the hotel lobby, through a large revolving door and out into the bustling street. But the initial impression created by this opening sequence is one of exhilaration: Murnau thrusts the spectator into a setting that is vibrantly alive, and by the use of forced perspective and a stunningly effective combination of real and fabricated props, buildings and people, packs what seems to be an entire city, deep and wide, into one flat film frame.

Most highly visible in this setting is the doorman (like the other characters in the film, unnamed), quite the largest figure here because of his extravagantly decorated uniform, which establishes him as an icon, representing the hotel's claim to be a high-class establishment. (Ironically, we soon find out that he is replaceable in part because as a signifier he is ultimately insignificant: disposable, easily replaced by another 'sign'.) It is evident from the way that he carries and grooms himself that he is proud of his position, and he takes his responsibilities very seriously: when a hotel guest's large trunk is unattended for a moment, he immediately steps in and with great effort takes it down from the top of a car. This exhausts him, and it takes him a few minutes (and a quick drink) to recover before he can go back to work, but far greater damage has been done: he has been observed by the hotel manager in an apparent moment of weakness and dereliction of duty (he looks like an image of reclining weariness rather than an upright and imposing advertisement for the hotel). Before long, as the saying goes, the doorman is history: no longer a respected reminder of an imagined golden era, but a relic of an age gone by discarded by an unsentimental modern age.

This action is delayed, though. First we see him return home, still in all his glory. In this section of the film, Murnau presents a brief vignette of the charming and comforting life of a small community. The doorman is welcomed cheerfully and respectfully as he walks down the street and into his apartment, shared with an older woman identified as 'the aunt', and a young woman, identified as his niece. Children play in the alley, friendly women beat rugs and converse happily, and work slides easily into celebration: the niece is baking a large cake for her wedding. The street lights are turned off, the houses and their inhabitants sleep peacefully, and then all wake as the sun rises and another bright new day begins. Life is good.

But when the doorman ventures out again from this protected domestic world he faces an unexpected shock: he arrives at work only to confront a new doorman, fully uniformed, in his place. Murnau captures the unsettling horror of this moment by making it seem like the eruption of the monstrous and the uncanny in a gothic or expressionist tale when a man suddenly faces his double. The old doorman responds physically, first by recoiling, and then by slumping deeper and deeper, particularly as the architect of this frightening moment, the hotel manager, coldly explains that he has been relieved of his position because of his 'infirmity'. It is no consolation at all to know that he is being moved to another job in the hotel. First we see that he is being moved to a space created at the expense of one of his fellow workers, a pathetic old codger shown in an inserted shot, let go completely from the hotel and moved to a rest home. Then we see exactly what this change in position entails for the doorman: a stripping off of his uniform, shown in agonising detail, and then a literal and symbolic journey downward, to his new place in the bowels of the hotel as a washroom attendant. The uniform is a complex image, signaling the doorman's vanity as well as dignity, but the scene in which he is disrobed – an action presided over by the first of a series of intimidating, even monstrous women in the film – is a deeply disturbing ceremony of humiliation that conveys the painful inevitability of aging, the pathos of historical transition (the 'new' not only replaces but crushes the 'old'), and the inhuman logic of modernity and bureaucratic capitalism. In moments like this (and there are others as well), *The Last Laugh* re-envisions Shakespeare's *King Lear* and takes on much of its tragic resonance.

The humiliation of the doorman initiates a marked change in the cinematic style of the film. There are more frequent insert shots, which disturb the linear orderliness and spatial continuity of the film, and there is an accelerating use of disorienting shots and special effects, highlighting the doorman's feelings of duress and alienation from the world. At the end of the workday, as he sneaks down a long corridor to steal back his uniform, the camera moves nervously and unsteadily, first with and then ahead of him, as if showing him both within and also observing the scene. Then, even more dramatically, after he takes back the uniform and runs away from the hotel, he pauses for a moment as the surrounding buildings seem to lean in on him ominously, visually conveying his sense that he lives in a hostile environment, and that his guilt and shame call forth inevitable punishment. (Collier focuses in detail on the Continental elements of Murnau's Romanticism, but this episode has a striking similarity to one of the key moments in British Romanticism, a pivotal 'spot of time' in Book I of *The Prelude*, where Wordsworth describes how after stealing a boat on a lake as a young boy he felt the surrounding mountains rise up and follow him accusingly.) Sadly, there is much more of this to come in *The Last Laugh*.

Murnau's special effects, though, are not used only to convey pain and judgement. When the doorman finally makes it home, dressed in his now-stolen uniform, he is, as always, welcomed warmly, and joins in the wedding celebration. He is almost completely rejuvenated by a combination of social companionship, drink and fantasy. Murnau gives a brief view of love, happiness and drunkenness from the outside – we see people embracing, smiling and staggering – but quickly turns to a variety of mobile point-of-view shots, unusual camera positions and distorted images to picture a world that is, for once, pleasantly reeling and unstable. This dream-like sequence is important for its affect – the doorman is happy and, like the camera, *entfesselt*, unchained – but also its content: he imagines himself back at work, but this time effortlessly lifting a trunk, to the applause of the patrons of the hotel.

The doorman's real return to work the next day, though, is anything but triumphant. Earlier his demotion was shown primarily as a spatial relocation, and even this was extremely painful; but now Murnau dwells on the specific indignities of this move, particularly the condescending way he is treated and his isolation from meaningful human contact. Patrons avoid looking at him and repay his careful attention to them with a trifling tip before they return to their gaiety and sumptuous dining upstairs, shown in all its splendor in Griffith-like intercut shots that are in stark contrast to the doorman alone with his poor bowl of soup in the toilet, as if excreted from and by high society. There is not only contrast and pathos but also insinuation and implicit judgement in these paired images: for any right-thinking observer, the coexistence of luxury and abject misery and poverty should shame the rich and underscore their selfishness and social irresponsibility.

Ironically, though, it is the doorman who is shamed, which completes the assault on his self, begun by his demotion and the loss of his uniform. The aunt comes to the hotel to bring him lunch, and after a suspenseful and mysterious search finally discovers him in his new role. Murnau structures this moment as a revelation of the monstrous, and the aunt runs back home shrieking. The doorman is even further broken and demoralised by this experience, and when he leaves work later in the day he moves through the streets as though in a trance. What awaits him at home, though, is not comfort but torture. The aunt has spread the news of the doorman's humiliation to a network of gossiping women, and Murnau uses some of his most powerful expressionist effects – multiple images of women forming a laughing chorus of contemptuous disapproval, extreme close-ups of their grotesque, mocking faces, and superimposed images of a cluster of eyes forming a frighteningly perfect emblem of a punishing gaze – to visualise his experience of shame. Even his immediate family shuns him, and he retreats, thoroughly dazed and demoralised, from his home back to work. The historical reference point for the doorman's shame may well be the nation's defeat in the war and the devastating terms of surrender enforced by the Atlantic alliance perhaps alluded to in the name of the hotel in the film. But Murnau's analysis of the origin and dynamics of shame goes far beyond this almost obvious topicality, and he insightfully exposes a long-standing social and familial culture of injustice and humiliation that cannot be blamed on foreign influences.

With nowhere else to go, the doorman returns to the hotel as his final resting place. On his final journey down to the washroom, he passes a night watchman, who in a touching irony is not a stern surveillance agent but rather a kindred spirit who comforts the doorman and covers him with his coat. Despite all the warmth and compassion of this final gesture, it is also funereal, and the doorman sinks motionless into a chair, near death as a result of natural and, as we have seen, unnatural causes.

The film, though, does not close here, as it perhaps should if it were to be truly honest and realistic about life as it is. An intertitle (a device that Murnau consciously avoided as much as possible elsewhere in *The Last Laugh*, opting for purely visual storytelling) reveals that the film's author too is sympathetic to the 'abandoned' doorman, and 'gives him an epilogue as a present, telling a story that usually doesn't occur in life – unfortunately'. What follows is a prolonged sequence of laughter, raucous and enjoyable rather than punishing, in response to a kind of cosmic joke: a millionaire has left all his money to the 'last man' with him at the time of his death, and in a dramatic revelation in the film that is, for once, not horrifying but miraculously wonderful, we see that this lucky last man is indeed our doorman, now dressed in a magnificent suit, seated at a table overflowing with food, waited on by the entire staff and accepted approvingly by everyone in the restaurant, including the hotel manager.

Despite all appearances, the doorman has only superficially become one of the happy and successful members of high society. In fact, everything he is and does shows that he subverts and transcends rather than joins or imitates them: he becomes not a rich man but a poor man with money and power. The ending of the film, in its spirit and its details, is carnivalesque, overturning the dour and oppressive conventions and conditions of everyday life, and envisioning a comic rather than tragically apocalyptic way that the last can become the first. The excess of the newly risen man's meal is not a sign of selfish over-indulgence or the conspicuous consumption of the elite but a celebration of the life of the body, and not only the individual but also the corporate body. He gets more pleasure sharing the meal with his guest, the night watchman, than he does eating alone. And during a break in the meal, he enforces 'justice' in the washroom, where he insures that the old man who now holds his former position is treated generously and fairly – and lovingly. In a spontaneous gesture, he suddenly kisses and caresses him. Finally, after the meal is over, he goes through an elaborate ceremony of giving money to the entire wait staff, and ends by blowing his whistle to summon his carriage, indicating that he is still and always will be the doorman.

Much of the ending takes on the form of a homoerotic fantasy, which – particularly given strong evidence of Murnau's own homosexuality – we should perhaps take both literally and figuratively. The lighting and smoking of cigars in the men's room is an obvious, and perhaps comically self-conscious image of male love-making. The night watchman is the doorman's date or partner, symbolised not only by the warmth with which he greets him but by the rose he places on his dinner plate before he arrives. And as the two men leave together, they are joined by a third man, perhaps suggesting the possibilities of a new form of interpersonal relationship beyond the couple or a new kind of family unit beyond the conventional mother-father-child configuration. Women are conspicuously absent. But I think that overall Murnau is less interested in prescribing specific (and exclusively homosexual or even homosocial) forms of behaviour than leaving us with a powerful dramatisation of a successful transcendence of the dehumanising relationships at work and home that dominate the first part of the film.

Critics often accuse Murnau of bowing to studio pressure and retreating to conventionality by adding a clichéd happy ending to *The Last Laugh*, but in almost all ways the ending is anything but conventional. The well-to-do patrons in the epilogue – perhaps like the viewers of the film – are amused and even somewhat puzzled by the curious spectacle that they witness, perhaps not fully aware that it is an enactment of ideals that once did and may yet again turn the world upside down: liberty, equality and fraternity. Murnau's carefully elaborated vision of the last man having the last laugh may not be 'realistic', but it is both a consoling and a sustaining fantasy, and an inspiring blueprint for what one may hope will be some not-too-distant future reality.

Sidney Gottlieb

REFERENCE

Collier, J. L. (1988) *From Wagner to Murnau: The Transposition of Romanticism from Stage to Screen*. Ann Arbor, MI: UMI Research Press.

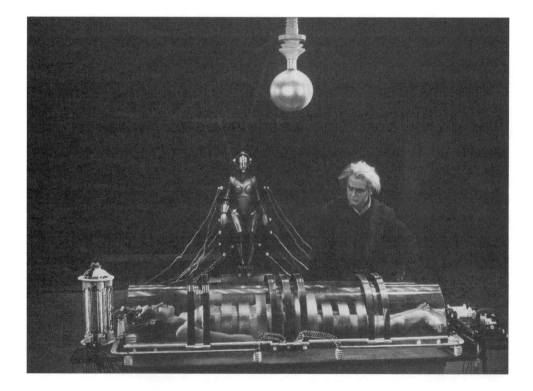

METROPOLIS

FRITZ LANG, GERMANY, 1926

Metropolis (1926) remains the albatross around Fritz Lang's neck, condemned, or at least partially condemned, by critics and filmmakers (including, at points, Lang himself). Since its first release, every generation seems to have found a new reason to be suspicious of this film, whether for its naïve romanticism about solving the problems of technology; its harbouring of – if not sympathies for – a susceptibility to Nazi ideologies; or its blatant gender stereotyping. While all these attacks hold some truth, what is hard to explain is why this rancour against *Metropolis* continues to be renewed. An even greater enigma in need of explanation is not the controversy the film inspires, but the development of its popularity. *Metropolis* ranked fourth in Germany's box-office listings for the 1927/28 season, but it was not an international success at the time. However, since the 1980s, it is constantly cited in international pop culture (Madonna's video *Express Yourself*; a London musical; the film *The Bodyguard*) as well as in highly regarded cultural sources (Rotwang's mechanical hand on *Dr. Strangelove*; the machine room explosion in Philip Glass and Robert Wilson's *Einstein on the Beach*; the references in Pynchon's *Gravity's Rainbow*).

Metropolis has remained a topic of heated discussion since its release, but its reception has hardly been stable and its current popularity cannot be attributed simply to the electro-pop makeover for its re-release by Giorgio Moroder in 1984. The very element that caused most critics to abjure it – the naïve resolution of the heart mediating between head and hand – was offered as the final words of wisdom in Madonna's *Express Yourself* video. I would claim that *Metropolis* was received as a postmodernist work in the 1980s. A new sensibility embraced its blend of kitsch and monumentality, mechanical sexuality and over-the-top melodrama, and powerful political critique matched by cartoon solutions, all conveyed through its exquisite sets and masterful visual style. In a postmodernist context, *Metropolis*'s contradictions could be seen not as an inherent flaw, but as the sign of a work divided against itself. Its schizoid nature found a home in the 1980s, on a level of appropriation, if not of critical evaluation, and its overt employment of allegory was intuitively – if rarely articulately – embraced by audiences and artists. Just as Walter Benjamin, writing his book on the baroque *Trauerspiel* in

Weimar Germany, felt that this seemingly archaic form held the key to the contemporary use of allegory in Expressionist art, I think the embrace of the allegorical in the postmodern has facilitated the contemporary revival of Weimar art and cinema.

Metropolis was Lang and Ufa's super-film, the most elaborate and expensive film made in Germany to that date and one which was to crown Germany's challenge to Hollywood as an international maker of films. However, *Metropolis* so overspent its budget that it drove Ufa into the red, and the mixed reviews *Metropolis* received at its opening led to the cutting of the film for its international release and for its secondary release in Germany. I will discuss Thea von Harbou's source novel in some depth, since it reflects much of the original design of the film.

An allegory can be defined as a text that uses tropes by grouping them into larger figures that regulate the whole text. If Benjamin's *Origin of German Tragic Drama* supplies the treatment of allegory both most contemporary and most revelatory for Lang's silent films, the most thorough contemporary study of the forms of the mode is Angus Fletcher's *Allegory: The Theory of a Symbolic Mode*. In *Metropolis* allegory, as well as the theme of the mechanical, lies on the surface, with the science fiction genre serving simply as the modern genre most attuned to the allegorical mode. Harbou makes clear in the epigram to her novel version of *Metropolis* that her tale is not intended as a simple prognostication of the future, but as a figural commentary on the present: 'This book is not of today or of the future. It tells of no place. […] It has a moral grown on the pillar of understanding.' It is important to remember that modern critical commentary on allegory began as condemnation. Samuel Taylor Coleridge perhaps said it most clearly, in 1816, when he translated the opposition between allegory and symbol into the conflict between the mechanical and the organic. Whether realist or romantic, nearly all of nineteenth-century aesthetics aligns itself with the organic form as opposed to the mechanical. In contrast, silent cinema – the 'art of the machine' – understood its affinity to allegory, and Lang perhaps more strongly than any other director.

Metropolis is the allegory of the future as the triumph of the machine. And the machine in a variety of manifestations becomes the central allegorical figure of the film. Freder in his vision sees the central machine of the city transform itself into a demon, the cannibalistic, pedophagic god, Moloch. But in many ways even more central to the film's allegorical structure is the figure of the robot. Fletcher, in his attempt to explain allegory's determinedly non-psychological, non-realist and non-organic approach to characterisation, not only describes allegorical characters as demonic, as if each were possessed by a monomaniacal force, but even declares: 'The perfect allegorical agent is not a man possessed by a daemon, but a robot.'

The image of the robot dominates *Metropolis*, not only in the false Maria created by inventor Rotwang, but also in the physical behaviour of the workers. *Metropolis* stands, therefore, as the Lang film that is most blatantly allegorical. It is the over-explicit nature of this film that makes many viewers, trained to hunt out subterranean meanings and organic symbols, so uncomfortable. But if Lang and Harbou's allegory at points appears too obvious, the process of reading it reveals, as in Freder's vision, demonic energies that pulse beneath the tropes and subvert any final comfortable interpretation.

Every allegory, and certainly every modern allegory, foregrounds the act of reading and even offers a lesson in how it should be read. *Metropolis* offers its lesson as instruction not only in the act of reading allegorical figures, but also in the specifically cinematic creation of tropes. The tutor text for this mode is revealed appropriately as a story within a story and as a visual parable: the story of the Tower of Babel. The selection of this particular Biblical text for visual translation and ideological re-interpretation marks *Metropolis*'s culmination of the millennial ambitions of the silent film. As Fritz Lang put it: 'The internationalism of filmic language will become the strongest instrument available for the mutual understanding of peoples, who otherwise have such difficulty understanding each other in all too many languages.' But as Miriam Hansen says, 'the Tower of Babel stands not only for the project of a universal language but also for its opposite, the impossibility of such a project'. Harbou and Lang's retelling of the Tower of Babel parable involves, as do all of the film's numerous Biblical references, not a pietistic reference but an allegorical refashioning of the original meaning.

Maria tells the tale of the Tower of Babel to the workers of Metropolis deep within the catacombs in the depths of the city. It functions primarily as a political parable about class and power divisions, introducing one of the oldest tropes in the history of allegory, the city-state as a human body, with workers conceived as 'hands' and planners as 'brains'. Rather than descending as divine punishment, the confusion in languages derives from a primal division in labour. Harbou's novel glosses this confusion in communication as a breakdown of the primal word 'Babel' into opposed meanings for each class: '"Babel!" shouted one, meaning: Divinity, Coronation, Eternal Triumph! "Babel!" shouted the other, meaning: Hell, Slavery, Eternal Damnation!' However, the limits of Harbou's political insight are also naturalised by her allegory: the division of labour is not questioned, nor are the power relations inherent in it revealed. The only problem is one of communication.

Many of these allegorical figures were commonplaces of Weimar culture. Harbou most probably adopted this image, as well as many others in the film, from Oswald Spengler, who had declared, 'the center of this artificial and complicated realm of the Machine is the organiser and manager. The mind, not the hand holds it together.' The portrayal of the natural masters of society as architects, planners or engineers occurs both in Weimar science fiction and in the 'reactionary modernism' of Weimar's right-wing engineers themselves. As Siegfried Kracauer commented, discussing the final scene of *Metropolis*, where the heart is proposed as mediator between brain and hand, '[Goebbels], too, appealed to the heart – in the interest of totalitarian propaganda'.

Although parsing the reactionary and progressive elements in *Metropolis* between Lang and Harbou seems to me suspicious (and possibly sexist), the articulated moral of the film seems to lag behind the play of figural language. If, generally, Lang can be held responsible for the visualisation of the film text, Harbou's mastery of allegorical figures within her novel shows a figural imagination that certainly inspired the film's visual style. At the same time, examples such as the visualisation of the Babel sequence in the film, although its basic figures derive from the parable as told in Harbou's novel, serve as a demonstration of the visual tropes at the command of a filmmaker as articulate as Lang (for example, the social hierarchy represented by the staircase, the columns of workers arranged like the five fingers of a hand, the image of the ruined tower). Visual emblems in *Metropolis* operate less as inert translations of a verbal moral than as a site for the play of opposed energies, or as Fletcher puts it, daemons.

If allegory employs demonic energies in explosive situations, what holds it together? For Fletcher containment comes from a specific type of allegorical figure that subordinates other figures into the central trope. He calls this central figure the *kosmos*. Fletcher uses this term for its two meanings, one familiar, the other forgotten: first a universe, and second, an adornment which reveals the wearer's rank within a hierarchy. In *Metropolis*, the *kosmos* is the city of Metropolis itself, which takes its spatial order from the Tower of Babel (in Harbou's novel the main building in which Joh Frederson has his offices is even called 'the New Tower of Babel'). The first third of the film basically traces and explores (and re-explores) the various hierarchical layers and levels. The prologue introduces the machines and the workers' lives, which are contrasted with the pleasure gardens of the rulers, including Freder, son of Joh Frederson, the Master of Metropolis. The hierarchy is disturbed when the pleasure gardens are invaded by Maria with a gaggle of urchins from the lower slums of Metropolis, who demands that Freder recognise the children as his 'brothers'. Freder's two voyages into the depths of his city (in one he dons worker's clothes) discover layers he had not known of before and raise new questions about who wields power in Metropolis.

Insufficient attention has been paid to the role of the clash between the gothic and the modern in this film, which often displaces the more manifest conflict between classes. While Lang indicated that he eliminated much of the gothic imagery from the film, plenty remains, radiating from two centres: Maria and the medieval Christian imagery associated with her, and Rotwang who drags along with him a whole baggage of medieval magic and demonic images. One can undoubtedly see the influence of Spengler's sweeping theory of history here, with its description of Western man as 'Faustian' and the impulses toward mastery of nature through the machine as having its roots in the 'gothic'. Metropolis is not simply a new modern city but a palimpsest whose layers contain the traces of previous belief systems (like the layers of ancient Rome that Sigmund Freud invokes as an image of the way the past persists in the unconscious). Lang makes it clear that these repressed layers are only slumbering and can be called back into life. The future as a return to the repressed and forbidden energies of the past – this constitutes one of *Metropolis*'s allegories of modernity.

American journalists had christened Thomas Edison 'The Wizard of Menlo Park', and Villiers de l'Isle Adam literalised this in his portrayal of Edison in *L'Eve Futur*, his symbolist novel of the creation of a female robot that greatly influenced Harbou. The ultimate sequence of gothic modernism takes place when Rotwang creates the film's synthesis of the energies of magic and technology, false Maria, the robot. This justly famous sequence employs all the spectacular resources of modern technology to produce the image of scientist as wizard. But, for all its heavy equipment, the means by which the robot is created remains mysterious: imagistic and metaphoric rather than technological. Raymond Bellour, in fact, describes the sequence as a whole as a reflection of the cinematic medium, 'the actual process of substituting a simulacrum for a living being directly replicates the camera's power to reproduce automatically the reality it confronts'. In *Metropolis*, Lang and Harbou bring the allegorical language of silent film to an end, bringing it to a climax and staking its high-water mark from which, in the years remaining to it, it can only recede. The mechanically driven figures of allegory in *Metropolis* confront and parody any attempt to revitalise the symbols of religion and magic and thereby tip the film into a sustained vision of the apocalypse.

Metropolis continues to produce visionary scenes of a more and more ambiguous nature and Freder becomes increasingly undone by them. When Freder sees the deceptive scene of (what he takes to be) Maria in his father's arms, quite simply, he freaks. The next ten minutes or so of the film are so bizarre, so fully loaded in their visual rhetoric, so complex and even contradictory that no analysis could ever exhaust them. But if we follow the thread of an alle-

gory-machine gone wild, spewing out a torrent of filmic rhetoric, we can follow its progression to the film's final apocalypse and its perverse destruction and reconstruction of its saviour
hero. The first hallucination sequence demonstrates Lang's alliance with the avant-garde of the
late 1920s, the 'pure film' montage experiments and the animation of Walter Ruttmann and
others.

Freder's attempt to bring his message of salvation up from the underworld here encounters its strongest check, a descent into madness, an almost classically Freudian nightmare
of Oedipal terror. The quick succession of close-ups at the centre of the sequence not only
provides a riddling answer to Freder's own disbelief at seeing his beloved in his father's
arms, but also addresses the central question of the film: who truly rules Metropolis? Freder,
however, cannot read or decode the message. The riddle of creation also proposes a succession
of 'masters' (and a mistress) of Metropolis: Joh, the robot, Rotwang, Death. But Freder does
not understand his vision and this leads to his complete regression. Cuts in the current version
of the film have obscured the back-story, but the primal forces are still very clear. Harbou
works as creatively with her Freudian themes as she does with the Biblical material.

In relation to the Christ myth Maria primarily plays the role of John the Baptist, the
forerunner of Christ. But her name and her association with virgin purity also align her with
the mother of God. But if the hero's romance demands the love for, and rescue of, a pure
maiden, Maria cannot be Freder's mother, without creating a scandal. But if the plot avoids
literally acting out this regressive Oedipal fantasy, Harbou constantly throws it back in our
face, and most obviously in this (primal) scene. What is this trauma-producing moment, as
Roger Dadoun was perhaps the first to point out, but Freder rushing into his parents' bedroom
to witness the primal act of darkness? The novel makes explicit Freder's longing for a mother,
more precisely for Hel, his biological mother who dies bringing him into the world. Maria
appears as the explicit reflection of this lost mother throughout the book. This dead mother
also broods over the creation of the robot. Hel was the wife of Rotwang; she was taken from
him by Joh Frederson, and the two men hate each other for this reason. At the film's climax
Rotwang has gone mad and believes Maria actually to be Hel and climbs the cathedral with
her in tow.

Joh (the invented first name intended to recall the God of the Old Testament) Frederson
corresponds to one Gnostic view of the Old Testament God as learning the lesson of compassion through his son's sacrifice. The film makes Freder's crucifixion explicit in his martyrdom
on the dial wheel of the machine room (crying out to his father), and Harbou in the novel lays

on Christ references with a trowel. But Freder's mission of salvation must also be an Oedipal revolt against his father, as his hallucination sequence makes clear. The need to reconcile Freder with his father, as well as the masters with the workers, strains Harbou's mythopoiesis to breaking point. The scenes of resolution and reconciliation remain unsatisfying partly because Harbou does not truly seem capable of thinking through (or accepting) any of the scenarios offered by her material.

Instead, imagery of breakdown and chaos dominate: the allegorical vision of Lang and Harbou remains an apocalyptic one, dominated by the figure of castration rather than identification with the father, Death rather than resurrection, capitulation rather than revolution. In the penultimate image of the delirium, Death is shown in front of the cathedral, his scythe in his hands, swinging the blade as he moves forward, swiping at the camera. The image of the Grim Reaper, the gothic image of death, derives partly from the reaping angels described in 'Revelations' harvesting the souls of the world. But his accoutrements, the hourglass and the scythe, also derive from a classical reference, the god Kronos, the Greek god of time, and father of Zeus. Kronos in Hesiod's *Theogony* castrates his father Uranos with a sickle given him by his mother. He in turn devours his own children until killed by Zeus. Beautifully, Lang images Death's attack as an attack on the film image itself: a huge arcing scratch appears over the image of Freder. The Freudian primal scene is the origin of castration anxiety. Behind the two extreme faces power assumes in this city of modernity – the rationalised image of the clock face and the devouring maw of the monster (both images associated with Kronos) – stands a figure of primal terror – lack and castration itself, and a desire for the absolute wiping clear of all representation, the scratching away of the film's emulsion, the desire not only for death but for the end of everything – apocalypse. One can no more read Freder's dream simply as an Oedipal fantasy and leave it at that, than decode its mythic references and ignore the psychoanalytical references.

The final third of this film chronicles the destruction of the city of Metropolis primarily by forces unleashed by the robotic Maria, and therefore with the collusion of Joh Frederson, and Rotwang. As almost all viewers have noticed, Joh Frederson's action seems to be lacking a motive (in fact the supplier of the English-language intertitles felt compelled to manufacture one not present in the English-language version, describing Frederson's desire to eliminate the workers and replace them with robots). In her novel Harbou responds theologically rather than psychologically to this lack with an allegorical scene in which Freder begs his father to save the city, but Joh Frederson declares it is his will that the city must be destroyed so that Freder can build it up again and redeem its inhabitants. Whether or not this scene was ever part of the original film, it still remains inconclusive. The motiveless destruction of Metropolis may reflect Lang's own vision, an attitude found in accounts of Lang's own titanic efforts during the film's production, as well as in the Tower of Babel parable: an unparalleled energy of creation matched by an equally powerful nihilism, a desire to smash creation into shards.

Although on one level the film can be seen as a reactionary, cautionary tale about the destructive power of workers' revolt, the film actually displaces its political discussion of power into a nihilistic denunciation of the world, expressing the melancholic world-denying nihilism that Walter Benjamin associates with the allegorical mode. Here lies the film's power. However, the film backs away from its nihilistic vision and attempts to reinstall Freder as an action hero. Resolution comes quickly to this film, as if the business of tying up loose ends should be accomplished as soon as possible. Within a single reel we see: the rescue of Maria; the destruction of Rotwang; the burning away of the illusory flesh of the false Maria; the accession to manhood of Freder; the transformation of Joh Frederson; and the pacification of the workers. Finally, we get the staging of Harbou's motto: 'The mediator between brain and muscle must be the heart.' The hierarchical stairs with Freder, Joh and Maria at the top and the orderly geometrical pyramid of workers seems designed to reverse the powerful image of revolt in the Tower of Babel sequence. The workers are led by Grot, the foreman. Maria urges Freder to emerge from the corner he has withdrawn into. Freder takes the hands of Joh Frederson and Grot and pulls them together into the handshake that now ends all existent versions of the film.

Everyone hates this ending. I will not try to redeem it, but there are things worth pointing out about it. The aspects of super-legibility and artificiality reflect the allegorical mode, so it would be inconsistent to fault this sequence for them. More complex issues are raised, however, if we scrutinise the personifications performed for us. In Grot, the workers are represented by a management spy and informer. And the heart is the boss's son. Kracauer, determined to discover the contraband concealed within this tableau, gave it this interpretation decades ago: 'The whole composition denotes that the industrialist acknowledges the heart for the purpose of manipulating it; that he does not give up his power, but will expand it over a realm not yet annexed – the realm of the collective soul.'

Are we supposed to read this sequence this way? Can we argue for an authorial intention? Nothing in Harbou's novel indicates cynicism about her motto (but this scene of reconciliation is also absent from it – it ends with Joh's reunion with his estranged mother). The Tower of Babel sequence ends with an inscribed motto ('Great is Man'), which is belied by the imagery of ruin beneath it. But Lang, for all his discomfort with the ending of this film, never claimed he visually undercut it. Perhaps the discomfort the ending causes most viewers comes partly from the film itself, an underlying nihilism, which it cannot articulate explicitly. Or if this tableau of reconciliation is not to be read against the grain, then it perhaps should be read cynically, as the fulfilment of Joh Frederson's master plan, with the revolt operating within the total system of Metropolis. Anton Kaes has also proposed to me another approach: that *Metropolis* is conceived basically as a series of sensations, a film of disparate attractions rather than narrative integration, and that Lang simply didn't care that much about pulling it all together in a final satisfying coherence. The final tableaux would then be a cinematic equivalent of the Looney Tunes proclamation of closure – 'That's all Folks!' Harbou (or Lang) does not seem capable of a truly feminist critique any more than of a Marxist, Freudian or Christian resolution. Instead, we have a text whose allegorical energies seem unable to coalesce into a single grand narrative, but rather ceaselessly generated reference to nearly all the narratives – political, religious, occult, aesthetic, sexual – that circulated through Weimar culture. The energy in *Metropolis* becomes increasingly centrifugal, images escaping from the grand narratives to which they belong – and therein lies its appeal to postmodern sensibility.

Tom Gunning

AUTHOR'S NOTE: In 2008 Paul Felix-Didier, the resourceful director of the Buenos Aires Film Museum, confirmed a long held suspicion that a 16mm reduction negative of *Metropolis* in their collection was the 1928 Buenos Aires release version, including scenes cut from the version widely circulated after the film's premiere. This is the closest version to Lang's original final cut, with at least twenty more minutes and dozens of small details and editing changes. After painstaking examination and restoration, we now have one of the holy grails of film history: a very nearly complete version of Fritz Lang's original version of *Metropolis*.

This essay is an abridged version of the chapter on *Metropolis* from my book *The Films of Fritz Lang: Allegories of Vision and Modernity* (British Film Institute, 2000), cut due to restrictions of space in this anthology, and readers intrigued by its argument should seek out the full version in that volume. It was originally written before this rediscovery and restoration. However, the essay fits the film as now exists. Allegory remains a dominant force, even if the restored version gives a fuller sense of the action of the film, especially the rescue of the children from the flood, which supplies a stronger sense of continuity. Since 2000 the critical recuperation of *Metropolis*

has also proceeded; the general scorn of the film no longer dominates its critical reception. The adoption of *Metropolis* as a pop icon continues as well, with references popping up in music videos, performances and CD covers of Lady Gaga, Beyonce, Kylie Minogue and Janelle Monae (I thank Katharina Loew for these references).

REFERENCES

Bellour, R. (1986) 'Ideal Hadaly (on Villiers' *The Future Eve*)', *Camera Obscura*, 15, Fall, 110–35.

Benjamin, W. (1977 [1925]) *The Origin of German Tragic Drama*. Trans. J. Osborne. London: New Left Books.

Coleridge, S. T. (1972 [1816]) 'The Statesman's Manual', in *The Collected Works of Samuel Taylor Coleridge, vol. 6*. Ed. R. J. White. Princeton, NJ: Princeton University Press.

Dadoun, R. (1986) '*Metropolis*: Mother-City – "Mittler" – Hitler', *Camera Obscura*, 15, Fall, 136–63.

Fletcher, A. (1964) *Allegory: The Theory of a Symbolic Mode*. Ithaca, NY: Cornell University Press.

Hansen, M. (1991) *Babel and Babylon: Spectatorship in American Silent Film*. Cambridge, MA: Harvard University Press.

Harbou, T. von (1963 [1927]) *Metropolis*. New York: Ace Books.

Kracauer, S. (1947) *From Caligari to Hitler: A Psychological History of the German Film*. Princeton, NJ: Princeton University Press.

Lang, F. (1994 [1926]) 'The Future of the Feature Film in Germany', in A. Kaes, M. Jay and E. Dimendberg (eds) *The Weimar Republic Sourcebook*. Berkeley, CA: University of California Press, 622–3.

Spengler, O. (1928 [1922]) *The Decline of the West, vol. 2: Perspectives on World History*. Trans. C. F. Atkinson. New York: Knopf.

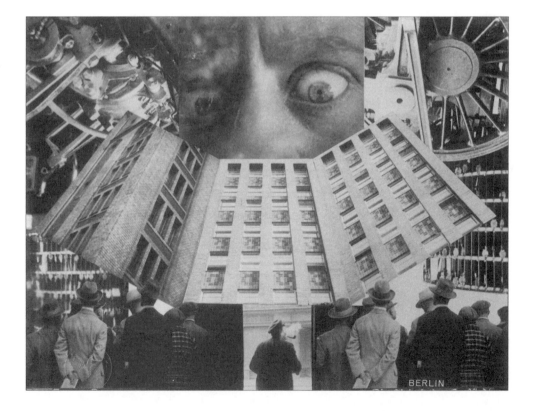

BERLIN – DIE SINFONIE DER GROSSTADT
BERLIN – SYMPHONY OF A BIG CITY

WALTER RUTTMANN, GERMANY, 1927

'No film has been more influential, more imitated.' When reading John Grierson's words quoted on the cover of a 1998 US video release (by KINO video) of *Berlin – Die Sinfonie der Großstadt* (*Berlin – Symphony of a Big City*, 1927), the reader might not realise that they were taken from a 1935 review that was not all favourable: 'Symphonies of cities have been sprouting ever since, each with its crescendo of dawn and coming-awake and workers' processions, its morning traffic and machinery, its lunchtime contrasts of rich and poor, its afternoon lull, its evening dénouement in sky-sign and night club. The model makes a good, if similar, movie.' In his famous earlier essay, 'The First Principles of Documentary', from 1932, Grierson had stated boldly: 'For all its ado of workmen and factories and swirl and swing of a great city, *Berlin* created nothing […]. I hold the symphony tradition of cinema for a danger and *Berlin* for the most dangerous of all film models to follow.'

Today, the film that brought fame to its director Walter Ruttmann is still one of the best known silent films and continues to influence students and filmmakers alike. It has been mentioned as a key influence in defining what is often labelled as 'MTV-style': the technique of fast cutting and use of candid material to match a rhythmic musical score. Even the reservations that Grierson held against the film proved to be productive: his objections helped define the ethics of British documentary filmmaking in the 1930s, which was committed to a social concern not found in the German film.

However, despite interest in the film still being so much alive, the misconceptions about its position towards filmic reality never faded away. In order to gain a better understanding, it is necessary to reconstruct the origins of this criticism as well as the film's contemporary context. The original version that passed censorship on 11 June 1927 seems to have survived in its entirety. According to information on the projection speed found in the published musical score by Edmund Meisel ('approximately 21 frames per second, not less then 20, not more than 22'), the original running time can be stated as approximately 61 minutes.

The film is divided into five movements by title cards. There are no other intertitles. Act 1 begins in a fast tempo, with moving water turning into abstract wave lines, which are then intercut with parallel lines that resemble railway tracks. The composer stated the tempo for this sequence as *Allegro*. Then a fast train is shown gliding through an early morning landscape. A sign reads 'Berlin 15km'. Tenement buildings and factory plants appear. The train arrives at Berlin Anhalter Station. This section lasts about five minutes. Act 2 (11.5 minutes) is dedicated to the morning hours and follows a much slower pace – *Andante*. A clock shows 5.00am. Empty streets come into view. Some of the shots last up to 45 seconds; they are the longest in the film. All in all the film is composed of 1,009 shots with an average length of only 3.7 seconds. (For comparison, Sergei Eisenstein's *Bronenosets Potyomkin* [*Battleship Potemkin*, 1925] has an even lower figure of 2.8 seconds.) Views of architecture with little or no movement are shown. Modern buildings are juxtaposed against older ones. The urban photography, dedicated to the common and unspectacular, is reminiscent of the work of Paul Strand. A remarkable shot of a paper bag being carried away by the wind adds some movement to an otherwise still street scene. The first people in the film appear: a guard with his dog, homecoming drunkards, patrolling policemen and a billposter. A locomotive engine leaves a garage, followed by shots of workers and clerks leaving their home for work. A two-minute sequence is composed of machines. More people are on their way now; children go to school.

Act 3 (*Allegro con fuoco*) begins with a clock showing 8.00am – opening hour for Berlin stores and workshops. The montage emphasises the differences of social groups without commenting on them. Shots of upper-middle-class employees beginning their office work are followed by images of the upper class riding in Grunewald. In a street, a man starts a fight stopped by the police. We see a ladies' shop, a couple getting married, Reichspräsident Hindenburg during a parade, while somewhere else a communist demonstration takes place. The Salvation Army collects money for the poor. A decorated funeral car heads for the cemetery; a beggar collects used cigarettes. After this 18.5-minute sequence, which is the longest of the film, the fourth movement – *Adagio* – begins. A clock shows noon. Lunch and coffee-break scenes are paired with a lion's meal in the Zoologischer Garten. The evening papers are printed. People gather and witness the suicide of a desperate woman, shown in close-up as she jumps from a bridge. The obvious staging of this scene contradicts one of the promises made in the premiere programme: 'No actors perform, but hundreds of thousands act.' At the end of this 12-minute sequence, a storm rises with heavy rainfall, as a fire brigade drives by at high speed.

Act 5 is dedicated to the evening and night hours: the 'finale' – *Allegro*. The working day has passed; machines stop one by one. The Berliners actively or passively participate in a variety of sports events. Others watch a Chaplin film (indicated only by a detail shot of his legs and feet). Actors and singers prepare for their stage performances. Curtains rise – the entertainment begins. Some workers are still busy repairing railway tracks. An elaborate shot of a packed bar, created with specially prepared film stock and special lighting, is followed by a revolving roulette wheel. In a great crescendo fireworks appear. Blinking lights from Berlin's landmark radio tower signal the end.

During its first European release, the film was presented with live performances of Edmund Meisel's original score. Since the score was conceived during shooting, it should be regarded as an integral part of the film. Meisel had won fame as the composer of the original score to the German version of *Battleship Potemkin* and the musical director at Erwin Piscator's theatre. He mixed industrial sounds with a symphony orchestra of 75 musicians, including a large percussion section. For smaller cinemas a version for a smaller orchestra or a piano extract were offered. In the beginning, wave-like music makes way for a memorable Leitmotif ('Berlin'), which is introduced as a distinctive choral in the brass sections. Slow chords accompany the sleeping city, and marches the work scenes. The heavy traffic at Potsdamer Platz set against a counterpoint to the city motif. The entire score is driven by pulsing rhythms developing to a crescendo. The traffic sounds and musical variations meet shortly before the finale in a powerful *fortissimo*. For the closing scenes the leitmotiv is repeated again. The composer positioned several musicians among the audience to create what he called a *Totalitätseindruck* ('an impression of totality').

Ironically, *Berlin – Symphony of a Big City* was not intended as a documentary film when it premiered in 1927. The term 'documentary' did not even exist – it was coined by Grierson in the essay quoted above. In the late 1920s in Germany, a theatrical non-fiction film was usually referred to as a *Kulturfilm* ('culture film'), a term for a certain type of educational short film, which for tax reasons remained a part of theatrical programming until the early 1980s. What Ruttmann and the production company Fox Europa had intended instead was a *Kunstfilm* ('art film') – though nevertheless an entertaining one aimed at a wide audience. 'A film should sell', Ruttmann wrote shortly before principal shooting began in July 1926. 'Meaning: It should not only please an elite community but many more people, hopefully everybody … We got accustomed to the belief that art is just for the educated few. But it [film] is art. Certainly not in all of its products, but it can be and will be art above all other things – not only because it speaks to everybody.'

The original advertising campaign did not announce *Berlin – Symphony of a Big City* as a documentary. Instead, it presented the film as a novel artistic experiment. A newspaper advertisement for the premiere at Berlin's Tauentzien-Palast read: 'A work was created that breaks with everything that film has ever shown. … There is no story, but there are numerous dramas to be found. … The powerful rhythm of work, the floating hymn of fancy, the desperate cry of misery and the thunder of paved streets – all of that was united in the Symphony of the Big City.'

In the past eight decades, the film has been widely discussed both as a pioneering effort in feature-length documentary filmmaking and as a key example of modernist avant-garde film. As the title suggests, the film presented itself as symphony, i.e. defined by the aesthetics of a classical musical structure. By referring to the high art form of concert music, the filmmakers ensured that their work would be regarded as a contribution to the contemporary German *Kunstfilm*-movement. This was no unconquered territory. Impressionistic montage-films composed of images of urban life had already been made by others (for example, *Manhatta*, 1921, directed by Paul Strand and Charles Sheeler; *Rien que les heures*, 1926, directed by Alberto Calvacanti).

As the newspaper sequence in the film suggests, the media industry played an important role in public life of the Weimar Republic. In 1928, 147 daily newspapers were published in the capital alone. *Berlin – Symphony of a Big City* was an opportunity to discuss the general status of film, especially in relation to the traditional arts. Noted critic Willy Haas of the leading trade paper *Film-Kurier* welcomed the departure from the 'actor's and director's cinema', but he also saw a 'danger of subjective capriciousness, of pictorial-musical impressionism'. Furthermore, he regarded the use of musical structures as inappropriate for film art: 'We do not want an adaptation of the possibilities of symphonic music, a Wagnerism in future cinema. Whatever will be: it will have to grow strictly and organically from the technology of cinematography. … In spite of that: it is the greatest, the most fundamentally important film-event for many years. How much of this must be credited to Carl Mayer, our only genuine film poet, cannot be determined.'

Mayer's role in the production has never been accurately reconstructed. According to producer Karl Freund, the film's 'only script was a single spoken question by Mayer: "Why don't you make a film about Berlin – without a story?"' Paul Rotha states: '[Mayer] disliked Ruttmann's inhuman handling of the idea and asked for his name to be removed from the credits.' If such a wish was expressed it was never fulfilled. On the contrary, Mayer's name was prominently featured in the advertising campaign. However, a detailed script provided by Ruttmann existed, even though in the experimental form of a set of cards, which were subject to ongoing rearrangement during the entire shooting and editing process, which lasted one year. In an article published under Mayer's name in the paper *B.Z.* ('Berliner Zeitung') four days after the premiere, the author calls the film 'a symphony of the real, orchestrated with the specific means of the cinema: movement, rhythm, shots and editing'.

Both Rotha and Siegfried Kracauer use Mayer's presumed unhappiness with the film to support their own judgement of the film as 'inhuman' in its depiction of life. Similarly, Jürgen Kasten, in his biography on Mayer, argues that the writer 'would have abandoned the hectic editing tempo and escapist cinematography. There are no such elements in any of the films to which he contributed.' Kasten concludes that the *B.Z.* article 'was probably not written by Mayer'. These efforts to defend a screenwriter's unwritten script against the final film may seem like a negligible curiosity. However, Mayer's name played an important part in marketing the film as an art film and gaining critical attention for the work of a little-known director.

Walter Ruttmann was a painter and graphic artist before he began experimenting with film. *Opus I* (1921), the first in a four part series, is regarded as the first abstract – or as he called it 'absolute' – film ever made. Ruttmann provided a dream sequence for Fritz Lang's epic production *Die Nibelungen – 1. Teil: Siegfried* (1924) and moving backgrounds for Lotte Reiniger's animation feature *Die Abenteuer des Prinzen Achmed* (*The Adventures of Prince Achmed*, 1926). Works following *Berlin – Symphony of a Big City* include the radio play *Weekend* (a sound montage without image executed on optical soundtrack), *Melodie der Welt* (*Melody of the World*, 1929; another feature-length montage film), *Feind im Blut* (1931; an educational feature on syphilis) and *Acciaio* (*Steel*, 1933; an Italian/German co-production). In 1934, Ruttmann's extensive work for Leni Riefenstahl's propaganda feature *Triumph des Willens* (*Triumph of the Will*, 1935) was cut in post-production. Ruttmann became head of the advertisement department at Ufa and directed several short films, including promotional films for the German war industry, such as *Deutsche Waffenschmieden* and *Deutsche Panzer* (both 1940). During his career Ruttmann maintained a concept of film as 'optical music' – but constantly adapted to the demands of technical innovations or commercial and ideological commitments. His later work can serve as a case study for discussing the involvement of avant-garde aesthetics in the national-socialist culture industry. In a short article published in May 1927, during the editing process of *Berlin – Symphony of a Big City*, Ruttmann gave a summary of his intentions with this film: '1. Consistent realisation of the musical-rhythmic demands of film. 2. Consistent avoidance of filmed theatre. 3. No staged scenes! ... Unnoticed filming resulted in a directness of expression. 4. Every action speaks for itself. That means: No intertitles!'

Ruttmann's artistic ambitions appear quite clear. But what motivated Fox Europa – a major American production company – to finance a German experimental film? This aspect received little attention, because the film was never credited as a US production. In 1927, distributors of foreign films were required to produce films in Germany as well. Fox had a special interest in German cinema, which at that time was noted for its technical and artistic innovations. The company had already employed director Friedrich Wilhelm Murnau and writer Carl Mayer for what was arguably to become the studio's most prestigious production, *Sunrise* (1927). Cinematographer Karl Freund was assigned as an executive producer of productions in Germany. The first film that Fox Europa produced in Berlin, *Die Abenteuer eines Zehnmarkscheins* (*Adventures of a Ten Mark Note*, 1926) resembled the later *Berlin – Symphony of a Big City*; it also dealt with an urban subject and contained montage editing as a major stylistic device. Based on a scenario by Béla Balázs, it showcased the aesthetic principles of *Neue Sachlichkeit* ('New Objectivity'). Assigning the leading role to an object – a small banknote – seems especially fitting. This style was of considerable influence in reshaping the design of both high art and popular artefacts, replacing the sinister, metaphysical worldview of Expressionism with nonchalance and straightforward facticism. A leading instrument in promoting the ideas of *Neue Sachlichkeit* was the magazine *Der Querschnitt*. Instantly, the term *Querschnittfilm* was coined by the press and later attached to *Berlin – Symphony of a Big City* as well. If audiences accepted a banknote in the lead, why not a city?

Producing art films not only matched the policies of William Fox's ambitious US company, which used profits from Tom Mix westerns to finance the artistic productions by famous directors such as John Ford, Howard Hawks and Frank Borzage. Julius Außenberg, general manager of the German Fox division, suggested another motivation for his involvement – patriotism: 'we created this film for the German audience who – due to its deep spiritual culture – is able to feel the cryptic depth that hides behind what seems banal and accidental in the surface world. … [O]ur German work should speak to the world of unbroken German power and untiring German diligence, which made Berlin a stronghold of work.' Indeed, considerable effort was put into the international release. Within one year, the film was shown in Austria, the United Kingdom, Czechoslovakia, France and Japan. But there was still another reason for this unusual commitment of a commercial company in promoting its product as an art film. In Germany, non-fiction films were not accepted as quota productions. It was essential that *Berlin – Symphony of a Big City* was categorised if not as an art film then at least as a work of fiction.

However, German officials did not share this opinion. The film was regarded as a *Kulturfilm*. They were not the only ones to think so. A number of film critics understood the film as a document of everyday life in Berlin. But as such, it was regarded as incomplete. Some aspects that were found missing were: the commercial activities of department stores and stock exchange, 'interior shots of the actual living conditions of the working class, in contrast to the twenty-room residences of the profiteers', and the suburbs and outskirts. Opinions were divided about Ruttmann's use of contrasting montage without taking sides on social issues. In his 1947 study, *From Caligari to Hitler*, Siegfried Kracauer concludes: 'Ruttmann's rhythmic "montage" is symptomatic of a withdrawal from basic decisions into ambiguous neutrality.'

Above all, one crucial item was found missing – Berliners. For this reason, Béla Bálazs regarded the film as a failure in both its artistic and documentary ambitions: 'the highly praised "film symphony" *Berlin* was with all its interesting qualities neither art nor even a popular success, and it did not even show reality. There is no reality without the humans, their emotions, moods, dreams.' But is the absence of the depiction of individuality reason enough to call the entire work inhuman? Indeed, the film shows more interest in portraying the outer appearance of modern city life than the inhabitants. The fascination with structures, semi-abstract patterns of movement and the organisation of time overlays the interest in the individual. Nevertheless, the film also has an equally clear ambition to represent the diversity of society. It can hardly be claimed that humans are shown as faceless members of a crowd, because the film assembles images of school children, Jewish citizens, a Christian couple getting married and so on. However, there is little spontaneity in these scenes – they rather give the impression of illustrating a pre-written 'want list'.

At the time of its making, the film was one of many attempts in German visual culture to represent modern-day life. Some of the most convincing examples appeared in photo-journalism. Ruttmann and Freund were well aware of these efforts. Their development of candid motion photography, by hiding the camera in cars or specially-built billboards, can be regarded as a response to the widespread use of Leica 35mm still photography. This small camera, which allowed the photographer to work unnoticed, was used and promoted by prominent photojournalists such as Erich Salomon and Paul Wolff. For promoting the finished film, the producers chose two outstanding photographers, Sasha Stone and Umbo, to provide special photomontages. By arranging various photographic and drawn images into dynamic compositions, these unconventional lobby cards aimed for a more appropriate representation of the film's artistic approach towards reality than the conventional still image could offer. In

1928, Ruttmann himself published two photomontages in *Uhu* magazine in a similar style on the Olympics. They may be all that is left of an announced second project for Fox Europa, titled *Sport*.

Though possibly inspired by photojournalism, the totalism of *Berlin – Symphony of a Big City* went far beyond the possibilities of printed news photography. The now famous efforts made by photographers in depicting modern-city life in the form of photo books were yet to follow (for example, by Albert Renger-Patzsch, Laszlo Willinger, Werner Gräff, Moi Ver, Paul Morand, Bill Brandt). It would not take long until other filmmakers presented more city symphonies that showcased the possibilities of montage cinema and candid cinematography. In 1929, the Soviet director Dziga Vertov celebrated the cinematic apparatus in *Chelovek s kino-apparatom* (*Man with a Movie Camera*). Again, documents of everyday life were assembled into an artistic composition, but this time the emphasis lay on the playfulness and artificiality of the individual filmmaker. In the same year, Vertov's brother, Mikhail Kaufman, directed *Wesnoy* (*Moscow*, 1927), a 'filmic poem' about Moscow in the springtime. John Grierson was proved correct in calling *Berlin – Symphony of a Big City* a successful model for shaping images of city life into a musically driven, feature-length montage film. The film and its maker should not be held responsible for what later became of their original ideas (for example, a disappointing remake, *Berlin – Symphony of a Big City*, 2002, directed by Thomas Schadt, even proved that the formula was not infallible). At the time of its original release, the film was groundbreaking in many ways. It developed new techniques of candid motion picture photography, while offering a formula to make them accessible to a broad audience. It was instrumental in launching experimental and documentary methods within the contexts of feature filmmaking. No lesser attention, however, should be given to the highly unusual success story, that a US major company produced a low-budget German avant-garde film and promoted it to worldwide recognition.

Daniel Kothenschulte

REFERENCES

Balázs, B. (1930) *Der Geist des Films*. Halle: Knapp.

Grierson, J. (1979) *Grierson on Documentary*. Ed. F. Hardy. London: Faber and Faber.

Kasten, J. (1994) *Carl Mayer: Filmpoet: Ein Drehbuchautor schreibt Filmgeschichte*. Berlin: Vistas.

Kracauer, S. (2004 [1927]) 'Wir schaffen's', *Frankfurter Zeitung*, 856, 17 November, in *Werke, vol. 6.1: Kleine Schriften zum Film 1921–1927*. Frankfurt am Main: Suhrkamp, 411–13.

_____ (1947) *From Caligari to Hitler: A Psychological History of the German Film*. London: Dennis Dobson.

Rotha, P. (1949) *The Film Till Now: A Survey of World Cinema, with an Additional Section by Richard Griffith*. Rev. ed. London: Vision.

DIE WEISSE HÖLLE VOM PIZ PALÜ
THE WHITE HELL OF PITZ PALU

ARNOLD FANCK AND G. W. PABST, GERMANY, 1929

Die weisse Hölle vom Piz Palü (*The White Hell of Pitz Palu*, 1929), produced by the German company Sokal and directed by Arnold Fanck and G. W. Pabst, was advertised by its Anglo-American distributor Universal Pictures as 'The greatest thriller of the screen!' when it was first shown in London on 10 June 1930. This version was synchronised with the music written by the experienced film composer Guiseppe Becce, while the original was released as a silent film with live music. The silent version premiered in Vienna on 11 October 1929 and was shown in Berlin on 15 November 1929. The first French screening followed shortly on 13 December 1929.

The film was an overnight success in Germany. More than 100,000 cinema-goers went to see the picture in the following four weeks in Berlin's Ufa-Palast am Zoo. The popularity of *The White Hell of Pitz Palu* is further confirmed by several contemporary film statistics. They chronicle that it was the second most successful film of the 1929/30 season, only surpassed by Fritz Lang's *Die Frau im Mond* (*Woman in the Moon*, 1929). The Ufa-Palast in Hamburg, at the time the largest cinema in Europe (2,667 seats), was inaugurated with this *Bergfilm* ('mountain film'). It also became an international box-office hit, and contemporary reviewers regarded it as one of the world's best films. In the USA it was shown under the title *Prisoners of the Mountain*. It was the first German film to which the huge New York cinema Roxy opened its doors. On account of the great success of the original, a re-edited sound version, which contained dubbed dialogue instead of intertitles, was released in Germany in 1935 and re-released in the 1960s, again to great success.

Only rarely is a popular film received equally well by critics. In his 1931 essay on Fanck, Béla Balázs describes the film's surprisingly broad acceptance across political factions, including writers from the communist *Rote Fahne* as well as the national-socialist *Völkischer Beobachter*. This positive response stands in contrast with film historians like Siegfried Kracauer, as this chapter will point out below. First, however, in view of these diverse judgments, the film itself requires analysis.

'The greatest thriller of the screen!' did indeed offer extraordinary suspense. The short prologue opens with breathtaking exhilaration as it presents the tragic past of Dr. Johannes Krafft (Gustav Diessl). Krafft (whose name is very close to the German word for 'strength'), laughing scornfully at the immensity of the alpine mountains, demonstrates his strength while holding a rope from which his wife Maria is suspended. In his overconfidence he ignores the power of nature and the danger of avalanches. But punishment for his arrogance is close: his wife is suddenly swept down a crevasse and to her death. Ten years later, another happy young couple arrive at the mountain hut 'Diavolezza' at Mount Bernina, situated south of St. Moritz and Pontresina. Maria (Leni Riefenstahl) and Hans (Ernst Petersen) are celebrating their engagement and receive a bottle of champagne from a passing aviator. The gaiety of the situation is disturbed by the entrance of Krafft, who has restlessly wandered, ghost-like, through the high mountains since the accident that took his wife. Maria's obvious attraction to this mysterious man completes the dramatic love-triangle. The next day, Krafft sets out to reach the summit of Piz Palü, followed by the jealous Hans, who resents both Maria's attraction to Krafft and his climbing skills. They are followed by Maria, who is drawn to both of them.

On the same day, a second crew of mountain climbers begins its ascent. This group of young Swiss students serves as both a subplot as well as a catalyst to the main plot, making the driving force ambition as well as jealousy. Both the suggested love-triangle and the rivalry with the inexperienced students are motives that jointly lead to the eventual catastrophe. During the ascent, Hans claims leadership of the trio's climb, despite his inexperience as a mountaineer. High up in the Alps, beneath the summit of Piz Palü, he slips, falls and is injured. Krafft then breaks his leg in an attempt to help him. Thus the trio are stuck in an icy altitude with no way of descending. They can see the students only a short distance below them, but the last hope of help seems dashed by a sudden avalanche that buries the students in its wake, plunging them into a crevasse. The trio have to spend several days and nights on a narrow mountain ledge, without food, and in a state of increasing despair. An impressive scene shows Krafft desperately sending signals for help with a lantern. Parallel to this struggle for survival, another subplot unfolds: a series of dramatic rescue attempts, all of which fail. Krafft decides to make an attempt to get help, at the cost of his own life, and is seen to disappear into the white hell below. Finally, the pilot of a light aircraft locates the small ledge in the rock face where Hans and Maria are stranded. The rescue team from the village succeeds in returning Hans and Maria to safety, but bitterness remains between them. The last shot shows the death of Krafft, buried in the ice that will be his coffin.

The plot of *The White Hell of Pitz Palu* develops with exceptional speed in the prologue's opening four minutes. The action scene is edited with remarkable swiftness; camera angles change nearly every second, demonstrating the power of the natural elements. In the sequences following the prologue, the plot undergoes a drastic retardation and change of atmosphere; instead of a dramatic adventure film, it becomes reminiscent of pastoral poetry, or romantic paintings of the Alps. The rocky and icy world of Piz Palü ('pale peak' in Rhaeto-Romanic) seems calm, innocent and peaceful, and the landscape of the Swiss Bernina massif is shown off to its best, in sunny weather. Like Adam and Eve, Hans and Maria exhibit a childish joy in their secluded paradise. The dramatic tension increases again, but the story unfolds slowly over the next thirty minutes.

Many contemporary reviewers criticised the film's length of 3,353 metres (127 minutes), particularly with respect to the treatment of the love affair in the first part of the film. The 1935 sound version was re-edited and shortened by 35 minutes (including the elimination of scenes with Kurt Gerron, following his flight from Nazi-Germany). On closer inspection, however, the dramaturgy skilfully develops suspense as well as symbolism. It is highly effective in resetting the narrative tension to a minimum in the (mountain) paradise with the conventional theme of a happy couple, then gradually (re-)building the tension towards its melodramatic climax, which is prefigured by the opening. The emotional development of the plot structure corresponds to the symbolic trajectory of mankind's innocence to its inevitable fall.

Throughout the film's history, reviewers have criticised the somewhat lacklustre construction of its storyline. Nonetheless, there was unanimity regarding the film's artistic achievements. It may well be that the plot, based on a screenplay by Fanck and Ladislaus Vajda, is neither fully engaging nor easily understandable at first viewing, especially given its religious metaphors of immutability and morality. The mountains do not simply serve as an attractive backdrop and romantic setting, as in the case of the popular German genre of the Bavarian and Tyrolean *Heimatfilm*. Instead, they become dangerous, ominous and threatening. Fanck turns the mountain into a principal player: literally the most powerful part in the film. Like a living character, the natural element changes its spirit, ranging from friendly to aggressive. But unlike the human protagonists, the mountains seem to be able to punish effectively. The simple moral principle that excessive pride precedes a fall is prefigured in the dramatic prologue and remains present throughout the story: the opposites of the power of nature and the weakness of the human who must surrender to the sheer might of the mountain, the true ruler of the world.

The co-director of *The White Hell of Pitz Palu* was none other than Georg Wilhelm Pabst, who had created milestones like *Die freudlose Gasse* (*The Joyless Street*, 1925), *Geheimnisse einer Seele* (*Secrets of a Soul*, 1926) and *Die Büchse der Pandora* (*Pandora's Box*, 1929). Pabst, the famous Austrian director of social realism, cooperated for the first (and also the last) time with Arnold Fanck, at the time the foremost director of nature documentaries. However, his most important contribution to Fanck's film was lending his name, as his actual input was comparatively small. He was in charge only of the indoor scenes shot in the Grunewald Studio, Berlin. The film derives its life not so much from these unspectacular sequences as from the documentary and semi-documentary scenes directed by Fanck.

Fanck's main stylistic device is repetition. One of the images frequently shown is that of icicles. They play an important role in linking the prologue with the rising tension and final catastrophe of the central plot. During the long wait for rescue, they constitute a visual metaphor for the inexorable passing of time and life-energy. Icicles are first shown when Krafft is sitting at the crevasse into which his wife has fallen, desperately waiting for help. The rhythm of ice-cold water drops falling and of his fingers drumming on his cheek are in unison. The monotonous, unrelenting rhythm drains Krafft's composure, almost to the point of madness. Later, icicles reflect Krafft's metaphorical impotence, reminding him of the death of his wife. At the end, icicles announce his death, when he finally finds redemption in the ice. Another recurring image shows the twisted caves with their many passageways. There are also numerous images of dark clouds, which foretell disaster; these images are reminiscent of Fanck's documentary *Das Wolkenphänomen in Majola* (*Cloud Phenomena of Majola*, 1924). Finally, there is the image of the summit of Piz Palü, shown in its majesty in the introduction. Fanck repeats the same take ten times to demonstrate the dangerous and foreboding nature of this towering peak. Over and over again Maria looks out of the window at the impressive massif, revealing the mountains as an unchanging constant unperturbed by human emotions such as ambition and desire.

The plot's weaknesses are more than made up for by stunning cinematography. It is without doubt the excellent lens work that gained the film so much attention and acclaim. There are extraordinary images of eerily beautiful landscapes, yawning abysses, frightening rock faces and imposing blizzards. Cameramen Sepp Allgeier, Hans Schneeberger and Richard Angst, as well as still photographer Hans Casparius, succeeded in capturing the inhospitable world of ice crystals reflecting light, snowflakes swirling around, and crevasses made of rock and ice. Casparius's stills were exhibited at the Berlin premiere and were praised by *Film-*

Kurier for their 'subtle impressionism' and 'high pictoreographic achievement'. Kracauer also praised the expressive, almost lyrical cinematography: 'As documents these films were incomparable achievements. Whoever saw them will remember the glittering white of glaciers against a sky dark in contrast, the magnificent play of clouds forming mountains above the mountains, the ice stalactites hanging down from roofs and windowsills of some small chalet, and inside crevasses, weird ice structures awakened to iridescent life by the torchlights of a nocturnal rescue party.'

The impressive visual achievement was heightened by aerial photography, used for the first time by Fanck. It portrayed modern technology in a highly symbolic shot: a light airplane high above the mountain peaks, demonstrating the triumph of mankind and technology over nature. This type of documentary shot was a rare stylistic device in silent cinema, particularly in the 1920s, when German films generally offered little more than the artificial world of studio decoration. Ernst Udet's aerial photography was surely an important factor for the enthusiastic reception the film received, especially in Germany, where Udet was well known. In World War I he had been a decorated fighter pilot and throughout the 1920s was regarded as a national hero. His participation in the film was heavily publicised. In Germany, billboards carried Udet's name as large as the film title itself. During shooting, Udet took on the double role of pilot and cameraman, and took great risks performing perilous aerial stunts close to the glacier. Not only Kracauer found Udet's 'daredevil flights' particularly memorable; the film's success motivated Udet to continue working with Fanck in his subsequent films, *Stürme über dem Montblanc* (*Avalanche*, 1930) and *SOS Eisberg* (1933). Udet's role never changed: appearing as himself, he performed aerial stunts and heroically saved human beings visible only as small dots from the height of his airborne plane. However, in *The White Hell of Pitz Palu*, his character only plays a minor part as a *deus ex machina*. After all, the most important actor in Fanck's films was nature.

The most remarkable feature of *The White Hell of Pitz Palu* is the location shooting, which was also stressed in the publicity, particularly by Fanck. Shooting took place in Switzerland from January to June 1929, at Morteratsch Glacier and Piz Palü. Cameramen as well as actors had to brave harsh conditions, such as avalanches and temperatures below 50 degrees Fahrenheit. Riefenstahl, the only woman amongst the cast and crew, worked with extreme commitment, for which she was highly admired by Pabst and Fanck. A former dancer, she learned climbing and skiing for the film. With no safeguards or ropes, she survived shoots that involved falling into a crevasse. In a contemporary film magazine, Riefenstahl related that she suffered frostbite while waiting several days for the right weather and light for optimal shooting. She described a climb into a crevasse thus: 'I hung there, the small crevasse between me and daylight 40 metres above me, and the darkness beneath me, scared to death as the glaciers melted groaningly and creakingly in spring. But what should I do? Is this not all part and parcel of a real, true *Bergfilm*?' These perilous stunts were so dangerous that when seen on screen, they appear implausible despite their authenticity. Audiences and experts found it difficult to believe that these were performed by the actors on location. These doubts explain why Fanck, originally a geologist, signed his films with his title 'Dr. Arnold Fanck'. He wanted to imbue the film with 'scientific authority'.

The White Hell of Pitz Palu is regarded as Fanck's undisputed masterpiece and the most important example of the *Bergfilm*. Although the cinematic fascination with alpine landscape has antecedents, the *Bergfilm*-genre is attributed to the pioneering efforts of Fanck. His debut, the educational film, *Das Wunder des Schneeschuhs* (1920), showcased a range of artistic skiing skills. His subsequent films, for example *Im Kampf mit dem Berge* (1921) and *Berg des Schicksals* (*Mountain of Destiny*, 1924), espoused a similar character. They were all shot in an authentic alpine terrain and incorporated excellent photography. The most characteristic feature of Fanck's work is the breathtaking footage of foolhardy skiing and mountaineering – aesthetically ambitious documentaries featuring daring alpine stunts. So impressive were Fanck's images that his films had a significant promotional impact: they probably kindled, and certainly overlapped, with the emergence of alpine tourism and of skiing in the high mountains. Late in his life, in the early 1970s, Fanck emphasised his contribution to ski and mountaineering tourism as his most outstanding achievement.

German film companies initially refused to finance Fanck's idea of documentaries set in the mountains due to the unpredictable expense connected with shooting on location in inaccessible, difficult terrain and the dependency on good weather conditions. Another reason for their scepticism was Fanck's ambition to show heroic sport performances in a full-length feature film. Consequently, Fanck initially produced and promoted his films alone, but the success led to a contract with Ufa. For them, Fanck directed the melodramatic *Der heilige Berg* (*The Holy Mountain*, 1925/26) and the mountain film comedy *Der große Sprung* (*The Big Leap*, 1927), both with Riefenstahl as the lead actress.

The participation of Riefenstahl, who gained fame and infamy as a director with propaganda films such as *Triumph des Willens* (*Triumph of the Will*, 1935), led to the association of *Bergfilme* with Nazi aesthetics. The genre was regarded as a nationalist phenomenon exploiting the German predilection for heroic characters, traditional culture and monumental settings. This argument goes back to the theory of Kracauer, who interpreted the *Bergfilm* as a typically German yearning for a time before modernity and as a symptom of the collective German soul caught between tyranny and chaos. Despite his admiration for the cinematography, he regarded the popularity of Fanck's films as a harbinger of Nazism. He wrote: 'The surge of pro-Nazi tendencies during the pre-Hitler period could not better be confirmed than by the increase and specific evolution of the mountain films. Dr. Arnold Fanck, the uncontested father of this species, continued along the lines he himself had developed.'

Even if Kracauer's claim of an ideological relationship between Fanck's films and Fascism were true, it would remain questionable if this association was specifically German. In any event, the international success of *The White Hell of Pitz Palu* indicates the film's wide and very general appeal. Most adventure dramas have heroes, and the conventional moral code of natural power and human weakness is neither Fanck's original idea, nor exclusive to *The White Hell of Pitz Palu*. For example, this narrative pattern is also well known from novels and adventure dramas, such as those made by the Swedish film director Victor Sjöström, a contemporary of Fanck's.

Today, film theory argues more cautiously and is less concerned with Fanck as the master of the *Bergfilm*, instead underlining the avant-garde elements of his films, such as dynamism and film kinetics. Fanck was a unique 'mountain maniac' amongst the film directors of the time. The mixture of ambitious, documentary-style photography and action-oriented spectacle gives *The White Hell of Pitz Palu* its specific quality, an idiosyncrasy equalled only in German film by Werner Herzog.

Annette Deeken

REFERENCES

Balázs, B. (1984) 'Der Fall Dr. Fanck', in *Schriften zum Film*. München: Hanser, 287-291.

Fanck, A. (1972) *Letter to Deutsche Kinemathek, Klaus Kreimeier*, 24 April, Deutsches Institut für Filmkunde, Frankfurt am Main.

Film-Kurier (1929) 273, 16 November.

Kracauer, S. (1974 [1947]) *From Caligari to Hitler: A Psychological History of the German Film*. Princeton, NJ: Princeton University Press.

Riefenstahl, L. (1929) 'Man friert sich durch', *Die Filmwoche*, 44.

DIE DREI VON DER TANKSTELLE
THREE FROM THE FILLING STATION

WILHELM THIELE, GERMANY, 1930

In *Die Drei von der Tankstelle* (*Three From the Filling Station*, 1930), three well-off bohemian friends, Willy (Willy Fritsch), Kurt (Oskar Karlweiss) and Hans (Heinz Rühmann), return from a vacation to find themselves completely broke. All they are left with is their dog and a car, in which they drive off. When they run out of petrol, they decide to sell the car and open a filling station. One of their regular customers is Lilian (Lilian Harvey), the pretty, witty and spoiled daughter of the rich consul, Gossmann (Fritz Kampers). Unbeknownst to each other, all three men fall in love with her, while she also finds herself equally attracted to all three of them. Finally, she realises that she is in love with Willy. Discovering that they all have feelings for the same woman, the men feel hurt and deceived. Their friendship falls apart. Lilian does not want to let that happen, so she tricks the three into becoming the executives of a chain of filling stations she has secretly set-up herself. When Willy finds out about this plot, at first he is outraged. But in the end, his tender feelings for Lilian win out. As Willy and Lilian become a couple, the three men vow that they will always be friends.

Three From the Filling Station is difficult to summarise, because its plot is full of incredible turnarounds. Yet, as its ranking in the film trade paper *Film-Kurier* shows, this musical comedy became the most successful film of the 1930/31 season in Germany. The songs, written by Werner Richard Heymann, were released on gramophone records and became enormously popular. 'Ein Freund, ein guter Freund' ('A friend, a good friend') even turned into a *Gassenhauer* ('popular song') that is still widely known and loved in Germany. Further indications of the enormous popularity of the film are a remake (*Die Drei von der Tankstelle*, 1955) and several films alluding to its title (for instance, *Die drei Mädels von der Tankstelle* [*Three Girls From the Filling Station*, 1997], featuring *Lola rennt* [*Run, Lola, Run*] star Franka Potente and television comedian Wigald Boning). Since 1993, PitStop, one of the largest German garage chains, has centred its television advertising campaign and general corporate design around elements of the original film, featuring three car mechanics dressed like Fritsch, Karlweiss and Rühmann and mimicking their comical dance movements, while the jingle is based on the film's essential tune, 'Ein Freund, ein guter Freund'. Furthermore, *Three From the Filling Station* is still regularly screened on television (particularly on local stations of the public broadcasters).

In addition, *Three From the Filling Station* marks the beginning of Heinz Rühmann's career, Germany's most popular film star. Up to that point, he had been a stage actor with only minor film appearances. The story goes that producer Erich Pommer saw Rühmann in the theatre and was electrified by his fresh and 'snotty' performance. When Rühmann first auditioned for the role of Kurt, he had changed his persona, much to the disappointment of Pommer. The producer invited him for a second audition, giving Rühmann clear instructions how he wanted him to act. Apparently, he was very satisfied, since he agreed to a much higher salary than usual for a newcomer. Although Rühmann's character is more like a comic sidekick than a starring role in the film, *Three From the Filling Station* was later regarded as a 'Rühmann film'. In fact, on film posters for its theatrical re-release as well as on the DVD, the order of names changed, with Rühmann surpassing Willy Fritsch and Lilian Harvey in the credits.

Although the relationship between intellectual film criticism and popular cinema (especially all types of comedy) has always been troubled in Germany, even Marxist writers from the former GDR could not deny the overwhelming entertainment qualities of *Three From the Filling Station*. Although almost every essay on this film brands it as escapism to some degree, there is always a notion that the escapism of *Three From the Filling Station* is a particularly charming, enjoyable and magical one. When the film premiered in September 1930, the US trade paper *Variety* ran a very favourable review: 'When leaving this charming talker operetta, one feels in good humor', 'constant laughter and enthusiasm', and concluding that an English language version 'would have proven worth while'. It seems that *Three From the Filling Station* is more than just another popular film; many other highly successful films of the period have since been forgotten. Rather, it became what one might call a cultural phenomenon, and most definitely a *Kultfilm* in Germany. A look at the academic discourse on the film may help to understand why.

While the traditional studies on Weimar cinema focus on expressionist masterpieces, such as *Das Cabinet des Dr. Caligari* (*The Cabinet of Dr. Caligari*, 1919), or the political implications of sinister films like Fritz Lang's *Dr. Mabuse, der Spieler* (*Dr. Mabuse, the Gambler*, 1921) or *Metropolis* (1926), *Three From the Filling Station* is, by contrast, an excellent example of a type of light comedy that was enormously popular at the time. Even though our understanding of Weimar cinema has become more nuanced in recent years, it is still noteworthy that all of the aforementioned films – 'from *Caligari* to *Tankstelle*', so to speak – were produced by the same executive, Erich Pommer, former head of Decla-Bioscope and then in charge of production at Ufa. Despite the fact that Pommer himself changed his attitude towards the relationship between high art and commercial entertainment (due to the near-bankruptcy of Ufa and his short visit to Hollywood), he remained a perfect example of how these often strictly separated paradigms of film production converged in Weimar cinema. Almost every discussion of *Three From the Filling Station* still reflects this ongoing debate to some degree, concerning its balance of conventional entertainment and artistically sophisticated experiment.

In the case of *Three From the Filling Station*, the debate begins with its genre. At the time, it was announced as a 'film operetta', a genre that was already highly successful in the silent era, when local orchestras and singers delivered the music for the play unfolding on the screen, at first often based on a popular stage production (for example, *Im weißen Rössl*, 1926). With the arrival of sound, the music simply wandered from the stage into the film. Contemporary film critics were used to a variety of film operettas, but they already noted that *Three From the Filling Station* was different from everything they had seen so far. Unlike many earlier examples of the genre, the film was not set in a historical period or otherwise distant world, but in the everyday here and now. However, this can be said for many sound film operettas that were no longer based on theatre productions, but featured original stories and songs (such as, *Ich bei Tag und Du bei Nacht*, 1932).

The musical numbers of these later operettas were not just *intermezzi* (in the traditional forms of solos, duets or chorus numbers) that do not contribute to the unfolding of the plot, but integral parts of the action, i.e. dialogue lines were substituted by song lyrics. For example, when Willy and Lilian seek shelter from a storm in the filling station, their developing romance is expressed in the lyrics of 'Mein Herz lässt Dich grüßen' ('My heart sends you greetings'). The singing and dancing in the film – aside of the coda scene – is not arranged in distinct stand-alone numbers, but interwoven in the flow with dialogue and sound effects, such as the distinct sound of Lilian's car horn, which becomes part of a tune. This is especially true for the final scene in the company office, when dialogue and song lyrics fully merge.

Due to this avant-garde approach, comparisons were even drawn with Bertolt Brecht's *Dreigroschenoper*. In another scene, Willy and Kurt are having a boxing fight, while their customers are waiting outside the filling station. The fight is accompanied by the song lyrics 'A friend, a good friend, that is the most beautiful thing in the world' and the rhythm is set by the knocking of the waiting car drivers and, later on, by punches. After Hans, playing referee to the fight, has been hit accidentally, he cools his eye with a wet towel and mocks their theme song by changing the lyrics into 'A black eye, a black eye, that is the most unfortunate thing in the world'. Such a usage of music achieved an unprecedented self-irony in the genre of film operettas. An even better example of this is the scene at the beginning, when the three friends are devastated upon finding the confiscation signs the bailiff has attached to their furniture. Since these signs are called 'Kuckuck' (cuckoo) in colloquial German, mocking the Prussian eagle that was pictured on them, the following song begins with the first bars of the well-known folk tune 'Kuckuck, Kuckuck, ruft's aus dem Wald' ('Cuckoo, cuckoo, is echoed from the forest'). David Bordwell and Kristin Thompson apparently miss the cultural reference when they call this piece a 'nonsense song'.

Thus, the film was originally categorised as an operetta, but with many contemporaries already regarding it as a parody of that genre. Today, most German film scholars call *Three From the Filling Station* a musical *avant la lettre*. However, the point here is not how the film should be categorised, but that despite its clearly designated genre-category, it was and is still perceived as transcending the established formula. Thus, *Three From the Filling Station* reveals the aesthetic richness and imaginative qualities of an entertainment-oriented, yet artistically ambitious cinema.

Another point that is widely discussed in academic studies is the question of escapism. One could argue that the story uses the background of world economic crisis, unemployment and impoverishment merely to tell a fairy tale about social rise, wonderful changes of fortune and romantic love that finally overcomes all obstacles. On the eve of the Nazi regime, *Three From the Filling Station* shows a singing bailiff, confiscated furniture flying away and three victims of bankruptcy, who do not act like victims at all. The film even features gags concerning anti-Semitism and the rise of the Nazis, in the form of the National Socialist German Workers Party (NSDAP). When Willy, Kurt and Hans telephone their apparently Jewish lawyer Dr. Kalmus (Kurt Gerron), he uses the word 'meschugge' (Yiddish for 'crazy'); they ask him how bad things have turned, proposing comparisons such as 'Worse than your wife having a blond baby?' or 'Worse than a change in government in Lippe-Detmold?' (a German region where the NSDAP was especially strong and gained power in 1932). Dr. Kalmus' answer to both is, 'Even worse!' Therefore, escapism is hardly a valid concept to describe the manner in which *Three From the Filling Station* entertained its audience. Surely, the film presents a kind of fairy tale, but it does not let its audience forget about their real-life problems or the disturbing times in which they live, contrary to what the concept of escapism suggests. The world of *Three From the Filling Station* is a world of crisis, where everyone can lose everything suddenly.

Of course, one could object that the main characters are far above a proletarian or even middle-class spectator: they mourn the loss of champagne and caviar, while many people in the real world were struggling to survive. But this is exactly the point that makes the film even more poignant. Three wealthy playboys are deprived of everything on which they have built their lives and which they have taken for granted. Realising that tennis or ballroom dancing will do them no good now, they must face the fact that they have absolutely no skills that would be useful for their new life. Thus, they are not even able to keep up with a proletarian, who at least knows how to earn his living. However, they are not depressed or angry. Since they obviously have no idea what it means to be poor and to have to work for one's living, their response to the new situation is one of unbroken optimism. Instead of worrying about their need for employment in times of wide-spread unemployment, they joke about going to work, as in the 'Kuckuck' song: 'We have seen work only from a distance, and even from a distance it was unpleasant!' They react to the catastrophe of losing their home with dancing and frolicking around. When they finally jump out of the window, which makes the bailiff fall over in surprise and amazement, they even look like the true victors. They beat the odds simply with their cheerful spirit. This is something to which the audience can relate emotionally, but is not made to appear as a realistic solution.

Three From the Filling Station does not let its audience dream away its troubles as the concept of escapism implies. It balances in a brilliant way the daydream of heroically facing one's problems with irony towards the miraculous solutions the plot presents. The film offers at least two different levels of interpretation and emotional involvement. On the first level, there is the story about friendship and love as the only reliable values in a world turning upside down. On the second level, there is self-ironic play with those wondrous operetta turnarounds, which does not ask for make-believe, but laughter instead. This is most evident at the end of the office scene, when the film does not finish with a kiss: Willy and Lilian move towards the camera, while the curtain falls behind them, and they acknowledge, directly addressing the cinema audience and thereby leaving the diegetic world, that the film needs a 'genuine' operetta finale, which is exactly what follows (traditional chorus line and all). This strategy allows the audience to enjoy the story without believing in what they see, which of course blatantly contradicts everyone's everyday experience. It is a playful, ironic and fresh way of dealing with the reality of the late Weimar Republic.

Taking into consideration that a French-language version of the film was simultaneously produced alongside the German film offers yet another perspective on *Three From the Filling Station*. Since most comments on Weimar cinema tend to focus on its social and political dimension in relation to German history (for example, Siegfried Kracauer's classic *From Caligari to Hitler* or Helmut Korte's *Der Spielfilm und das Ende der Weimarer Republik*), it is noteworthy that many films were made for an international market. While there were indeed nationally specific genres that were not very suitable for selling abroad – for example, the military comedy – it was a strategy of the German film industry and especially of Pommer to produce high-profile films that might be successful in foreign markets. With the spread of sound film and the audience (as yet) unwilling to accept dubbing or subtitles, there was only one solution to the problem of film export: to produce multi-language versions. As the budget did not allow major changes in settings, costumes and so on, few alterations were made to the story. As Pommer pointed out, even the first sketch of the concept had to prove that the film could also be understood and enjoyed outside Germany.

Since most multi-language productions included French versions, this was also the case for *Three From the Filling Station*. The French version, *Le Chemin du Paradis* (*The Way of Paradise*, 1930), directed by Wilhelm Thiele with Max de Vaucorbeil, was shot on the same sets and at the same time as the German version. It tells the same story, but has a different cast: Henri Garat took over for Willy Fritsch (as Willy), Jacques Maury for Oskar Karlweiss (as Guy) and René Lefèvre for Heinz Rühmann (as Jean) – with one exception: Lilian Harvey kept her role, although she was initially nervous that her 'school French' might not be good enough. In fact, at least 90 per cent of *The Way of Paradise* is a shot-by-shot re-enactment of *Three From the Filling Station*: the same types of actors were cast (René Lefèvre would almost pass as a double for Heinz Rühmann), wearing identical or similar costumes, following the same choreography. Since every scene was shot on the same set first in German, then in French (and sometimes, when Thiele noticed something about the latter version that he liked better, in German again), the actors of each nation could watch each other closely, so that in many cases even gestures and facial expressions match exactly. The lyrics of the songs were translated as closely as possible, for example, 'Ein Freund, ein guter Freund' became 'Avoir un bon copain, voilà c'qu'il y a d'meilleur au monde'.

However, there are some differences between the two versions that reveal cultural adaptation. The French characters are more strongly typified than the German characters: Jean, the pendant to the Rühmann character Hans, is a constant and therefore piteous loser. The first customer of the filling station pays him less than the others. Later, when he and Guy hail a cab in order to get to the night club, he is left behind. In the German version, Hans gets paid as much as the others and wins the fight over the taxi. A possible explanation for this typification is that it makes the characters easier to distinguish: the weak Jean, the flirtatious Guy and the gentleman Willy, which makes it more likely that Lilian will end up with the latter. This becomes even more plausible if one compares the first meetings between Lilian and the boys in the two different versions: while in *Three From the Filling Station* it seems like all three get a fair share of Lilian's attention, in *The Way of Paradise* there is a clear emphasis on the meeting with Willy. After their conversation they perform the musical number that Lilian had with Kurt in the German film. They even share a quick kiss. Thus, there can be little doubt for the audience which of the characters are destined for each other from the very beginning. The German version makes this less clear, for the simple reason that it did not have to, since Lilian Harvey and Willy Fritsch (who even kept their first names for their roles) were an established film couple (with three films together by that time, including *Liebeswalzer* [*Love Waltz*, 1929], also directed by Thiele, one of the most successful pictures of the 1929/30 season). Thus, the narrative could focus on strengthening the dramatic conflict. By contrast, Harvey and Garat worked together for the first time, so they had to be introduced to the audience in a manner that would reduce the confusion of whom Lilian should choose. This development is also reflected by the change of title, which slightly shifts the connotations from the friendship-drama towards the romance.

Another remarkable difference between the two language versions is the elimination of all Jewish references in the French film. In the German film, their use of Yiddish expressions clearly indicates that Kurt and Dr. Kalmus are Jews, but there are none in the French version. It is possible that these changes were made by Pommer in accordance with what he felt were the preferences of the French market, since anti-Semitism was an issue in France at the time as well. It is also possible that co-director de Vaucorbeil made these changes simply because Yiddish words are less common in France and thus the allusions were difficult to translate.

Apparently, *The Way of Paradise* was as popular in France as *Three From the Filling Station* was in Germany. According to polls, Harvey and Garat both gained enormous popularity through it. While Harvey and Fritsch became the *Traumpaar* ('dream couple') of German cinema and made eight more films together, she and Garat teamed up for another five films (mostly French-language versions in which he replaced Fritsch). In 1955, there was a remake of *The Way of Paradise*, which again was produced alongside the German remake. Since multi-language versions were long out of fashion (due to the acceptance of dubbing), this certainly shows how popular the original must have been in France.

What these comments on *Three From the Filling Station* suggest may come as a surprise: German cinema produced artistically innovative, popular and – at least in the case of *Three From the Filling Station* – even internationally marketable comedies. They owe their specific quality to the talents of German-Jewish filmmakers, such as the directors Ernst Lubitsch (e.g., *Die Austernprinzessin*, 1919), Richard Eichberg (e.g. *Die keusche Susanne* [*The Innocent Susanne*, 1926]) and Alexis Granowksy (e.g. *Die Koffer des Herrn O. F.* [*The Trunks of Mr O. F.*, 1931]), or screenwriter Billy Wilder (e.g. *Ihre Hoheit befiehlt* [*Her Grace Commands*, 1931]). The key personnel of *Three From the Filling Station* were also German Jews: from the screenwriters Franz Schulz and Paul Franck, director Wilhelm Thiele and composer Werner Richard Heymann to producer Erich Pommer. They were mostly forced to leave Germany by 1933. For some, even that did not save them. Actor Kurt Gerron was captured and later killed by the Nazis when Germany invaded the Netherlands. Some of the emigrated filmmakers, like Wilhelm Thiele, returned after the war. But the strong tradition of German-Jewish film comedy was irretrievably broken.

Christian Junklewitz

AUTHOR'S NOTE: I thankfully acknowledge the assistance in translating of Jennifer Scott and Annemone Ligensa (English) and Ilil Land-Boss (French).

REFERENCES

Bordwell, D. and K. Thompson (1994) *Film History: An Introduction*. New York: McGraw-Hill.

Korte, H. (1998) *Der Spielfilm und das Ende der Weimarer Republik: Ein rezeptionshistorischer Versuch*. Göttingen: Vandenhoeck & Ruprecht.

Kracauer, S. (2004 [1947]) *From Caligari to Hitler: A Psychological History of the German Film*. Princeton, NJ: Princeton University Press.

Magnus (1930) 'From the Gas Station', *Variety*, 15 October.

OLYMPIA – TEIL 1: FEST DER VÖLKER; TEIL 2: FEST DER SCHÖNHEIT

OLYMPIA – PART 1: FESTIVAL OF THE NATIONS; PART 2: FESTIVAL OF BEAUTY

LENI RIEFENSTAHL, GERMANY, 1938

The XIth Olympic Games of 1936 in Berlin were a significant media event. For the first time the Olympic Games were broadcast on the radio internationally, with live commentary by 105 reporters. It was also the first time that television participated: the moving images were transmitted live to 28 public TV rooms in Berlin, Potsdam and Leipzig, to around 160,000 spectators. However, film was still the dominant medium for moving images at the time, with approximately 33,000 cinemas in Europe alone.

Previous reports on the Olympic Games in the form of moving images were integrated into newsreels. But in 1936, a feature-length, two-part documentary film was made: *Olympia*, directed by Leni Riefenstahl. It cost 2.8 million Reichsmark, which was eleven times the average budget of a German production at the time. With an enormous investment in labour and logistics, 240 hours of film were shot, mostly during the 16 days of the Olympic Games, and it took 18 months of post-production to assemble the 217 minutes of finished film.

Olympia was realised upon Adolf Hitler's personal request, financed with public funds and produced by the Olympiade-Film GmbH, which was founded in 1935 to cover up the Nazi regime's backing. Hitler allowed Riefenstahl total artistic and organisational control, which already during shooting she exploited for her self-presentation as an artistic genius. She suggested that the film should premiere on Hitler's birthday, 20 April 1938, in Berlin. Subsequently, it was distributed throughout Germany through 120 prints, a large number for the time. Riefenstahl had established herself with the Nazi regime through her films of the *Parteitage der NSDAP* ('conventions of the Nazi party'). In particular *Triumph des Willens* (*Triumph of the Will*, 1935), a documentary on the Nuremberg convention in 1934, demonstrated that she knew how to film a political mass event in accordance with the regime's concepts and aims.

The International Olympic Committee (IOC) had chosen Germany as site for the XIth Olympic Games in 1931. The Nazis, who came to power in 1933, passed more than fifty laws that eliminated Jews from Germany's public sphere, before the systematic genocide was begun in 1941. Hitler recognised the Olympic Games as an opportunity to 'raise foreign currency as well as our international standing'. In reaction to international concerns and threats of boycotts, Nazi Germany aimed to present itself as a tolerant and peaceful country: anti-Semitic propaganda temporarily disappeared from public view. But behind the scenes, the situation was quite different: only 'Half-Jews' who were already established athletes were permitted to participate. Victor Klemperer, a professor in Romanic languages and literature, who had lost his position at the Technische Hochschule Dresden due to his Jewish background, recorded in his diary on 13 August 1936: '[T]he silver medal in fencing that went to Germany was won by a Jew, Helene Mayer (I do not know where the greater shamelessness lies: in her appearance as a German of the Third Reich or in the exploitation of her achievement by the Third Reich). [...] Nazi chants are forbidden (for the duration of the [games of the] Olympiad) and agitation against Jews, warmongering, everything offensive has disappeared from the newspapers until 16 August; but also until that day, everywhere, day and night, swastika-flags are hissed. In articles written in English it is endlessly pointed out to "our guests" how peaceful and joyous our country is, while in Spain "communist hordes" commit robbery and manslaughter.'

For the Nazis, the Olympic Games of 1936 were a major political event. A film of the Olympic Games that explicitly transported the Nazi's ideology by glorifying the 'Aryan race' as superior to others would have been detrimental to the aims described above. Instead, the film's propagandist function would be furthered by depicting athletes of all nations and ethnicities in a free and fair contest. And the more this was elaborated aesthetically, the more culturally civilised the 'new Germany' would look, and the more prestige it would acquire.

In Germany, *Olympia* became the second most successful film of the 1937/38 season (the biggest success was the comedy *Der Mustergatte* [*Model Husband*, 1937], featuring one of Germany's top stars, Heinz Rühmann). *Olympia* was banned in the USA and UK for reasons external to the film, after the so-called *Reichsprogromnacht* on 9 November 1938, when the Nazis destroyed synagogues, vandalised and robbed Jewish shops and murdered many Jews. However, in the countries in which the film was shown, it was seen by large audiences and favourably received by many critics. In the foreign market it made more money than all the German films released in 1938 combined. International critics celebrated it as a 'masterpiece' and as the greatest sports film of all time. It won many international awards – in Fascist countries such as Italy (*Coppa Mussolini* at the Venice film festival) as well as democratic countries such as Sweden (Polar Prize). How can this international success of a film that was financed by the Nazis and that celebrated an event that was of great political significance be explained?

Concerning the basic understanding of documentary filmmaking, *Olympia* does not significantly differ from other documentary films of the 1920s and 1930s. Like Robert Flaherty with his films *Nanook of the North* (1922) and *Man of Aran* (1934), Riefenstahl was not a distanced observer, but a creative constructor of reality. 'Legitimate' devices included the staging of events as well as the addition of sound in post-production. For example, Riefenstahl used material filmed during training for the representation of competitions, such as the shots of the rowers from the perspective of the coxswain. With the exception of Hitler's opening speech, the film's voices and sound effects were entirely dubbed in Berlin sound studios. Two of the best-known German radio reporters of the day, Paul Laven and Rolf Wernicke, commentated. The music by Herbert Windt is a mix of late romanticism and early expressionism, further dramatising the events.

The film is formally divided into clearly separated segments, most of which present competitions from the various Olympic disciplines. Others visualise concepts, such as the prologue of Part One, on the origin of the Olympic idea, and the apotheosis of Part Two, on the beauty of athletic achievement. The film only presents a selection of the official 19 sports and 119 disciplines. Significantly, this selection is not representatively based on the rank of the countries according to the medals table. (Germany was the top-ranking country, followed by the USA, Hungary, Italy, Finland, France, Sweden, Japan, the Netherlands and the UK.) It is based on the principles of showing the 'classic' disciplines, for example, the 100-metre sprint, the marathon and the decathlon, focusing in particular on those disciplines that display the beauty of athletes' bodies. The order does not follow the chronology of the Olympic Games, but is an arrangement according to aesthetic and dramatic principles.

The aesthetic innovations of the film can be more fully understood by comparing it with previous newsreel reports. They only ever showed a selection of competitions in static shots, because there was no material available with which to represent the drama of the events. The main reason for this was that before 1936 only a few cameras were allowed on the site of the Games, and their positions were strictly regulated. According to the official report on the Olympic Games of 1932 in Los Angeles, only 'four News Reel concerns were permitted to have one motion picture camera each on the fields or platforms of the various Stadiums where competitions were being held. Inasmuch as most of the motion picture film was taken in sound, and the necessary equipment could not easily be moved from place to place, these pictures were mainly taken from fixed positions agreed upon in advance of the Games.'

In contrast to *Olympia*, which was shown 18 months after the Games had ended, the newsreel films reported on the events shortly after they had taken place. However, on the order of the Ministry of Propaganda, the newsreel companies accredited for the Olympic Games – Ufa, Tobis-Melo and Fox – were supervised by Riefenstahl, who privileged her own camera-team in jockeying for the best positions. Riefenstahl did everything to obtain a myriad of extraordinary images. She shot almost all of the scenes without sound so that she could use light, mobile cameras. She demanded the development of new devices, such as a camera on tracks for parallel movements with athletes, a tiny hand-camera for shots from the perspective of athletes, and an extreme telephoto lens for unobtrusive filming of athletes and spectators. Furthermore, Riefenstahl chose a multitude of highly unusual camera positions, for which she often fought bitterly with the IOC and the local organisational committee. She used steel towers, cranes, captive balloons and zeppelins for shots from above, and trenches were dug for shots from below. She also employed dozens of cameramen. There were six head cameramen (Hans Ertl, Walter Frentz, Guzzi Lantschner, Kurt Neubert, Hans Scheib and Willy Zielke), with at least 38 cameramen (as far as are known by name) working under them. Riefenstahl perfected the efficiency of the team by delegating specific tasks to each division: Ertl was the specialist for underwater shots, Frentz and Lantschner for the hand-camera, Neubert for slow-motion shots, and Scheib for telephoto shots; Zielke filmed and edited the prologue.

Thus, Riefenstahl obtained many types of images that were new to audiences at that time – but are now the common language of TV sports reporting. Such images include the faces of athletes before the competition, close-ups of the competitions themselves, travelling shots parallel to runners, circling shots around discus-throwers, underwater shots of divers, the cheering audience and overhead-shots of the stadium where the events are taking place.

But these unusual images were only the material on which the even greater aesthetic innovations of *Olympia* were based. Riefenstahl created an experience of presence for the film audience, which was previously reserved for live spectators of the Games. In contrast to the newsreel reports, which focused on results, Riefenstahl's film was process-oriented, in order to recreate the drama of the competitions. Thus, even when the results of the competitions were already known, the spectator could become emotionally involved in the events. For this purpose, Riefenstahl used techniques established in narrative fictional films to promote iden-tification with athletes and build suspense. The 100-metre sprint may serve as an example.

Three qualifying runs and the final run are shown. From the beginning, suspense is built by the comment that 'the USA's fastest runner, Jesse Owens' is among the athletes. We see him achieve a world record in a qualifying run, but it is revoked because of tailwind. The emotional involvement is promoted through shots of the concentrated and nervous faces of the athletes, whose names and nationalities are stated. We see the phase of preparation, the signal-giver, the athletes on their marks, but also failures such as a false start – and then the climactic final run.

Riefenstahl not only dramatised the sports events, but also idealised the Olympic Games as a 'Festival of the Nations' and a 'Festival of Beauty' (the subtitles of the two parts). In contrast to the fictional films of the Third Reich, in documentaries, including *Olympia*, swastika-flags, the political leaders, especially Hitler, and Germans giving the Hitler-salute are shown. In contrast to *Triumph des Willens*, in which Hitler is idealised as a 'saviour', in *Olympia* he mostly appears as an individual who freely expresses his emotions. Hitler is shown as an easygoing, average sports fan, who cheers the Germans' successes and is disappointed in their failures – an image connoting *Mitmensch* ('fellow human being') rather than *Übermensch* ('super-human').

Some sequences do not deal with the competitions between nations, but stress the commonalities of the athletes, such as the morning training during the opening of the film, or the apotheosis at the end of Part Two, which shows divers without mention of national origins or results. The divers seem to transcend gravity when their feats are composed into movement-images in the style of 'abstract films'. Such images do not convey competition, but the beauty of athletic prowess for its own sake. Riefenstahl's depictions of athletic, strong and beautiful bodies may be fascist in their context, even though they were common before and after the Third Reich. The functionalisation of these 'body aesthetics' for fascist ideology is a frame of reference not made explicit in the film and therefore dependent on the spectator – thus, these aesthetics could also be appreciated by others with a different frame of reference. Whereas Riefenstahl's technical innovations and semi-fictional devices had a lasting, international influence on sports reporting, this was not the case for her distinctive aestheticisation of the body inspired by abstract film.

To enable the film's success in as many foreign countries as possible, several versions in different languages – French, English and Italian – were produced. The German version was not only shown in German-speaking countries, but also exported to countries speaking none of the other languages. Only the Italian version was produced in the Cinecittà studios in Rome; the other versions were made in Berlin.

Furthermore, the different versions were not just linguistic translations. The presentation of the Olympic Games was 'nationalised' for different contexts. Mostly, the same film material was used, but significant replacements and additions were made. In newsreels produced by the different countries themselves, orientation towards local preferences had always been the rule: they predominantly reported on the athletes of their own country, favourite sports, and so on. Such variations had usually been the result of different producers, but for the 1936 Olympics total control over the different versions lay in the hands of Riefenstahl.

For several years after the introduction of sound in 1929, the production of 'multiple language versions' (separate films with more or less the same story, but with local actors, and sometimes different settings) was a common and successful practice for exporting fictional films, because it made domestic productions more understandable, culturally acceptable and popular abroad. Smaller countries subtitled films, but several larger countries – Germany, France, Britain, Italy and Spain – produced versions, which were more expensive and only economically viable for large markets. For example, since national audiences of the time favoured their own stars, using local actors made these versions much more popular than dubbed productions. Similarly, the export versions of *Olympia* employed the sports reporters of the respective target countries as voice-over commentators. The reporters also appear on-screen: they are shown commenting in actual presence at the Olympic Games, which gives the 'nationalised' reports a feel of authenticity.

The export versions partly show different events or show the same events differently. Competitions won by the target country were given priority in the respective export version. For example, a sailing regatta and a fencing match that the Italians won is shown in the Italian version, but not in the German one. The Anglo-American version does not include fencing at all, because neither the British nor the Americans won any medals in that sport. Disciplines with a strong tradition in a specific country are shown only in the version made for them, for example, wrestling in Greco-Roman style is only included in the Italian version. Athletes who did not win any medals are usually only shown in the version for their country of origin.

However, the nationalisation of the versions never went so far as to contradict the internationality of the Olympic idea. Even though local athletes feature more prominently in each version, all of them feature American athletes Jesse Owens and Glenn Morris as the top stars, because they won the most medals. For example, Morris's triumph at the decathlon is elaborately presented as a dramatic individual struggle against his countrymen Bob Clark and Jack Parker. Furthermore, the Afro-American Jesse Owens is given 'star treatment' in the presentation of the 100-metre sprint, in which he won the gold medal. From the 19 competitions, Riefenstahl selected four, among them all three in which Owens participated. She shows the events not in chronological order, but in a dramatic progression, suggesting that Owens steadily improved with each event. Not only is his status as favourite emphasised verbally from the beginning, he is also portrayed in a higher number of close-ups than any of the other runners. The only event without Owens that is shown is the one in which a German, Erich Borchmeyer, qualified (although he ended fifth in the final, which the film does not mention). By comparison, even when taking into consideration some racist remarks in the film's commentary, the local German radio reports blatantly portrayed the 100-metre sprint as a fight between races (black vs. white) and worlds (USA vs. Europe).

How successful this international marketing strategy of *Olympia* was can be demonstrated by the reactions of Luxembourg critic Evy Friedrich in the daily newspaper *Escher Tageblatt*. At first (17 June 1938) he vehemently complained about the second part of the German version: '[S]everal sports are completely missing, including bicycling, wrestling and heavy athletics. That is all the more deplorable, because France is not given the opportunity to show its achievements. Thus, we must observe what we did not believe was the case a week ago in first part, that a certain tendency was smuggled into the film, namely the clear tendency to present Germany once again as the best and strongest country, at least of Europe.' Which it was, at least in the medals table. One month later (15 July 1938), Friedrich changed his opinion: 'Some time ago we observed here that in the two *Olympia*-films all the competitions that the French won were missing. That was true for the original German version. But recently, first in Brussels, then in Paris, the French version, called *Les dieux du stade*, was shown. Behold: in this version, not made for Germany, all the competitions that the French won are included.' Friedrich goes on to recommend that the Luxembourg exhibitors should show only the French version.

Riefenstahl's *Olympia* is propagandistic in a manner that is frequently underestimated – especially by the critical theorists of the 1960s and 1970s, who criticised their parent generation for their role in Nazism and rejected all films of the Third Reich as symbolic representations of Fascism. No matter how one interprets and judges *Olympia* with regard to Nazi ideology, the film's two main aims were, as Hitler put it, to 'raise foreign currency as well as our international standing'. To achieve this, Riefenstahl adapted two strategies from fiction films for her documentary. Firstly, she developed aesthetic devices that were innovative, compared to prior filmic reports of the Olympic Games, which gave spectators the feeling of actually being present at the dramatic events by involving them emotionally. Secondly, export versions catering to the preferences of the target countries were produced, which nationalised the presentation of the Olympic Games, but also represented the Olympic idea of a fair international contest. Since *Olympia* earned more money in foreign markets than all other German films of 1938 combined, Riefenstahl clearly reached the first aim. Whether the film also achieved its second aim, to internationally disseminate an image of the XIth Olympic Games that made Nazi Germany look like a cosmopolitan and peaceful country, is more difficult to estimate. The 'success' of the film in this respect depended on contemporary spectators, and thus varied with different contexts and individuals. While the film probably did not change Germany's image with spectators who knew what was happening in Germany and were opposed to Fascism, spectators who were oblivious of Nazi politics may have come to believe that all was well in the state of Germany.

Joseph Garncarz

Translated by Annemone Ligensa

REFERENCES

Klemperer, V. (1999) *Tagebücher 1935–1936*. Berlin: Aufbau.

Lesch, P. (2002) *Heim ins Ufa-Reich? NS-Filmpolitik und die Rezeption deutscher Filme in Luxemburg 1933–1944*. Trier: WVT.

Radio report on the 100-metre-sprint, 3 August 1938. On-line. Available HTTP: http://www.dhm.de/lemo/html/1936/index.html (accessed 3 February 2006).

Picker, H. (1993) *Hitlers Tischgespräche im Führerhauptquartier*. Frankfurt: Ullstein.

Xth Olympiad Committee of the Games of Los Angeles (1933) *The Games of the Xth Olympiad Los Angeles 1932: Official Report*.

ZARAH LEANDER
Die große Liebe

DIE GROSSE LIEBE THE GREAT LOVE

09

ROLF HANSEN, GERMANY, 1942

From June 1942 on, not long after the Allies began massive air strikes against German cities and shortly before the ill-fated German offensive against Stalingrad began, the German public flocked to the theatres to see a picture entitled *Die große Liebe* (*The Great Love*), which told of a love affair between a singer and a German air force pilot. The film starred the highest paid and most popular actress of the Nazi period, Zarah Leander, offering her the opportunity to sing songs like 'Ein Leben für die Liebe' ('A life for love'), 'Davon geht die Welt nicht unter' ('That isn't the end of the world'), or 'Ich weiß, es wird einmal ein Wunder gescheh'n' ('I'm sure a miracle will occur someday'), which were popular then and are still well known today.

Thus it might seem that pure escapism drew the public into this musical love story in increasingly grim times. However, the film was officially rated as having 'outstanding political and artistic value'. Postwar reception tells a different story as well, as *The Great Love* is commonly listed among political films. It is seen as bolstering morale and the will to fight, making it a prime example of specific Nazi wartime genres, the *Heimatfrontfilm* ('home front film') and the *Durchhaltefilm* ('hold out film').

Thus, *The Great Love* is marked by ambivalence between escapist entertainment and a political message, making it typical of German cinema in the Nazi period. Audiences even consumed films such as *Jud Süß* (*Jew Suess*, 1940) as entertainment, though they could not fail to recognise the propagandistic intention. Nazi ideology was, however, part of everyday life for most Germans, found in schoolbooks, magazines, the daily newspaper, radio, and on the streets, and not just in the rabidly anti-Semitic *Stürmer*, published by the party. The most effectively ideological films were those that integrated their message into popular entertainment. Films were never free of ideology, even if they appeared apolitical. They still presented models of behaviour and fostered the public's acceptance of the dominant ideology. *The Great Love* did this through the central love story and through a number of scenes referring to reality. It is one of the few films to directly show the war at all, even if, as Mary-Elizabeth O'Brien suggests, it was depicted in a harmless and trivialising way, turning it into a 'catalyst for the love story' or romanticising it as a kind of fairy tale world that makes it possible for the characters' wishes to come true.

While not the most-seen film of the Nazi period, as has sometimes been claimed, *The Great Love* was extremely popular. The war-time period showed a strong increase in cinema attendance, with ticket sales reaching 1,116,500 in 1943, over three times the prewar level. At the same time, fewer films were produced, which increased an individual film's chances of reaching a large audience. Even so, there were great differences in the success of individual pictures. Factors such as the number of copies, the extent of advertising and promotion, budgets, stars, and even tax breaks for films rated as politically or artistically valuable had an effect, as did the production planning of the film companies. During the war, international competition dropped and German companies gained privileged access to European markets. From 1938 on, the industry underwent a process of indirect state ownership, so that production was increasingly co-ordinated. Still, individual films competed with each other at the box office, leaving audiences to decide which films they wanted to see. Cinema-going in the Third Reich took place within a complex field of forces, involving taste, class, gender, marketing and politics.

The Great Love was a film that audiences wanted to see; it grossed 8 million Reichsmark in the first 18 months and ran a record of 91 days straight in its Berlin first-run theatre. There are various possible explanations for this popularity. One factor is certainly its star, Zarah Leander, who had already appeared in a number of hit films. However, as relative flops like *Der Blaufuchs* (*The Blue Fox*, 1938) or *Das Lied der Wüste* (*The Desert Song*, 1939) show, she did not always guarantee an audience. She had to play the right role in a story the public liked. *The Great Love* provided a topical love story that accomodated Leander's image and effectively touched audiences emotionally. Music was another important element. The songs and her unmistakable contralto voice were attractions of their own, a feature of all her films.

In Nazi cinema, it was unusual that the war or current events were depicted. Most films were set in historical periods or in an indeterminate peace-time society, often even copying American genre films. The war appeared in newsreels that made up part of every cinema programme and occasionally in propagandistic documentaries such as *Sieg im Westen* (*Victory in the West*, 1940) or *Feldzug in Polen* (*Campaign in Poland*, 1940) and in a few war films like *Stukas* (1941), *Kampfgeschwader Lützow* (*Combat Squadron Lützow*, 1941) or *U-Boote westwärts!* (*Submarines Westward!*, 1941). Generally, though, few films were set in wartime or explicitly in Nazi Germany and the uniforms, flags and Nazi insignia of everyday life were seldom shown.

Films were intended to support the war effort by maintaining good spirits and teaching proper behaviour, albeit in less direct ways. The home front films such as *The Great Love*, *Wunschkonzert* (*Request Concert*, 1940), *Sechs Tage Heimaturlaub* (*Six Days Leave*, 1941), *Fronttheater* (*Theatre at the Front*, 1942) and *Zwei in einer großen Stadt* (*Two People in a Big City*, 1942) were popular, probably because they showed the audience an illusory world, but one that was recognisable as a transfigured version of their own, often grim, reality. *Wunschkonzert* portrayed the successful *Blitzkrieg* against France and integrated more war scenes, including newsreel footage and a montage sequence of combat at the end, but *The Great Love* reflected a more difficult phase of the war. While it focused on private life, critics like Walter-Hugo Senske and Harald Feddersen emphasised its 'topical subject' and that it was 'filled with the atmosphere of the times'. A key episode takes place in an air-raid shelter. The threatening situation in the cellar turns into a scene of fun and sociability, and captures family life, when Wendlandt and Hanna play Pachisi with the children. Wendlandt makes fun of one of the residents (a stereotyped *Meckerer* ['complainer']), and even manages to come up with a ration of 'real coffee beans' for all the occupants, tricking the owner into donating it to the *Volksgemeinschaft* ('community'). The film refers to very real problems; secret Security Service reports showed that food shortages and bombing had led to seriously low morale by the time the film was playing. That *The Great Love* tries to make bombing attacks, scarce goods, familial separation and worrying about loved ones seem harmless is not surprising; what is surprising for Nazi cinema is that they are shown at all.

The 'home front films' played a political role by connecting the homeland and the front. As Jo Fox explains: 'Film provided a link to brothers, fathers, husbands and loved ones, confirming their heroism and the necessity of their absence, as well as boosting morale for a population enduring wartime hardships. [Reich Film Administrator – S.L.] Hinkel communicated in an August 1944 report, entitled *Film und Totaler Krieg* ('Film and Total War'), "The fact that in the last year over 1.1 million people visited German cinemas, gives us an indication of the meaning of our film production for the care of our fighting and producing peoples."'

While the war is at least latently present throughout the film, it is the private sphere and personal feelings that motivate most of the plot. The film was particularly aimed at women and their experiences. Not heroism, but coping with privations, waiting and deferring the fulfilment of desires dominate the film's emotional register.

The film tells the story of the romance between a German air force pilot, Paul Wendlandt, and a music hall singer, Hanna Holberg. The war brings the lovers together – they meet when

Wendlandt is on leave in Berlin. He sees her on stage, follows her, and an air raid brings them closer, forcing her to take him into the shelter in her house. They spend the night together, but he disappears the next day without having revealed his identity to her. Weeks later, he turns up again, now telling her that he is an air force pilot. He proposes marriage and she accepts, but the war tears them apart again and again, even on the night before their planned marriage. They meet again in Rome, where she has a singing engagement, and once more make wedding plans. However, when Paul decides to return to his unit, just because another officer suggested it would be the thing to do, Hanna loses her patience. They separate in strife, since she expects him to stay with her, and he is disappointed that she does not understand what it would mean to be an officer's wife. Only later does she realise that it was the attack on the Soviet Union that called him back to the front. But it is too late, since the death of a comrade has convinced Wendlandt that it is better to face death alone, without having to worry about loved ones. But then he is wounded and Hanna rushes to visit him in hospital, and finally they look forward to the future together, even if it means duty and separation.

The film depicts many aspects of wartime reality, but what is more important is the way the characters learn to handle these situations. As Jens Thiele and Fred Ritzel point out, the protagonists have to learn to adapt their expectations to wartime life, postponing hopes of individual fulfilment until peacetime, but not giving them up entirely. Instead, as Martin Loiperdinger and Klaus Schönekas explain, knowing *for whom* one lives, fights or endures hardships becomes a part of morale, distinguishing this film from most war pictures that centred on soldierly heroes and male bonding.

The narrative process of the film plays out the transformation of the characters. They – and particularly she – must learn to fulfil their roles in a particular way and to relinquish their desires. However, in doing that they become truly themselves, casting off false wishes and poses to become a model couple.

Transformation might seem unnecessary for Wendlandt, who is a hero from the very beginning. The start of the film clearly establishes his bravery, coolness and sense of duty and dedication when he risks his life to get his plane back onto the ground in one piece, despite defective landing gear. Furthermore, the film stresses his masculinity: in Berlin he appears to be an undaunted womaniser, not afraid to try to seduce a famous star. What he has to learn, however, is to connect his emotional life with his duty and to give up a bachelor's freedom, but that turns out to be just a superficial role, not really part of his character. It proves harder to reconcile marriage with his soldierly life. But since an exemplary sense of responsibility is his defining characteristic, the burden of accepting the privations of military service is left with Hanna.

Hanna Holberg is a typical role for Leander, who frequently played apparently libertine divas, who turn out to be good-hearted women and self-sacrificing mothers. As Antje Ascheid has shown, Leander's star image was complex and contradictory. Her performances embodied disparate elements, many of which seem to go against Nazi ideology. Thus she played (and was) a glamorous star, a working woman and a symbol of erotic desire, all things the official ideology impugned. These characteristics were emphasised in the popular press: 'Zarah Leander, in her stance as an actress, is the epitome of "transcendental sensuality". Her inner being is as dark as her wondrous deep alto voice, which so enticingly expresses women's hidden desires.' A Swedish actress playing independent women with sex appeal, careers and 'questionable' morals would seem to be just the opposite of what Nazi cinema would tolerate. But exactly this image was used to build up Leander as a star in a number of high-budget films. She was intended to be a glamour star and an ersatz Marlene Dietrich, though the active sexuality and androgynous elements in her image were nowhere near the level of Dietrich's persona. This image had a strong popular appeal, making her the top female star of Nazi cinema. Still, there are reasons to argue that this side of her persona was just an 'illusory image of transgression' as Helma Sanders-Brahms puts it, or even a 'fascist illusion of female autonomy' as Heide Schlüpmann argues. The melodramatic stories are responsible for this, making her give up career and independence to take her place in society as wife and mother in the end, even if some of the films – particularly those directed by Detlef Sierck (Douglas Sirk) – do retain a certain ambiguity.

A common plot pattern in Leander's films is the transformation from apparent vamp to a marriageable woman. Typically, in *The Great Love* she is first shown as a singer with sex appeal, but this is immediately revealed to be just a stage role. Still, she has to undergo a stronger transformation than Wendlandt – she has to learn to accept and even take on 'male' obedience to duty, subordinating herself to the greater good. She undergoes a metamorphosis into the Nazi stereotype of a good comrade, wife and future mother. First she has to learn to wait, then she takes on an active role, singing for the troops at the front, but most of all, she must learn to take what comes without placing demands on the man or questioning his duty. What is involved, then, is the domestication of individual desire.

The film embodies its message in its visual qualities as well as in the plot. A comparison between the first and last stage performances of Hanna Holberg clearly shows the trajectory of her development. These scenes also show how the film tries to engage the audience's feelings and re-channel them in ideologically preferred ways.

In the first stage scene, Hanna sings 'Mein Leben für die Liebe'. Amongst rows of male dancers, wearing a low-cut dress and a blonde wig, she appears to fit Leander's standard role at the beginning of her films: the erotic woman. This characterisation is supported by the staging and music: rows of darkly dressed dancers carrying out irregular, chaotic movements, a background chorus that sounds like shouting, and stage decorations suggesting flames place her in the midst of a complex of signs suggesting passion, chaos and unbridled desire. This position is confirmed by the way she is made the object of the (male) gaze – that of Wendlandt and his comrade in the audience and, through their eye-lines, also the gaze of the camera (here the film seems to present an exemplary case for Laura Mulvey's analysis of the male gaze in cinema). That this view is a voyeuristic one is confirmed when the men exchange looks and a nod, expressing their appreciation of the woman as an erotic object and confirming their male role. Her song, described by *Film-Kurier* as 'a humorously pointed chanson with sex-appeal', with lyrics stating 'Mein Wahlspruch heißt: Erlaubt ist, was gefällt' ('My motto is: do as you please'), reinforces this view of Hanna as an openly erotic woman, an impression heightened by her looks and posture. She appears as the active woman, with – at least for the mentality of that time – strong male components or even a phallic staging of her body. Her performance as *femme fatale* is certainly effective for Wendlandt, who immediately sets off to try to get to know her, or as he says, to 'fly reconnaissance', whereas his comrade says it is pointless to go up against 'superior forces'. Their dialogue sets up Wendlandt as the reckless go-getter and the woman as game to be hunted, or as the opponent in the 'battle of the sexes.' This continues in the following sequence, but in this scene she drops the role of *femme fatale* as soon as she is offstage. The 'real' Hanna is 'softer' and more 'feminine' – and closer in appearance to the usual image of Leander – as soon as she takes off her wig and changes into her ordinary clothes. This, however, also means she is more vulnerable, as shown when Wendlandt and another man follow her from the theatre into the subway, where she is made the object of open stares and male jokes, but is – in contrast to her stage role – unable to look back or assert any power. In real life Hanna is far from the *femme fatale* that her performance suggested, and even her status as diva proves not to be a viable role.

It is also one that she is forced to give up – even in its most rudimentary forms of desires of her own – in the course of the film. Repeated separation from the man she loves, frustration of their plans to marry, and finally Wendlandt's decision to renounce private happiness in order to face the threat of death, bring her to suppress her own wishes. She is gradually 'purified' of her individualistic impulses. By the final stage scene she is willing to subordinate herself to the war – and to the man and his duties. This is visualised by a *mise-en-scène* that reverses the iconography of her first appearance.

The contrast between the opening stage scene and the final one could hardly be greater. Darkness, high contrasts, flames, rows of male dancers and the foxtrot have been replaced by white sets and costumes, high-key lighting, the organic forms of plants and flowers and a slow waltz with female singers humming like an angelic chorus in the background. The lyrics, 'Ich weiß, es wird einmal ein Wunder gesch'n' ('I'm sure a miracle will occur someday'), overtly reverses the opening song. Leander no longer sings, 'I don't want to dream, don't want to miss anything … I live my life to the full', and is now reduced to the purely passive (feminine) role of waiting and hoping. This immobilisation of female desire also determines staging and camera work. Throughout most of the sequence, Leander is shown frontally in medium close-up, then the camera travels into a long close-up. The white background, costume and the light skin tones meld her into the background, an effect heightened by the limited depth and tight framing of the shot. When she lifts her arms above her head in the close-up, the impression that she is pinned to the background becomes even stronger. That this occurs while she sings about believing in a miracle and a tear rolls down her cheek makes the emotional impact as well as making the meaning of the song all too clear. The 'great love' is one that can defer satisfaction, one that is made up more of unending longing than of desire. We know that this form of love will be rewarded, as the song concludes: 'Our souls are one / And that is why a miracle will occur / and I know that we will meet again.' The melodramatic moment of the narration coincides with the musical climax and a lingering 'glamour' shot of the star's face. At the visual and semantic levels, connotations of purity, faith and hope come together with the reduction of the woman to a passive, immobilised position. The camera takes on the function of an 'evil eye' with a mortifying, petrifying gaze, as characterised by Karsten Witte as a tendency in Nazi cinema. With this image, the story has reached its goal, at least in terms of re-aligning the woman with a role defined by passiveness, sacrifice and the renunciation of any desire of her own.

In terms of the film's political aim, however, there is more to be done, so it follows Hanna to a hospital in the mountains, where she is re-united with Wendlandt. He says that because of his injury they will have three weeks together and asks her if they should try one more time to get married. After a kiss, she asks, 'Three weeks, and then …?' Wendlandt answers with a glance up at a formation of airplanes flying over. She looks up with him, exactly repeating the direction of her look during the last stage performance, underscored by an instrumental version of the song 'Ich weiß, es wird einmal ein Wunder gescheh'n'. Thus, as Loiperdinger and Schönekas argue, the film manages to find a synthesis of the signifying systems woman, music, and love on the one hand and man, duty, military, and airplanes on the other – two codes referred to throughout the film, but shown in collision thus far. The apparent synthesis actually represents the subordination of private, female desire to the male military system. *The Great Love* mobilises desires for autonomy, love, happiness and private satisfaction only to re-contain them through the development of its story and even through shifts in visual representation. The ideological work of the plot is to re-define male and particularly female gender roles, and also to aim at manufacturing consent to the hardships of war. The film shows that the way to happiness, and even to a greater love, is that of renouncing individual desire and submitting to discipline and the war effort.

But what did audiences make of this message? Was the film able to educate them in the sense of the 'invisible propaganda' that Goebbels favoured, re-aligning feelings, gender roles and subjectivity to produce conformity or even enthusiasm for the regime and its war efforts? Or did they see through the propagandistic intention, but perhaps still learn their lesson, accepting wartime privations as a necessary evil? Or did the wishes for personal happiness resist their containment through narrative closure and remain a latent moment of not opposition, but at least passive resistance? Without any real documents of film reception, and in light of the common distortion and repression of memories of the Third Reich, it is impossible to reconstruct what effect the film had. Most likely a mixture of very divergent outcomes, since the audiences and popular culture in Nazi Germany were more heterogeneous than was often thought. The film's enormous popularity does indicate that it touched the feelings of many people and did serve as a reflection of their lives during the war period. It may well have helped them 'hold out' in hard times and hope for a 'miracle' – whatever that might have meant for each of them. It definitely offered them role models in the main characters, but there again, combined with some of the ambiguity involved in any melodrama.

Stephen Lowry

REFERENCES

Ascheid, A. (2003) *Hitler's Heroines: Stardom and Womanhood in Nazi Cinema*. Philadelphia: Temple University Press.

Feddersen, H. (1942) 'Ein neuer Zarah-Leander-Film', *Steglitzer Anzeiger*, 17 June.

Film-Kurier (1941) 'Kammerspielszene mit Zarah Leander', 13, 262 (7 November), 3.

Fox, J. (2000) *Filming Women in the Third Reich*. Oxford: Berg.

Loiperdinger, M. and K. Schönekäs (1991) 'Die große Liebe – Propaganda im Unterhaltungsfilm', in R. Rother (ed.) *Bilder schreiben Geschichte: Der Historiker im Kino*. Berlin: Wagenbach, 143–9.

Mulvey, L. (1975) 'Visual Pleasure and Narrative Cinema', *Screen*, 16, 3, 6–18.

O'Brien, M.-E. (2004) *Nazi Cinema as Enchantment: The Politics of Entertainment in the Third Reich*. Rochester, NY: Camden.

Sanders-Brahms, H. (1992 [1981]) 'Zarah', in *Das Dunkle zwischen den Bildern*. Frankfurt am Main: Verlag der Autoren, 57–64.

Schlüpmann, H. (1988) 'Faschistische Trugbilder weiblicher Autonomie', *Frauen und Film*, 44/45, 44–66.

Senske, W. H. (1942) 'Der neue Zarah-Leander-Film *Die große Liebe*', *Bremer Nachrichten*, 5 August.

Thiele, J. and F. Ritzel (1991) 'Politische Botschaft und Unterhaltung – Die Realität im NS-Film: Die große Liebe (1942)', in W. Faulstich and H. Korte (eds) *Fischer Filmgeschichte, Band 2: 1925–1944*. Frankfurt am Main: Fischer, 310–23.

Witte, K. (1995) *Lachende Erben, Toller Tag: Filmkomödie im Dritten Reich*. Berlin: Vorwerk 8.

DER WEISSE TRAUM THE WHITE DREAM **10**

GÉZA VON CZIFFRA, GERMANY, 1943

Der Weiße Traum (*The White Dream*) premiered on 5 October 1943 in Vienna and was shown in Berlin for the first time on 11 November 1943. As a contemporary reviewer wrote,

> The audience of the Berlin premiere of the Wien-Film *The White Dream* at the Ufa-Palast am Zoo experienced the first European ice show on film. Géza von Cziffra, the film's writer and director has without doubt created a masterpiece, which through unheard-of verve and exceptional Viennese charm will take the audience by storm.

The film tells the story of a figure skater who dreams of becoming an actress. This dream seems to come true all of a sudden, when by chance and confusion she is engaged as the lead in a stage show. A love story develops between the young woman and an ice-hockey player, who works as a stage designer for the show. After the first night, the company is thrown out of the theatre due to quarrels with the owner, and decides to put the show on ice.

Since dancing and singing in the style of a revue are integrated into the plot, this film is commonly regarded as a 'revue film'. Films of this kind were not uncommon, and some of them – *Frauen sind doch die besseren Diplomaten* (*Women Are Better Diplomats*, 1941), *Immer nur Du* (*You Only You*, 1941) and *Die Frau meiner Träume* (*The Woman of My Dreams, 1944*) – were among the most successful films of the early 1940s. *The White Dream*, too, attracted extraordinarily large audiences, like the above-quoted reviewer predicted. Gerd Albrecht lists it as the most successful film of 1944. Boguslaw Drewniak calls attention to an unpublished note by the Ministry of Propaganda, dated 13 January 1944, in which *The White Dream* is mentioned as the commercially most successful black and white film, and that an exceptional number of copies were produced. He adds that the film was also successful abroad, for example, in Italy, Denmark, Sweden, Albania and Turkey. Von Cziffra speaks of 35 million viewers and 140 million Marks revenue.

Why did this production become the box-office hit of the season? To what extent was this film typical of the films of the early 1940s or of a certain genre? Was the audience drawn by new visual attractions, or did the film rely on well-tried elements and patterns? Looking beyond the contemporary context: which developments in German cinema does the remake of *The White Dream* by the same writer/director, *Kauf dir einen bunten Luftballon* (1961), represent? Finally, is today's assessment of the film typical for a certain view of films made during the Third Reich?

Albrecht also stated: 'Diversion, entertainment, relaxation, combined with music, glamour, flirt, dallying, love, impressive landscapes and sets – that is what the audience was looking for on the screen towards the end of Hitler's war.' This is reflected by the genres of the Nazi-era: comedies of different types, including *Schwank* ('low' comedy) and *Lustspiel* ('high' comedy), amounted to almost half (48 per cent) of the film production in the Third Reich, and musical comedy was one of the most popular genres. In 1943, the share of comedies rose to a new high (55 per cent).

At the beginning of the 1940s, on the one hand, films were oriented towards children, adolescents, women and elderly people, i.e. those not directly involved in the war and thus able to go to the cinema as usual. However, they were also oriented towards soldiers at the front. Drewniak claimed, 'In the year 1941, the RPL [Reich's Ministry of Propaganda], according to press releases, had around 1,140 travelling cinemas in service, showing films and news reels to more than 92 million viewers.' Revue films were likely to be attractive to both groups. Since, in most cases, a female protagonist was at the centre of the story, they offered female audiences a potential for identification. Furthermore, the love story, together with music, dancing and lavish costumes, were likely to appeal to many women. For the men at the front or the military hospitals, it was probably edifying to see attractive women dancing and singing popular songs. Typically, these songs were also broadcast on the radio and sold as records; film studios and music industry were closely connected, so both parties profited from cross-marketing. Even though the supply of films at this time was monitored and influenced by the Nazi regime, popular taste could not be controlled, so the film industry's commercial interests had to take the audience's preferences into account.

The concept of merging a story with singing and dancing had proven successful in the *Tonfilmoperette* ('sound film operetta') of the early 1930s. This subgenre combined traditions drawn from operetta, comedy, cabaret and music hall revue, and usually featured ordinary people. As Thomas Elsaesser has pointed out, 'many composers being Jewish, Ufa changed the formula after 1933, switching to *Revuefilme*'. For revue films, the well-established pattern was extended by opulent revue numbers, like those found in elaborate stage revues. The theatrical genre had been especially popular in the 1920s, but some of the revues still filled theatres, such as the 3,000-seat Berliner Scala, even in the 1930s, despite the Great Depression. The revues often included 'mass ornament' choreographies, for which most theatres maintained their own ballet troupes. Whereas the main emphasis of the theatrical revues was on the show elements, and these were usually only loosely connected, the revue films integrated the song and dance numbers into the plot. This is also noticeable in early 1930s US film musicals, which possibly provided a model for the German revue films, of which *The White Dream* is an example.

After the introduction of the sound film, Broadway became interesting for Hollywood for several reasons. Firstly, the stage provided actors with trained voices. Secondly, many Broadway plays could be used as templates for film plots. Thirdly, the theatre milieu was an entertaining setting. Thus, as early as 1929, three backstage film musicals were produced: *The Broadway Melody* (one of the earliest sound films and the first musical to win the Academy Award for Best Film), *Applause* and *On With the Show*. The success of *The Broadway Melody* led to a vast number of imitations trying to benefit from the Broadway flair, for instance, *The Broadway Hoofer* and *Broadway Scandals* (both 1929). Then 1933 saw the beginning of the era of Busby Berkley, who staged the dance scenes in three legendary musicals in the same year: *Gold Diggers of 1933*, *42nd Street* and *Footlight Parade*. All three films tell amusing stories of the stage milieu and feature a number of Broadway insider gags. MGM continued the tradition begun by *The Broadway Melody* with *Broadway Melody of 1936* (1935), *Broadway Melody of 1938* (1937) and *Broadway Melody of 1940* (1940), all with Eleanor Powell, who also starred in many other MGM musicals.

The number of US films in German cinemas had declined since 1933 and from 1941 onwards, no foreign films were screened at all. However, by then some US backstage musicals had already been shown: *On the Avenue* (1937), *Broadway Serenade* (German title: *Irrwege der Liebe*, 1939), *Broadway Melody of 1936* (1935) and *Broadway Melody of 1938* (1937). The two 'Broadway Melodies' were the most successful films in Berlin first-run cinemas, judging by the number of showings.

Apart from the screening of US films for the general public, there were special screenings, even of forbidden films, for filmmakers, state and party officials, army leaders, police and so on. In 1943, the *Reichsfilmarchiv* owned approximately 29,000 German and foreign fiction films and documentaries. As of mid-1942, around 3,500 feature-length sound films, of which only half were German productions, were catalogued and prepared for screening. Thus, the idea of producing German adaptations of US film musicals may have emerged from different contexts. The positive response of audiences to films like those starring Eleanor Powell may have inspired German emulations. Or the idea to produce films for the German market in the style of US backstage musicals may have arisen during special screenings, where such films were shown (for example, a screening of *Coney Island* [1943] is documented).

Whereas theatrical revues, US musicals and film operettas may have served as models for film musicals like *The White Dream*, there were also likely sources for the film's figure skating elements. For example, Hollywood produced ice revue films with international figure skating star Sonja Henie, such as *One in a Million* (1936) und *Happy Landing* (1938), which were among the most popular films in the USA during their respective seasons. In 1940, live ice revues were shown in New York's Center Theater. Furthermore, in the early 1940s, travelling entertainment shows such as *Ice Capades* (founded in 1940) and *Holiday on Ice* (founded in 1943) began their tours.

Around the same time in Austria, the *Karl-Schäfer-Eisrevue* was set up, named after its founder, the seven-time world champion and two-time Olympic gold medal winner in figure skating. Between 1938 and 1939, Karl Schäfer worked as trainer in the USA and could have seen ice revue films while there. In Germany, of the ice revue films, only *Happy Landing* was shown. However, since this film was criticised by the Nazi press for the 'racial sympathies' of the lead actress, it may not have been in cinemas for long.

Apart from the viewers who had seen *Happy Landing* and the visitors of the *Karl-Schäfer-Eisrevue*, which was only staged in Vienna, it was *The White Dream* that brought the ice revue to a wider German audience. The skating spectacle was combined with popular motifs of contemporary German film musicals. These usually contained two story lines: the successful rise of a hard-working show talent to revue stardom, and a love story complicated by confusion and misunderstandings. In the case of *The White Dream*, the plot is set, for a large part, in a theatre during preparations for the premiere of a stage show. The backstage milieu was not only the setting of many US musicals; it was also typical of contemporary German revue films. The attractions of this scenario are obvious. Firstly, the world of circus, music hall or theatre provides glamorous scenery. Secondly, it is plausible to incorporate dancing and singing into the plot. In German films, song and dance numbers were usually motivated by a performance situation, whereas in Hollywood films, characters sometimes suddenly burst into song in everyday situations. Consequently, the protagonists of German revue films were conceived accordingly: in 28 film musicals between 1933 and 1945, among the female protagonists there were 17 dancers, eight singers, a show whistler, a card girl and a figure skater, i.e. all of them working in show business. Of the male protagonists, eight work on stage (as bit player, singer or artiste), ten work backstage (as lighting technician, stage manager, set designer, playwright or composer), and ten work outside of this milieu (as scientist, engineer or member of the armed forces). Thus, almost two thirds of the male protagonists also work in show business.

With this emphasis on characters from the performing arts, it is hardly surprising that their preparations and performances feature prominently in the films. In *The White Dream*, we see an audition, several rehearsals, the beginning of the revue's ill-fated first night and finally the premiere at the ice rink. The latter sequence at the end of the film covers twenty minutes, showing – with some minor interruptions for dialogue scenes – a short version of the ice revue.

A notable quality of *The White Dream* is that the revue scenes are organically embedded and directly motivated by the plot. And the audience follows not only a certain career, but also a revue's production from first rehearsals to premiere. As Dietrich Steinbeck states, 'story and revue scenes … are organically developed from each other and thus not randomly interchangeable'. Furthermore, the musical numbers are not fragmented into extracts but, at the end of the film, shown as a complete revue.

Opulent revue scenes were quite common; exotic designs were especially popular; as Steinbeck has noted: 'Japanese next to Spanish … the inevitable tap dance scene next to … white tails, see-through tulle and waltzing groups in an open, columned hall, bathed in starlight.' These typical elements also can be found in *The White Dream*: a tap dance on skates, in tails, in front of the stylised skyline of Manhattan, the colourful hustle and bustle at the Vienna Prater, a Spanish bullfight, Venetian gondolas, Hungarian folk dances, and so on. The press especially commended the 'glittering, fantastic images' and 'lavish splendour'.

The significant difference between this film and other German revue films is the staging on ice. A performance of this kind presented new visual attractions: an ice rink provides a larger and more innovative creative space than a theatre stage. Moreover, the movements of figure skaters are much smoother than those of dancers, and the choreography gains in tempo, because the actors are faster on ice skates than in dancing shoes. The audience, however, is carefully prepared for this new feature: at first, revue and ice skating are shown as parallel worlds. One part of the story takes place on the ice rink, with emphasis on sporting activities, such as figure skating training and ice hockey matches, the other part in the theatre. Because the protagonists live in both worlds, the link between revue stage and ice rink is finally established. The audience is thus not immediately confronted with a revue on ice, a sight that would have been completely new for large parts of the German audience; instead, it is witness to the evolution of this new attraction within the film itself.

The White Dream was the first German film to combine the typical elements of German revue films, accompanied by the music of a hit songwriter (Anton Pofes), with figure skating and its stars; the film's success created a precedent for many more productions like it. The concept of combining sports and theatrical performance demanded much of the actors and thus influenced the casting. The female lead is played by the Austrian ice-dancing champion Olly Holzmann, who was also an actress. In the revue scenes, her partner was figure skater Karl Schäfer, whose ice revue troupe staffs the largest part of the final ice revue. Due to the demands on the actors, the casting significantly differed from other revue films. These featured mainly popular stars like Martha Eggert, Zarah Leander, Anny Ondra, Ilse Werner or La Jana. Marika Rökk was cast more often than any other actress, with leading roles in at least eight successful film musicals of the 1930s and 1940s, followed by Johannes Heesters playing the male lead in at least seven productions of that time. Engaging a female lead unknown as an actress and a chorus without previous film experience certainly was a risk, but one that paid off.

One indication of the lasting popularity of ice-revues in Germany (and Austria) in the 1950s and 1960s is the continued existence of the Karl-Schäfer-Eisrevue after World War II as the *Wiener Eisrevue* ('Viennese ice revue'). Holiday on Ice was also very popular, especially in Berlin in 1952, with Sonja Henie. Some figure skaters appeared in both troupes, such as Marika Kilius and Hans-Jürgen Bäumler or Hanna Eigel. Furthermore, the *Wiener Eisrevue* appeared in many films after World War II, which reveals a continued demand: in 1951, *Frühling auf dem Eis* was released, followed by *Der Bunte Traum* in 1952, *Symphonie in Gold* in 1956, *Traumrevue* in 1959 (with three European figure skating champions from Vienna), *Kauf dir einen bunten Luftballon* (the remake of *The White Dream*) in 1961 and, in the same year, *Ein Stern fällt vom Himmel* (*A Star Falls from Heaven*). Several of these films, including the remake of *The White Dream*, were again written and directed by von Cziffra. A few years later, two films were produced with the famous ice-dancing couple Marika Kilius and Hans-Jürgen Bäumler: *Die große Kür* in 1964 (the third most successful German film of the season) and *Das große Glück* in 1967.

Obviously, the concept that was first realised in Germany with *The White Dream* did not go out of fashion, because the later films also dealt with putting on an ice revue, but with less exposition and more obstacles for the sake of narrative suspense and variety. Furthermore, it was a general strategy until the mid-1960s in Germany to produce exact remakes of successful films, adding technical innovations established in the meantime, such as sound and colour. At least 20 per cent of the German top-ten films in the 1950s were remakes, mostly in colour, of pre-war black and white films. The remake of *The White Dream* was also shot in colour and is thus a typical example of this strategy.

Since *The White Dream* and its remake are twenty years apart, a new cast was engaged (except for Oscar Sima, who appears in both films); the leading roles were played by two famous athletes, figure skater Ina Bauer and skier Toni Sailer. With popular comedian Heinz Erhardt as the theatre manager, another marquee attraction was added to the list. The remake's title, *Kauf dir einen bunten Luftballon*, quotes a song of *The White Dream*'s protagonist, which had become an evergreen and was used again in the remake, as well as one other piece from the original film. However, both melodies are updated with swinging rhythms, and the lead character sings 'Ich bin die flotte Susi' ('I'm snappy Susie'), more 'hip' than the original 'Ich bin die Pratermizzi' ('I'm Mizzi from the Prater', an allusion to a famous Austrian silent film character). The rest of the score was newly composed in the popular style of the 1960s. In addition, at the beginning and the end of the film, skiing scenes are included to showcase the talents of Toni Sailer. Apart from these variations concerning technology, cast and music, the story (including all characters) was left intact, most of the dialogues were retained verbatim, the *mise-en-scène* is very similar, and even most of the shots are nearly identical. The rationale for this is certainly the wish to repeat the huge success of *The White Dream*, by creating a remake as close to the original as possible.

The close similarities between the original and the remake are of interest for another reason as well: for interpretations of the original film on the basis of its political context. Although many remakes of films from the 1930s and 1940s were produced after the war, and although in the case of *The White Dream* neither story nor dramatic structure were changed. Drewniak, amongst others, has alleged that even (or especially) 'films of a light character, like *Operette* (*Operetta*, 1940), *Schrammeln* (1940), *The White Dream*, *Seine beste Rolle* (1944) or *Es lebe die Liebe* (1944), contained more or less subtle intentions to control'. It is argued that these intentions are expressed, firstly, in implicit sexist, nationalist and racist ideologies, and secondly, in the production of uncritical entertainment as diversion. The latter is regarded as 'in no way apolitical', for one always has to bear in mind why, and from what, people were to be distracted.

This assessment is based on the fact that the regime's ruling elite had a strong influence on the film sector and explicitly pursued the goal of utilising films for political propaganda. Indeed, the existence of far-reaching control mechanisms, which functionalised the film industry according to the will of the Nazi-regime, is indisputable. The explicit propaganda films most obviously show how films were exploited for ideological purposes, but other films, too, were subjected to the maxims of the Ministry of Propaganda. But was this always the case?

There are grounds to question the notion that all directors and their staff were so dedicated to the Nazi worldview that their work inevitably showed traces of that ideology. One also wonders how far the regime's control mechanisms reached in practice, especially for films not produced in Berlin. *The White Dream* was produced in the Vienna Studios of Wien-Film GmbH during the Nazi annexation. Nevertheless, von Cziffra describes the Vienna-based film industry as an oasis, in which many people longed to work: far away from the Ministry of Propaganda, one could escape not only the Allied bombers, but also demands to support contemporary political tendencies. One may dismiss such statements, as Gerhard Stahr has observed, as 'apologies of those responsible for the production'. However, von Cziffra's account of the situation may at least give rise to some doubts as to what extent the regime's principles were automatically put into practice by filmmakers, who were not necessarily in agreement and separated from the RPL, not only by large distances, but also by several ramifications of a complex organisational structure. Historians have repeatedly pointed out the limits of Nazi influence on the film sector. Furthermore, there is strong indication that the production of popular and thus profitable films continued after the Nazi regime's rise to power, as long as the content was not in direct contradiction to official ideology.

The White Dream – like any other light entertainment film of this kind – may, of course, be accused of escapism. But films transporting their audience to fantasy worlds existed both before and after the Third Reich. The Nazis certainly furthered this branch of film production. That does not mean, however, that all light entertainment films were politically exploited and imbued with Nazi ideology *per se*. Despite the regime's programmatic demands, the system in which films were produced cannot be seen as completely cut off from foreign trends and homogenously compliant. Furthermore, a film that cost a fair amount of money would have failed to pass censorship only if it expressed outright anti-regime tendencies. Due to the fact that *The White Dream* could be remade in 1963 without major changes, there is every reason to regard the film primarily as well-made entertainment – a film that presented likable characters and hit songs, skilfully adapted elements typical of its genre, and impressed audiences with a tightly woven dramatic structure and innovative visual attractions.

Anna Sarah Vielhaber

Translated by Michael Ross and Alexander Rindfleisch

REFERENCES

Albrecht, G. (1969) *Nationalsozialistische Filmpolitik: Eine soziologische Untersuchung über die Spielfilme des Dritten Reichs.* Stuttgart: Enke.

____ (ed.) (1979) *Film im Dritten Reich.* Karlsruhe: Doku.

____ (1995) 'Kino am Abgrund', in C. Hackl, K. F. Reimers and B. Scherer (eds) *Unser Jahrhundert in Film und Fernsehen: Beiträge zu zeitgeschichtlichen Film- und Fernsehdokumenten.* Konstanz: Ölschläger, 99–115.

Cziffra, G. von (1989) *Ungelogen: Erinnerungen an mein Jahrhundert.* Frankfurt am Main and Berlin: Ullstein.

Drewniak, B. (1987) *Der Deutsche Film 1938–1945: Ein Gesamtüberblick.* Düsseldorf: Droste.

Elsaesser, T. (ed.) (1999) *The BFI Companion to German Cinema.* London: British Film Institute.

Stahr, G. (2001) *Volksgemeinschaft vor der Leinwand?: Der nationalsozialistische Film und sein Publikum.* Berlin: Theissen.

Steinbeck, D. (1979) 'Oper und Turnen. Zur Rolle des Tanzes im nationalsozialistischen Revuefilm', in H. Belach (ed.) *Wir tanzen um die Welt: Deutsche Revuefilme 1933–1945.* München: Hanser, 53–72.

DIE MÖRDER SIND UNTER UNS

11

THE MURDERERS ARE AMONG US

WOLFGANG STAUDTE, EAST GERMANY, 1946

It is symptomatic of the bifurcated history of post-1945 German film that Germany's first postwar domestic feature, Wolfgang Staudte's *Die Mörder sind unter uns* (*The Murderers Are Among Us*, 1946), figures as the simultaneous point of departure for two distinct narratives of national cinematic development. In the history of GDR cinema, the film enjoys pride of place as the title that launched East Germany's national film studio, DEFA, and ensconced the anti-fascist film as DEFA's defining genre in the studio's first decade. In West German cinema history, by contrast, the protagonist's struggle with issues of guilt and complicity secured for *The Murderers Are Among Us* a reputation as the founding text of a characteristically West German tradition of cinematic *Vergangenheitsbewältigung* ('coming to terms with the past'): a tradition seen to reach its apogee in the New German Cinema of the 1970s and 1980s, when films investigating continuities between the nation's fascist past and its conservative present secured for West German directors a place in the international pantheon of *auteur* film.

The film's significance as a stepping stone to German cinema's postwar rehabilitation was prefigured already by the choice of venue for its premiere. The film had its opening screening on 15 October 1946 in the Berlin State Opera House at the heart of the former capital's Soviet-occupied central sector. The prestige launch was widely applauded in the German-language press as a fitting celebration of a new beginning for German film. In November 1944, Allied military command had responded to the film medium's key role in fascist cultural politics with a ban on German film production, distribution and cinema exhibition. On 12 May 1945, prohibition was superseded by a directive foreseeing a limited revival of the German film industry, but within the framework of a licensing and censorship system designed to suppress activity by film personnel politically implicated in, or ideologically sympathetic to, National Socialism. Though the effectivity of licensing was questionable – directors Veit Harlan and Wolfgang Liebeneiner were only two of the most prominent among the many politically compromised figures swiftly denazified after 1945 – the license system, together with the material difficulties presented by film stock shortages, bombed-out studios and the absence of raw materials and equipment for set construction, costume or props, had until autumn 1946 significantly delayed the revival of German film production in the four zones of occupation under Allied control.

The first screening of *The Murderers Are Among Us* signified on one level, then, a successful overcoming of material obstacles by the combined forces of director/scriptwriter Staudte and his main collaborator, the cinematographer Friedl Behn-Grund. As contemporary reviews were quick to indicate, the film broke new ground most significantly, however, in its rejection of the themes and aesthetic strategies of Third Reich film. Against a Third Reich industry increasingly committed to extravagant cinematic fantasies – recent examples perhaps recalled by contemporary audiences might have included Josef von Báky's adventure fantasy *Münchhausen* (*The Extraordinary Adventures of Baron Munchhausen*, 1943), the revue spectacular *Die Frau meiner Träume* (*The Woman of My Dreams*, 1944) or Veit Harlan's war blockbuster *Kolberg* (*Burning Hearts*, 1944) – Staudte posed a starkly topical narrative of crime and punishment. The film's two protagonists share the prototypical traumas of the war experience. Hans Mertens (Wilhelm Borchert) returns from the front a broken man, drinking himself into an oblivion that suppresses memories of atrocities he witnessed but could not prevent. Susanne Wallner (Hildegard Knef) is the (improbably well-groomed) concentration camp survivor who returns to Berlin to find Mertens squatting in her flat. In what becomes a romance narrative, we witness Susanne by turns forgiving and despairing over Mertens' mood swings and secretive ways. Susanne herself has returned to work both as model housewife – she cleans continually – and as a graphic artist whose 'save the children' poster pays telling stylistic homage to the World War I pacifist and socialist Käthe Kollwitz. Mertens, by contrast, dissipates his days in weary stumbling across the ruined city from bar to bar.

The enigma of Mertens' alternating anger and despair is resolved when Susanne discovers a letter to a certain Frau Brückner, wife of Mertens' former commanding officer, who has apparently fallen in combat and committed his last written words to Mertens' care. Susanne's subsequent visit to Frau Brückner (Erna Sellmer) reveals that her husband, unbeknownst to Mertens, is alive and kicking – profiting, indeed, from the war by recycling army helmets as cooking pots. Mertens' fury at this apparently happy news is explained in the film's denouement, when we witness Brückner (Arno Paulsen) in a flashback to the war, demanding of Mertens that he carry out an order to massacre Polish civilians on the Eastern front. Mertens' first postwar impulse – to extract revenge by shooting Brückner – is checked when Susanne intervenes. 'We do not have the right to judge!', she says, before agreeing with her lover that it is their shared duty 'to accuse'.

The message of the film's didactic closing passage is unequivocal. While on the one hand *The Murderers Are Among Us* demands of German audiences that they bring to justice those responsible for war crimes and Nazi terror, on the other the film sends out a clarion call to fellow filmmakers for a politically engaged revival of a German cinema capable, as the reviewer Peter Kast put it, of 'proving … that forces are at work in the new, democratic Germany which will not rest until punishment is meted out to war criminals who have sullied the German name'. This was a topical demand indeed. On the day of the film's release, Hermann Goering, on trial since November 1945 at the International Military Tribunal in Nuremberg, and under sentence of death since 1 October 1946, committed suicide by swallowing cyanide. On 16 October, the day after the film's premiere, ten other war criminals were hanged at Nuremberg. Audiences in the film's opening week would thus have seen it in tandem with Allied newsreels in which the Nuremberg trials were headline news. What distinguished the film from the newsreels, however – and this was a fact much commented on by audiences and press – was the specifically German inflection of its response to issues addressed at Nuremberg by an international tribunal under Allied control. Against the US interpretation of war crimes as the product of a collective German guilt, Staudte pitted a vision of a German people, embodied allegorically in the figures of Susanne and Hans, that could build its own route to national renewal by seeking out and bringing to justice fellow Germans responsible for Nazi crimes.

The Murderers Are Among Us gained acclamation, accordingly, from those German critics for whom the film's call for justice needed to be made 'by and for Germans alone'. The film's insistence on German self-determination, however, may have been one source of the distrust that Staudte encountered from Allied authorities. A further cause, for the Western Allies at least, may have been the film's critique of free market economics as the correlative of political democracy. Relevant characters here are the war criminal Brückner, whose depravity is accentuated in the film by the alacrity of his pursuit of personal wealth; and the charlatan astrologist Timm, a minor but significant figure whose bulging wallet betrays a sinister proclivity to profit from others' misery.

In any event, the film met initially with only negative Western Allied response. Staudte, already active before 1945 as both minor actor and director, had penned the treatment for *The Murderers Are Among Us* in the final wartime months and laid plans with cameraman Behn-Grund to realise the project after the war's end. When Staudte circulated his draft first to the British, later to the US authorities, finally to the French, it was turned down, before finally gaining approval from the Soviet licensing authority, albeit under condition that the director both change the title (originally *Der Mann, den ich töten werde* – 'The Man I Will Kill') and discard the original ending, in which Mertens, in a moment of passion, shoots Brückner dead.

From the outset, then, responses to Staudte's film prefigured the East/West division that was to mark forty years of German film after 1949. The opposing reactions of Western and Eastern military authorities to Staudte's treatment are explicable, indeed, by divergences in Allied cultural politics from the very earliest stage. In Germany's western zones of occupation, an early tension emerged in Allied film policy between the ideological goal of re-education for democracy and the commercial aims in particular of the US to win German markets for Hollywood film. Despite the postwar scarcity economy, revival was rapid in the cinema sector after 1945. As causes for the cinemagoing boom – annual box-office figures rose from 150 million in 1945 to 474 million in 1949 – historians have pointed to the exemption of cinema tickets from rationing, cheap tickets and a popular thirst for entertainment. The US majors also exploited the US military administration's initial faith in the ability of Hollywood features to inculcate in German audiences a sympathy for democratic ways of life by sending to Germany films from their back catalogue that had been barred entry during a five-year import ban. Though film officers in the western zones did entertain as their medium-term goal the reconstruction of a domestic film and media sector, that policy was slow to take effect, and cinema programmes remained dominated in the early postwar months by a combination of Allied newsreel and documentary, Hollywood and other foreign features and second-run German films produced before 1945, but declared ideologically neutral by Allied censors.

The rather different situation in the Soviet sector sheds light on the motivation underlying that administration's more favourable response to Staudte's approach. As early as November 1944, émigré politicians and artists had begun to sketch a cultural policy for a liberated Germany in whose reconstruction pro-Soviet German cultural practitioners would play a central role. Their vision of a cultural sector dedicated to the construction of a post-fascist German consensus came to early fruition with the founding of the DEFA studio in spring 1946. DEFA's commitment in its founding programme to 'expunging the remains of Nazism and militarism from the conscience of every German' sat well with Staudte's narrative of a personal and national redemption achieved by the pursuit of those who, like Hauptmann Brückner, had escaped retribution for wartime crimes. Indeed this dovetailing of Staudte's message with DEFA's anti-fascism was to situate *The Murderers Are Among Us* as an exemplar for the anti-fascist film, DEFA's prototypical genre after 1946. Among the DEFA productions following in the film's wake were Kurt Maetzig's *Ehe im Schatten* (*Marriage in the Shadows*, 1947), a melodrama built around the true story of a marriage between, and ultimately joint suicide by, the actor Joachim Gottschalk and his Jewish wife; Erich Engel's thriller exploring anti-Semitism in the post-World War I police and judiciary, *Affäre Blum* (*The Blum Affair*, 1948); and Staudte's own *Rotation* (1949), the tale of a printworker producing anti-fascist leaflets as a favour for his brother-in-law, and of the family tragedy that ensues when he is denounced by his Hitler Youth son.

After 1949, German division and the advent of Cold War, DEFA's anti-fascism shifted from the exploration of a shared German political history towards more polemical representations of Western capitalism as the seat of German fascism's crimes, including, for example, Kurt Maetzig's *Rat der Götter* (*The Gods' Advice*, 1950), a story of intrigue and war crimes in the chemical concern IG-Farben. In West German cinema, it was not until the early 1960s that critics and historians fully acknowledged the significance of Staudte's film. After 1959, when *The Murderers Are Among Us* was revived for its first-ever screening in the Federal Republic, Western commentators came to see in Staudte a director remarkable at least for his efforts to achieve not only an ideological, but also an artistic break with Third Reich film.

The most immediately arresting signal of that aesthetic rupture is the transformation of Berlin's rubble landscape into modernist *mise-en-scène*. The canted framing of the opening sequence, its stark black-white contrast and heavy symbolism – a wooden cross in the foreground and brooding shadows around the hunched figure of a shambling stranger (Mertens) – bespeak from the outset this film's affirmation of cinematic expressionism as a tradition ripe for reclaiming in post-1945 German film. Staudte's debt to the Weimar silents becomes yet more visible in Behn-Grund's use of oblique framing, underlighting and jagged silhouette to transform the urban ruins into allegorical figures for the inner torment of a broken man. In his performance of Mertens, Wilhelm Borchert reaches back similarly to the hyperbole of expressionist acting style; hence his maniacal laughter at crisis moments or his tortured face, frozen in close-up, as Mertens flashes back to the massacre he could not prevent. Vocally too, Borchert's guttural delivery suggests a modernist understanding of language as the bodily expression of emotions that words cannot convey, but that are captured instead in modulations of rhythm, volume, tempo, pitch and tone. All this, in tandem with lighting that situates Mertens in a shadowy zone between the dark forces of such figures as Brückner and the brilliant white of redemption, evoked by lighting that bathes Knef as Susanne in perpetual light, prompted the *Berliner Zeitung* – among others – to hail *The Murderers Are Among Us* as a film reminiscent of 'those great [Weimar] productions which earned German cinema its international reputation'.

There are limitations, though, to this reading of *The Murderers Are Among Us* as a homage to Weimar. When on the film's release critics talked in the same breath of its debt to silent cinema and of its topicality as a 'film of our time', they touched on a tension in the film between its retrospective visual style and a narrative that is squarely situated in the socio-political moment of 1945–49. The feature that roots *The Murderers Are Among Us* most obviously in its contemporary moment is its urban setting. In 1945/46, despite extensive bomb damage, sections of Berlin's film studios remained at least potentially open for use. Staudte and Behn-Grund set the tone for the *Trümmerfilm* ('rubble film') when they selected nonetheless to film on location in the ruins of Berlin. In part a repudiation of Third Reich film's claustrophobic studio aesthetic, this use of bombed-out cityscapes as film set was not so much realist, however, as allegorical. Staudte deployed the urban ruins in part as realist milieu, but more centrally as a visual metaphor for individual psychic collapse – the rats that Mertens sees streaming across the rubble thus become the symbolic embodiment of memories he cannot contain – and for the collective condition of socio-political fracture his film explores. That a return to studio interiors would have entailed a refusal of the moral and political challenges of Germany's ruined present is, indeed, inferred in Staudte's film through the visual opposition he establishes between the restored bourgeois order of ex-Hauptmann Brückner's home and the bullet-scarred walls and shattered windows of Susanne Wallner's tenement block. When the ruined house becomes the scene both of Susanne and Mertens' emerging redemptive love and of a painful but necessary exploration of Mertens' war memories, the message (as critics who disparage Staudte's heavy symbolism often note) is all too clear: it is only by sifting through the literal and metaphorical ruins that litter postwar landscapes that both the film's protagonist and its audience can chart a route to the future.

Alongside this allegorical deployment of rubble landscapes, *The Murderers Are Among Us* roots itself secondly in its contemporary moment through its unconventional organisation of narrative time. The film's narrative is non-linear, the forward movement of both romantic plotline and mystery blocked by flashbacks that return Mertens to the recurring trauma of the Polish massacre. Mertens' problem is not amnesia; as he himself avers, 'I have forgotten nothing.' The issue instead is the acutely topical one of how a soldier stranded in the stasis of war trauma and guilt can become again the agent both of his own life story and of the collective narrative of Germany's socio-political restoration. The film's flashbacks thus delineate with increasing clarity the precise contours of a war experience that traps Mertens in the inertia of unemployment and alcoholic excess. In the first flashback, a barroom chess game becomes unbearable when his opponent's move to save the king reminds Mertens of his own frontline insight that the leader is always saved, invariably at the cost of innocent lives. At this stage, as in a second flashback when Mertens suffers nervous collapse in a hospital at the sound of patients' moans, the film audience remains unenlightened about the source of his distress. Revelation begins only when Brückner returns the pistol Mertens had left with the war-wounded officer when he assumed him on the brink of death. The pistol triggers a sound flashback to stuttering gunfire and a woman's screams: a scenario fleshed out visually in the fourth and final flashback when a celebration in Brückner's factory at Christmas 1945 provokes in Mertens, in full at last, the memory of a previous wartime Christmas celebrated by Brückner and his officers to the accompanying sound of their soldiers gunning down civilians in the snow outside. The film's narrative structure approximates, then, to the therapeutic process whereby fragments of a traumatic memory are recalled, to be 'overcome' only when remembered in their original immediacy, and in full.

When critical interest in Staudte's film was finally reawakened in the West, attention often centred on these parallels between the film's narrative mirroring of psychotherapeutic memory work and films from such 1970s and 1980s directors as Alexander Kluge, Hans Jürgen Syberberg or Edgar Reitz, who understood their work as undertaking what Eric L. Santner has called 'elegiac labour' for Germany. *The Murderers Are Among Us* prefigures later West German work, however, not only in its structuring around achronological narrative patterns of personal remembering. The feature that both situated Staudte's film as a model for later films and that (paradoxically) roots the film in its late 1940s context, is a narrative structure in which the protagonist's struggle to remember becomes at the same time a process that submits the memories of others to historical repression. Most marked in *The Murderers Are Among Us* – and in this sense the film has been described as paradigmatic for what the social psychologists Alexander and Margarethe Mitscherlich famously termed West Germany's collective 'inability to mourn' – was the film's privileging of a point of view that obscured memories from the victims' perspective. There is clear evidence in the film's final flashback of Mertens' complicity in a war atrocity: he intervenes on the massacre victims' behalf, but capitulates in the end to Hauptmann Brückner's command. Repeatedly throughout the film, Mertens is figured nonetheless as fascism's victim: for instance, in his childlike nestling for comfort against Susanne's shoulder, his tormented raging or his description as a 'poor soul' by a neighbour, Mondschein (Robert Forsch), whose comments are validated by his status as Susanne's confidant and closest friend. *The Murderers Are Among Us* deftly sidesteps the Nazi genocide also, referencing it only in a breakfast scene when Brückner's ebullient absence of repentance is underscored by his avid munching of a hearty breakfast, his boiled egg only partially obscuring a newspaper headline reporting the gassing of millions in the Nazi camps.

As critics of the New German Cinema were later to comment, the point of view structure elaborated in *The Murderers Are Among Us*, in which the perspective of fascism's victims is radically obscured, was to become entrenched in later reworkings of fascism in German film. So too, finally, was a last feature that locates *The Murderers Are Among Us* as a film of its time. Reviewers in 1946 spilt little ink in their accounts of Hildegard Knef as Susanne Wallner, noting only her status, at age 21, as a young actress of unsullied reputation, despite bit parts for Ufa in the final war years. Unforeseen in October 1946 was the flourishing of Knef's career that *The Murderers Are Among Us* would provoke. The film paved the way for further titles that cemented Knef's screen persona as German film's archetypal *Trümmermädchen* ('rubble girl'): the resourceful Kat of *Zwischen gestern und morgen* (*Between Yesterday and Tomorrow*, 1947), a displaced person, who makes what living she can from black market trading, and wins the heart of the film's male protagonist Michael (Viktor de Kowa) when she solves the mystery of a theft of which he is wrongly accused; or the sassy housekeeper Christine in *Film ohne Titel* (*Film without a Title*, 1947/48), whose refugee suitor is transformed, like Mertens in *The Murderers Are Among Us*, by Knef whose love redeems her partner Martin by transforming him into a practical man.

The acclaim Knef later won as West Germany's first major postwar female star is explicable in part by the iconic status these three films establish for 'Hilde' as a woman of her time. So-called *Trümmerfrauen* ('rubble women') were set to work in their thousands after 1945 to clear German cities in preparation for the physical and economic reconstruction of the two postwar German states. Knef, first as Susanne in *The Murderers Are Among Us*, but equally in her later roles, epitomises the rubble generation first in her enthusiasm for physical labour. 'To work, to live, at last to live', declares this camp survivor to her neighbour Mondschein on her return; so she dons scarf and apron in a subsequent scene, cleaning her flat here and later with a gusto that borders on the obsessional.

As feminist critics have stressed, Knef becomes emblematic, too, for postwar cinematic representations of women through an amnesiac relation to her concentration camp past that enables her all the more readily to serve as a catalyst for the process of remembering embarked on by her men. Thus in *The Murderers Are Among Us*, it is Susanne, not Mertens, who pieces together the fragments of his troubled past; it is she who discovers the letter to Brückner's wife, pushes him to visit Brückner, reads Mertens' diary, and uses its insights to force from him an acknowledgement that due judicial process, not murder, is the route to change. Knef's performance style, which shifts from an easy naturalism in scenes of Susanne at work in her flat to the studied blankness she assumes in Behn-Grund's numerous facial close-ups, replicates, moreover, this oscillation in her narrative position between realist embodiment of a contemporary rubble woman active in the historical process and allegorical figure for an ahistorical femininity that absorbs, heals and soothes men's historical wounds (it is not by accident, in this context, that an early shot in *The Murderers Are Among Us* lingers on a statue of the Madonna and child artfully juxtaposed with the figure of Susanne as she navigates the ruins on her first return home).

Staudte's sternest postwar critics have reproached the director, in sum, by turns for the film's ponderous and inconsistent visual style, for its sexual-political conservatism and, most consistently, for its early delineation of narrative models of filmic memory work that are as notable for the perspectives they repress as for the insights they enable. However, the film's inconsistencies are, finally, perhaps its greatest strength, leaving open as they do the question of the appropriate relation at any given moment between the historical present and Germany's fascist past.

Erica Carter

REFERENCES

Kast, P. (1946) 'Tiefernste Mahnung zur Wachsamkeit', *Vorwärts*, 17 October.

Mitscherlich, A. and M. Mitscherlich (1975) *The Inability to Mourn: Principles of Collective Behavior*. Trans. B. R. Placzek. New York: Grove Press.

Santner, E. L. (1990) *Stranded Objects: Mourning, Memory and Film in Postwar Germany*. Ithaca, NY: Cornell University Press.

R. N. Produktion   Grün ist die Heide.   EUROPA

GRÜN IST DIE HEIDE THE HEATH IS GREEN

HANS DEPPE, WEST GERMANY, 1951

In September 1951, the small town of Bleckede, a war zone during the final phase of World War II, surrendered to a civilian, but not less effective, conquest – by the cast and crew of *Grün ist die Heide* (*The Heath Is Green*, 1951). The team employed by the production company, Berolina, included Hans Deppe, director of propaganda and light entertainment films during the Third Reich, who had also written the script with established screenwriter Bobby Lüthge, and the major stars, Rudolf Prack and Sonja Ziemann. Within the film industry, Prack and Ziemann were mockingly called *Firma Zieprack* ('Zieprack Inc.') expressing their pole position in one of the most popular German postwar genres, the *Heimatfilm*.

As added attractions, the regional heath landscape was to play an essential part, captured on state-of-the-art colour film, and crowds of locals, hoping to secure a place 'in the movies', were cast as extras. The set, which included trees adorned with plastic flowers and green paint, made it blatantly obvious how synthetic this verdant heath actually was. But neither the recorded folk music nor an uptight star like Sonja Ziemann, who felt encumbered by the noise from the cowsheds, could dampen the spirit that pervaded the production. Even today, witnesses recall the general feeling that 'we all wanted to be part of it'.

Contemporary criticism articulated a similar yearning for a filmic homeland replete with 'all creatures great and small of the heath'. From its first screening at the Berolina-Filmpalast in December 1951, with its 'opulent shots in surprisingly lush colours', as the *Evangelischer Filmbeobachter* enthused, the film attracted entire towns as audiences. The fact that the film won the *Bambi* award of 1953 for 'greatest commercial success' and drew an audience of approximately 14 million between 1951 and 1954, and 20 million by 1961, can be regarded as a verification of this judgement. Films like *Schwarzwaldmädel* (*The Black Forest Girl*, 1950), with an audience of 14 million by 1952, *Der Förster vom Silberwald* (1955), with an audience of 22 million by 1958, or *Die Trapp-Familie* (*The Trapp Family*, 1956 – on which the hit film and multiple Academy Award-winner *The Sound of Music* [1965] is based), with an audience of 28 million by 1962, were to follow.

This chapter aims to show why and in what way the *Heimatfilm* managed to become one of the most popular genres of West German postwar cinema. Firstly, it will look at how perfectly a film as early as *The Heath Is Green* responded to contemporary concerns about reviving traditional value systems, while not overlooking the problematic aspects of such a 'renaissance'. Secondly, it will examine the postwar obsession with *Heimat*, at a time when *Heimat* seemed an extremely unrealistic concept, and look at the whys and wherefores of this trend. Thirdly, it will consider what could be called the paradox of a modernism clothed in the pseudo-traditional garb of the *Heimatfilm*. Finally, it closes with some controversial ideas about how an essentially artificial construct like *Heimat* was able to evoke such a strong emotional response in its audience.

In one key scene of *The Heath Is Green*, we see a long shot of a woman, dressed in fashionable riding breeches and boots, riding a white horse from the shore of a lake into the heathlands. This is Nora von Buckwitz (Maria Holst), who has lost everything in the war and now works as a dressage artist at the circus, with which she plans to emigrate, via Hamburg, to the USA. On the heath, she encounters Helga (Sonja Ziemann), an expellee, who has found refuge with her uncle (a character dressed strangely like an old-fashioned Bismarckian). She lives in his castle with her father, a broken man after their expulsion from one of the former German provinces (apparently East Prussia). Helga is visibly singled out both as a receiver and giver of aid. She works as an assistant pharmacist, where, according to her employer, she 'gives away more than she sells' to the children (which says much about her real vocation in life). Dressed in a remarkably delicate blue-ringed dress and picking a heather bouquet for an unknown recipient, she harbours affection for the new forester (Rudolf Prack), as the more experienced Nora immediately notices. This forester, markedly older, meets the two women while out with his dog and gun. Nora now leaves the scene, claiming that she 'has to get to the circus', and the forester and Helga are left to amble among the heath.

During this walk, filmed with remarkable slowness, Helga is introduced as an affectionate and appealing yet cautious young girl, while her rather stiff and formal forester is shown in full professional dress, replete with almost all the paraphernalia of an officer's uniform, such as collar patches, epaulettes, riding breeches and army boots. The gun, which is not casually slung across the forester's shoulder, but held at an angle in front of his chest in nearly all scenes, further emphasises his appearance of being equipped with all the insignia of armed masculinity, even though it is noteworthy just how tightly he clutches this phallic symbol throughout the film. Even the prewar authorities, village pub regulars, who reminiscence about times gone by ('Oh, the good old days!'), are strategically placed in front of the barrel of the forester's gun, which – it is useless to try to suppress the obligatory Freud quotation here – like all 'long and sharp weapons' appears destined to 'represent the male member'.

Thus, the forester embodies (maybe still rather tentatively) an ideal of authoritative, uniformed masculinity, which has been purged of almost all warlike attributes in the aftermath of the Nazi dictatorship. During the course of the film, this masculine principle is increasingly called upon to come to the succour of a femininity left stranded amidst psychologically broken war and prewar authorities. Helga only once takes action, when she admonishes her father, whose emotional degeneration has led him to take up poaching, by asking him if he 'wants to go to jail' and locking away his purloined gun (!). All this allows for an interpretation of this *Heimatfilm* as the typical 'boy meets girl' story whose protagonists were to reinstate family harmony in so many examples of the genre.

However, *The Heath Is Green* is also remarkably straightforward about how problematic the traditional gender roles needed for the re-establishment of such a family model could be. In a contrastive subplot, Nora, whom we have already come across earlier, takes a decisive and tenacious stand by staying true to her plans to emigrate ('I want to go to America, to look for a new home'), despite the wooing of an elderly magistrate and confirmed bachelor, played by Willy Fritsch, one-time heartthrob of Nazi cinema (who in this role looks rather worse for wear). Dressed in fashionable and tight-fitting outfits, which in the semantics of the *Heimatfilm* denotes urbanity, Nora's determined refusal to act according to the cliché of feminine helplessness earns her the admiring, if not envious comment of her childhood friend Helga, 'How bold you are – but then, you were always like that!'

In this context, it comes rather as a surprise at the end of the film to see Nora, who stubbornly adheres to her notion of 'having passed the sentimental stage, thank God', or who tells the magistrate that his 'heathlands' hocus-pocus doesn't do it for me', fail to act according to her maxim of 'always carrying through what I've once decided to do'. One could call it a backlash that Nora is married off to her elderly admirer, after having repeatedly insisted on how independently this experienced and mature woman coped as an impoverished refugee ('Everything's gone' is her one laconic comment on this). At least her conversion is only fully accomplished after she falls off her proud white stallion and breaks a leg.

The contrast between Nora's and Helga's story is another trademark of 'Zieprack Inc.': the protagonists do not simply re-create patriarchal families, but they acknowledge the conflicts and contradictions of this model. Furthermore, the psychological troubles of Helga's father, the old-fashioned antics of her castle-dwelling uncle, or the bachelor magistrate's trick of seducing experienced women by serving them sweet liqueur and playing the piano, leave no doubt that the unquestioned authority of the patriarchal forefathers belongs to the past. The foresters, country doctors, landowners and farmers of the 1950s *Heimatfilm*, perennially challenged as they are by the failure of their forefathers, cannot simply count on women to fall off horses anymore.

But then why do these films revert to administering such a strong dose of *Heimat* sentiment? This is not the place to trace in detail the history of the German concept of *Heimat*, which has its roots in the Romantic period around 1800. But it should be mentioned that this concept does not represent a regressive and thus ideologically questionable emotional disposition *per se*. Younger cultural historians, such as Ina-Maria Greverus, argue that the basis of *Heimat* is an emotional link with a territorially limited space 'offering shelter, serving identity development and delineating the sphere of activity', which serves as a precondition for the development of a sense of self, both on the individual and collective level. Furthermore, *Heimat* in this sense is not, according to Johannes von Moltke, 'a territory excluding any considerations of the spaces beyond its reach. On the contrary the historical purpose of *Heimat* … was precisely to articulate the link between inside and outside on the level of lived, local experience.' Thus, the loss of *Heimat* leaves people not simply at an economic disadvantage, but impairs them socially and psychologically.

In early postwar Germany, around 45 per cent of housing in cities was destroyed or desolate, and nearly seven million POWs were still detained or on their way home to a devastated country. Add to this the 'displaced persons', i.e. former forced labourers or other victims of the war that had been abducted to Germany, who (often without valid identification) were left wandering the streets. There were also around twelve million expellees from the former German or German-occupied eastern territories, of whom nine million managed to reach West Germany by 1950. When we take into consideration that all this was more than familiar to the contemporary audience, through direct experience, press and/or newsreels, we can hardly be surprised at the directness with which *The Heath Is Green* takes up the troubles and estrangement of such a *Nation ohne Haus* ('unhoused nation', as Adolf M. Birke put it). Nevertheless, the film is remarkable for the comprehensiveness with which it addresses these losses, while (more or less successfully) providing filmic therapy for the traumatised. This set standards for the *Heimatfilm* genre.

For example, there are the three 'rovers', who – in the words of the eldest local authority, the head forester – 'have simply drifted here'. By day they roam perpetually sun-drenched panoramic long shots of the heathlands, singing songs by Hermann Löns, and by night they 'make themselves a bed of moss and a blanket of sky', as one of them puts it. Since it never seems to rain on this lush filmic heath (which may have puzzled local audiences), and the three wandering singers are reliably regaled by the vicar, the head forester and the squire according to a precise weekly schedule, it does not come as much of a surprise when they decline an offer to emigrate to the USA with the circus, after a successful performance there. Instead, they opt for a decidedly patriotic variety of a regionally delineated 'vagabond' life. Only their refusal to take on even casual work, because they are unwilling to 'take away what little work there is from the many unemployed', might be perceived as a hint towards social tensions between the locals and the 'vagabonds'.

Social conflicts are more directly expressed in the story of Helga's father, the displaced landowner, who, as he himself says, has taken to poaching not because he wants 'the heat of the chase' but because he needs to 'forget all the misery'. The character of the ex-landowner is cleverly calculated for identification: his story represents expellees, who feel 'barely tolerated' by society, despite all efforts to commit and conform. For even after they have just 'rebuilt an entire agriculture' (as the cousin of the homeless baron sees it), they tend to be overwhelmed by 'moods of homesickness' and appear so 'devastated' that nobody 'can find any use' for them.

How traumatic the loss must be is expressed by the fact that the poaching baron hunts through ominously lit forests not for game, but 'the antlers – the trophies', which he tears off the stags he has shot – 'a fatal passion', as the rather passionless Rudolf Prack character blankly remarks. We do not need to quote Freud again to interpret the removal of the animals' secondary sex characteristics as displaced aggression meant to distract from personal failure. In this reading of the film, the father's plea, spoken off-camera after his daughter has locked away his gun – 'Yes, lock it away … Maybe if I don't see the thing anymore…' – can be understood as a half-conscious desire to find salvation in auto-castration, acted out on a substitute object. In this way, as von Moltke asserts, 'the morbid baron' remains 'an irritating presence in the *Heimat* idyll'.

In order to dramatise the depth of the trauma with visual and auditory means, *The Heath Is Green* introduces yet another invaluable motif to the *Heimatfilm* genre: a traditional shooting club and festival, in which people of different regions and different social backgrounds meet and mingle. This not only gives expellees and locals opportunity to show off their magnificent traditional costumes, they can also assure each other of the vital importance of regional bonds by singing and dancing. In one key scene, which was to recur in many examples of the genre, the formerly reserved and anxious baron makes a speech. The camera moves towards him from medium-long-shot to close-up, as he speaks in emotional yet firm tones, 'on behalf of myself and all those many others who have found a second home here', explaining how they are different from people who never had to leave their *Heimat*: 'someone who did not have to abandon his native home cannot comprehend what it means to be so deprived'; in this, 'we have been most grievously punished'.

However, since words do not seem to be enough to express this sentiment, the film then stages the performance of the 'Song of the Sudeten Mountains' by one of the vagabonds; the lines 'how beautiful this spot of land is / and this is what I call home' serve as a musical reminder of how inextricably territorial space and social familiarity must be interlinked to create a feeling of *Heimat*. One could – and the contemporary audience was probably supposed to – interpret this as saying that the loss of their original *Heimat* predestined expellees to re-animate a sense of community on a regional level, in order to lay the emotional foundations for a new sense of national togetherness, purged of the burdens and iniquities of the Nazi past. This, however, makes it all too clear that what we are now dealing with is the rather dubious attempt to conjure up a clean slate of national innocence for a people who elected their Nazi dictators and had to be liberated by foreign troops. Thus it does not come as a surprise that territorial claims are renewed: the chorus, which is sung by the entire congregation, marks out the Sudeten mountains as German ('Giant Mountains / German mountains').

Added to this is the plotline around an animal warden at the circus, who is referred to as 'half human' in one of the first scenes, because he has no documents. At the end of the film, it turns out that he has also taken up poaching, out of personal greed, and he kills the country constable who catches him red-handed – thus proving that it is better not to trust Displaced Persons without home or documents. Although this may not quite be the 'terror of an idyll', as Claudia Beindorf describes, it is notable that this contrastive action close to the conclusion of the film amounts to a plea for preventive violence to secure the community against outsiders. However, a sentimental collective as emotionally charged as this *Heimat* is, seems to have no other way of reacting. What external influences are really being struggled against will be made apparent in one last look at this reliably revealing film.

Without tracing in detail the developments that have been thoroughly explored elsewhere, it is relevant to note that a longing for *Heimat* was already evoked around 1900, at a time when not only big cities but small towns and villages were already affected by modernisation. This may explain why we find an attempt to blend modernisation into *Heimat* and to create a kind of rural 'reactionary modernism', as Jeffrey Herf calls it, whose exponents were dreaming of a reconciliation between modernity and tradition. How resilient this yearning for a modernism that could at least be made to *look* traditional turned out to be can be seen by the way in which the *Heimatfilm* of the 1950s represents the paradox of a modernisation within tradition.

In the case of *The Heath Is Green*, we can gather just how much suspension of disbelief is required to go along with this concept by considering the fact that, although the baron has single-handedly 'knocked the local agriculture back into shape', we never get to see any of the highly efficient working methods necessary to achieve this. This is mainly because nobody in the film ever seems to work or indeed lead any sort of ordinary life. Hence we do not see tools, let alone modern machinery, and vehicle traffic only features in one scene in the form of an automobile. This sunny heath landscape seems to be made exclusively for outings on horseback or musical performances. One might almost get the impression that, in order to 'find something to do', people who are tired of 'sitting around all day' have no other option but to go to town, as the expelled landowner says.

Structural gaps like these permit the head forester to criticise the squire's plan to move to the city (motivated by a fear of discovery). Although his rhetorical figures are rather skewed, the head forester still proves to be maliciously prophetic regarding the impossibility for town and country to harmonise in any way, even when the city strives to emulate the country: 'You know, if I had to go live in town, I'd die – just shrivel away, like an oak in a flower pot – high buildings – chimneys – smoke, pale faces, noise. […] No sun, no greenery – if you come across a tree you have to dust it first to know it's a tree.' What the head forester refers to might today be called the attempt to restore nature where it has been thoroughly destroyed, which allows us some momentary sympathy with an otherwise remote character.

If we apply the words of the head forester to the *Heimatfilm* itself, we can again see that our difficulties today in approaching the genre are not owing to the fact that these films deal with such an essentially German concept of *Heimat*. What seems to be the main problem is that a filmed *Heimat* is inextricably linked to the media world of urban modernity, where, according to its own supposed logic, *Heimat* cannot but appear as recycled, as a restored and thus denaturalised version of itself. This would be in line with Theodor W. Adorno's comment that 'no *Heimat* survives being filmed'.

But if we look at how much enthusiasm the film was able to generate both during production and reception, it becomes probable that not only urban cinema audiences, but also many of the local extras (for reasons discussed in the beginning) were each in their own way more than happy to consciously implicate themselves in an entirely artificial *Heimat* conjured up by filmic means. In this sense, the *Heimatfilm* would have delivered lasting proof for the idea that the emotions generated by films are sometimes felt to be not just real, but more real than real, precisely because they have been so painstakingly constructed. That this is only valid for as long as there is an audience receptive to this particular sort of emotional construct is in the 'nature' of such cinematic effects.

Harro Segeberg

Translated by Anna Wille

REFERENCES

Adorno, T. W. (1997 [1963]) 'Résumé über Kulturindustrie', in *Kultur und Gesellschaft*. Frankfurt am Main: Suhrkamp.

Beindorf, C. (2001) *Terror des Idylls: Die kulturelle Konstruktion von Gemeinschaften in Heimatfilm und Landsbygdsfilm 1930–1960*. Baden-Baden: Nomos.

Birke, A. M. (1994) *Nation ohne Haus: Deutschland 1945–1961*. Berlin: Siedler.

Freud, S. (1972 [1900]) *Die Traumdeutung*. Frankfurt am Main: Fischer.

Greverus, I.-M. (1979) *Auf der Suche nach Heimat*. München: Beck.

Herf, J. (1984) *Reactionary Modernism: Technology, Culture, and Politics in Weimar and the Third Reich*. Cambridge: Cambridge University Press.

Moltke, J. von (2005) *No Place like Home: Locations of Heimat in German Cinema*. Berkeley, CA: University of California Press.

DIE BRÜCKE THE BRIDGE

13

BERNHARD WICKI, WEST GERMANY, 1959

Bernhard Wicki's anti-war film *Die Brücke* (*The Bridge*, 1959), was showered with awards internationally on its release and is doubtless one of the most honoured films of postwar German cinema. Throughout his long and eventful career as a filmmaker and actor, Wicki never again caused such a sensation with any of his other films as he did with *The Bridge*, which was only the second film he directed. *The Bridge*, the fourth most successful German film of 1960, was awarded several *Bundesfilmpreise* ('national film award'), the *Bambi* (awarded for popularity), and the *Deutscher Jugendfilmpreis* ('German youth film award'); but internationally, too, the film was one of the most successful German films of the postwar years, winning the Grand Prix and the International Film Critics Award (the FIPRESCI Prize) in Mar de Plata, as well as the Golden Globe for Best Foreign Film.

Critics were enthusiastic: 'Manfred Gregor's modest *opus one* [the 1958 novel on which the film was based] was turned into one of the toughest, most unrelenting and severe anti-war films ever shown on screen. [...] This film is an instant masterpiece. It is, if ever a film was, 'particularly valuable' [the certification mark of the *Filmbewertungsstelle* ('German board for film rating'), which grants tax reductions for films of particular merit], because it brings home to us once again the shock that we experienced and forgot fourteen years ago', wrote Hans-Dieter Roos in the *Süddeutsche Zeitung*. Similarly, Enno Patalas remarked, 'Of all recent German films, this one undoubtedly goes furthest in denouncing the war. The authors refused to make the slightest compromise, even on an unconscious level; war is represented as the absolute horror that it is. [...] The battle scenes at the end of the film are staged in such a way that the terror retains its shocking effect to the very end. Short, uneventful interludes let the "heroes" as well as the audience catch their breath before the horror takes over completely. [...] In this episode [of the war], "not mentioned in any military report", as the credits inform us, there is neither room for meaningful heroism nor for "dying a sweet and glorious death for one's country". Scenes such as the German civilian burning alive or the horrifying dying of the American soldier have never been shown in German cinema in such a drastic manner; they unmistakably and thoroughly deny the [conservative] myth of the German soldier's "heroic death". An indifferent presentation would hardly have achieved the unmasking that the film accomplishes.' Accordingly, in the context of the *Oberhausener Manifest* of 1962, which declared the end of '*Papas Kino*' ('Daddy's cinema') and founded the New German Cinema, Alexander Kluge and Laurens Straub, among others, called Wicki's *The Bridge* the 'first new German film' – a label that Wicki rejected.

At least some contemporary German politicians were less enthusiastic than the critics and filmmakers. Even though Wicki's film received five of thirteen honours at the *Bundesfilmpreis*, the Minister of the Interior, Gerhard Schröder, responsible for awarding the prizes, did not attend the ceremony – a gesture that was and is readily interpreted as protest. Instead he sent his Secretary of State, Georg Anders, who insinuatingly spoke of the 'fatal pathos' of certain films. Thus was occasion for the critical news-magazine *Der Spiegel* to print the following comment: 'In the future everyone will know: if, at the Berlinale, Gerhard Schröder looks at you from the TV screens, the majority of the films receiving awards respects the Christian-democratic point of view and doesn't hurt any Nazis. If, however, Doctor Anders can be spotted, this means: one should go to the cinema.'

To go to the cinema to watch *The Bridge*, as *Der Spiegel* suggested, was as recommendable for aesthetic as for political reasons, because Wicki's film came as close to Italian Neorealism as few other German film of the 1950s had been able to. The majority of the young actors (all of which, except Günther Hoffmann, had careers in West German television afterwards, most notably perhaps Fritz Wepper in the hit crime series *Derrick*) were amateurs. Only Michael Hinz and Folker Bohnet came direct from acting school. The others were cast with the help of a talent scout and screen tests. As Wicki noted in an interview with Robert Fischer: 'The actors chosen were not necessarily the best; it was more important that they fitted into the group as a whole. Because we didn't really have any money, those screen tests were silent. I had come up with a few standard situations to which the young people had to react.' Not only the use of amateur actors, but also the sparseness of the images, the unusually drastic representation of the war scenes, the very limited use of music, the sound design (for example, in the train station scene the noise of a departing train drowns out the argument between father and son) and the film's humanistic message call to mind the influence of Italian Neorealism, to which Wicki himself repeatedly referred.

The film, which runs for almost two hours, tells the story of seven boys, all of whom are around sixteen years of age, who are drafted into the German army during the last days of the war. Trying to defend a bridge in their hometown against the advancing Allied Forces, all but one (Albert Mutz) are killed. The film rewrites the story of Gregor's book considerably – a fact Wicki emphasised: 'In the novel, the boys are true heroes: a general positions them by a bridge and orders them to defend it, so that the Americans won't be able to besiege his division, and these boys give their lives for that. In my film it's completely different: they die because they have been raised that way. That is a significant difference. They defend this bridge, too, because this is where they used to play: this is where they grew up. That sets a completely different course. […] In the film, I changed the basic set-up entirely, and the screenwriter, Michael Mansfeld, who was a holder of the *Ritterkreuz* ('Knight's Cross'), completely went along with that. I always said: I can and want to make this film only if I can make it as an anti-war film, if I can change essential parts of the book, not just the story, but the attitude behind it.' The crucial change Wicki makes concerns the strategic importance of defending the bridge. In the film, the boys are ordered to secure the bridge precisely because it has lost its military importance: well-meaning father figures give the adolescents, drafted in the final days of a war everybody expects to be over soon, a phoney task instead of shipping them to 'the front'. In a viciously ironic twist of fate, six of the seven boys die in the mission that was supposed to save their lives. A written epilogue, inserted before the credits, laconically comments: 'This happened on 27 April 1945. It was of so little importance that no army report mentioned it.'

Thus, film critics and film historians have unanimously categorised Wicki's *The Bridge* as an anti-war film, a genre comprised of only few films from 1950s Germany. However, this genre classification needs to be amended. Wicki's film is also reminiscent of what today would be called a 'teen movie'. The overlong exposition, which takes up two thirds of the film's running time, is typical of the teen film, because it introduces us to the boys' lives and families: we witness their Oedipal battles against their fathers, their relationships with their mothers, torn between love and the need to loosen the bond, and their first feelings of infatuation.

At least one of the boys has some experience with the other sex: Walter Forst (Michael Hinz), the son of a Nazi officer, has an affair with the girls' gym teacher. He openly revolts against his father, the *Ortsgruppenleiter* (the local chapter leader of the National Socialist German Workers Party [NSDAP]), without, however, breaking with his father's ideology of war. The washerwoman's son, Sigi Bernhard (Günther Hoffmann) is, by contrast, uninterested in girls. The 'chicken' of the group, he is still occupied with childlike hobbies, such as taking care of his pet rabbits Wotan and Alberich. He is the first to die on the bridge, because – in an effort to prove to his friends that he is not a coward – he does not run for cover during a low-level attack. Jürgen Borchert (Frank Glaubrecht) comes from an upper-class family (the film is obviously interested in creating a socially differentiated group), whose male family members have all embarked on a military career. His idealised father, a major, has already died in action; with his mother's approval and his father's gun, Jürgen volunteers as an officer cadet and joins the ranks. Karl Horber (Karl Michael Balzer) does not have a mother anymore; his father, a barber, lost his right hand in combat, which makes his work difficult. Karl witnesses a rendezvous between his father and Barbara, his father's assistant, whom Karl adores and whose portrait he secretly draws. Infuriated, the son breaks with his Oedipal, paternal rival – the emotions dramatised in this scene are of the same intensity as those evoked in the battle scenes around the bridge. While Karl is largely driven by his emotions, Hans Scholten (Folker Bohnet) and his friend Albert Mutz (Fritz Wepper) are mellower. Hans is characterised as thoughtful and artistic (in English class, he recites one of the protagonist's monologues from *Romeo and Juliet*) and as more sensible than the other boys (he is the only one who recognises the futility of defending the bridge, and he would like to send everyone home, if the others would let him). Corporal Heilmann puts Hans in charge of the group when he leaves (much to the anger of Walter and Jürgen, who subsequently question his leadership). Finally, there is Klaus Hager (Volker Lechtenbrink). He is a close friend of the only girl in class, Franziska (Cordula Trantow), who is – besides the boys' mothers and quasi-mothers – one of the few female protagonists of the film.

The film presents these seven protagonists as a group of idealistic young men – or rather, children – who are enthusiastic about the idea of fighting for their country. Their project is a patriotic one, modelled on Friedrich Hölderlin's poetry. In a conversation, Captain Fröhlich and the English teacher quote 'Tod für's Vaterland' ('Death for the Fatherland'): 'The battle is ours! Live on high, O Fatherland, and do not count the dead! For you, beloved, not one too many has fallen!' The boys' project is not decidedly National-Socialist, even though it is infected by Nazi propaganda. While the Nazi officials turn tail and the more or less disbanded regiments flee from the enemy, the group of teenagers (occasionally called a 'Kindergarten' by Germans as well as Americans) 'hold the fort' and do not run from what they believe to be their duty. The familial situation of each of the boys is precarious for different reasons; none of the families can be called 'intact'. The fathers are at war, if they have not already been killed in action. Those who have not been drafted appear as either castrated/disabled (like Karl's father) or as corrupt and cowardly. And when Walter's father, the *Ortsgruppenleiter*, places his wife in safety, it seems to his son (and one tends to agree with him), that he only does so to be free for his numerous extramarital affairs. He takes advantage of his position to help himself to extra rations, and he flees from the approaching Allied troops while his son reports for duty.

The characterisation of the child soldiers, disappointed by corrupt and disillusioned adults, as a group that enters upon a fight for noble ideals even though these ideals have been perverted by demagogues, has been criticised, because it allows a reading of the film unintended by the director. Would the adolescents' deaths have been justified, if it had been for a better cause? Pauline Kael remarked: 'Bernhard Wicki directed this brutally cool and lucid account of how German schoolboys were drafted in the last days of World War II and insanely and absurdly sacrificed. Oddly, the film has acquired a following among conservatives and militarists who think the massacred innocents died nobly.' Even though Wicki repeatedly emphasised that he had intended to deconstruct heroism, it is possible to read *The Bridge* in a 'revisionist' manner. This, however, is not that surprising, since it is characteristic of the anti-war film to tip over into its opposite – its politically incorrect brother, the war film – and vice versa. Every anti-war film is also a film about war and usually stages representations of war (this 'tug-of-war' can be demonstrated with any given example of the genre, such as Michael Cimino's *The Deer Hunter* [1978] and Barry Levinson's *Good Morning, Vietnam* [1987]); and every war film, no matter how inflammatorily and glorifyingly it might be staging its subject, necessarily evokes moments that cross out the genre and evoke its antithesis: the anti-war film.

In any case, it is important to consider the film's historical context. Comparing Wicki's treatment of World War II and Nazism with the rest of postwar German cinema and what it had to offer on these themes, one cannot but state the exceptional importance of *The Bridge* (even though the Holocaust and the crimes of the *Wehrmacht* [Nazi Germany's armed forces] are not mentioned and representations of Nazi symbols are mostly avoided). The sensation the film caused in the *Adenauerrepublik* ('Adenauer's Republic'), where many official posts were still held by (former?) Nazis, was already illustrated above by the scandal surrounding the *Bundesfilmpreis*. In fact, hardly any other film of the 1950s and 1960s dealt with Nazi Germany as radically: while the successful *Heimat-*, *Revue-* and *Schlagerfilme* usually blanked out National Socialism, and while the films made by returning emigrants that dealt openly with it were mostly unsuccessful (for instance, Peter Lorres' *Der Verlorene* [*The Lost One*, 1951]), the majority of German war films (the descendants of the very successful mid-1950s *08/15* trilogy), in an apologetic tenor, presented a few convinced Nazis against which the apolitical, tragic heroes were powerless. *The Bridge*, by contrast, focused on pointing out the fatal consequences of Nazi ideology and indoctrination – without appeals to easily forgive and forget.

The re-issue trailer (which is included on the German DVD) reveals the connection to the teen film genre, which emerged in the US as well as in Germany in the 1950s (regarded as having originated in Richard Brooks' enormously successful *Blackboard Jungle* [1955]; for the German context, Georg Tressler's *Die Halbstarken* [1956] is central). The trailer begins as follows: 'Nobody, nobody should ever forget what happened. Never! Much has been said about the terrors of the war that lie behind us. But have you heard about the seven children by the bridge who thought they could save their country through a last-minute manoeuvre?' And later: '*The Bridge*: a film with new faces! A film of the young!' It becomes clear here that the film not only focused on teenage protagonists and their problems, but also specifically addressed a young audience. Accordingly, Wicki was especially pleased when young conscientious objectors told him that his film had influenced their decision not to become soldiers. As recently as 2003 a team of experts commissioned by the *Bundeszentrale für politische Bildung* ('The National Centre for Political Education') included *The Bridge* in a canon of films recommended for screening in schools.

Wicki's decision to make adolescents his protagonists produces a generic hybridisation. *The Bridge* is not only an anti-war film, but also a 'teen movie' (and a melodrama, and a historical epic). This, however, is not specific to this particular film: all genre films operate with patterns of various genres. Thus, a genre does not precede the genre hybrid; rather, it is the genre hybrid that is prior – and the singling out of individual genres requires the simplifying reading of a configuration that always already transgresses single genres.

The decision to deal with the Nazi regime and World War II by representing the idealistic, but entirely futile, mission of a group of adolescents is precarious because (as mentioned above) it allows the viewer to (mis)read the film as representing or even promoting the abysses of National Socialism. The story calls attention to the inhumane practice to draft young people as a last resort (compared to the Holocaust, however, this appears as one of the regime's 'marginal' cruelties) – thus, the representation Wicki chose may act 'only' as a metonymy, not as a fundamental critique. However, as precarious as this may be, in other respects the focus on teenagers is very fruitful, even clever (not just for commercial reasons). In a thorough manner, it not only brings into play the basic narrative constituents of the war film as well as the anti-war film, but it also puts them up for discussion, particularly the concept of war as a rite of passage, a *Stahlbad* (a 'bath of steel') which produces 'real men' (the difference between the war film and the anti-war film being, that the former regards 'brave' soldiers as 'real' men, while the latter's 'real men' are those who develop a critical stance towards the war machinery). This 'masculinity'-producing rite (with regard to the war film) includes self-victory, proof of bravery and the killing of the 'enemy' who threatens the integrity of self and country. Wicki's *The Bridge* counters this programme of initiation for the simple reason that six of the seven boys 'to be initiated' die a fast and meaningless death; the boys do not become 'real men' but only dead bodies.

Furthermore, by focusing on child soldiers, *The Bridge* exposes an implicit equation of war films: war is often staged as a 'sporting' event, a game even, allowing 'bands of brothers' to perform masculinity rituals – just like soccer or other 'combatant sports'. The child soldiers in *The Bridge* understand war as a 'game', simply because playing games – whether it is 'General Staff' or 'Cowboys and Indians' – is what they do every day. One of their favourite 'playgrounds' happens to be the very bridge that they are assigned to 'defend' (and they do so from the tree house they once built for their games). Wicki's film wants to demonstrate the deadliness of the 'game of war'. The various performances of war and masculinity that the boys try out might at first seem relatively harmless: the power struggles between them, the bonding rituals, even the intimidation of civilians.

However, the game (remarks such as 'War in weather like this should be declared illegal' clearly illustrate that the boys initially regard it as such) suddenly becomes very serious, tests of courage have unexpected, fatal outcomes. Instead of shooting at tin cans, the boys shoot at humans; and the game goes awry: we are – quite unexpectedly – confronted with intestines and burned faces. The protagonists cannot cope with this sudden change any better than the audience, who is made to share the children's horrified look at the horrifying events. Albert expresses everyone's thoughts and feelings when he screams: 'I want to get out of here! I want to get out of here! I want to go home!' The American soldier who calls out to the boys, 'Go home, I don't want to shoot at a kindergarten' seems to echo the words of Karl's father, who said that his pubescent son did not belong in the barracks, but in a kindergarten. It is in line with the film's logic that the GI's 'humanitarian' gesture is his undoing. When Karl hears the word 'kindergarten' he is filled with hatred (towards his father), and he shoots at the very person who is trying to save the young soldiers – the 'enemy'. The images of the civilian burning alive and, even more strongly, those of the dying US soldier, whose intestines are spilling out of him, rupture the viewing habits of the 1950s. No other contemporary war film contains scenes of this kind – they mark the exceptional standing of Bernhard Wicki's *The Bridge*.

Claudia Liebrand and Gereon Blaseio

AUTHORS' NOTE: We would like to thank Katrin Oltmann for numerous valuable suggestions and for translating this chapter. [The editors add their thanks to Adrian Del Caro for his assistance in translating the Hölderlin quotation.]

REFERENCES

Fischer, R. (1991) '"Mit dem fertigen Film ist der Kampf erst einmal gewonnen". Interview mit Bernhard Wicki', in R. Fischer (ed.) *Sanftmut und Gewalt: Der Regisseur und Schauspieler Bernhard Wicki*. Essen: Filmwerkstatt, 9–52.

Kluge, A. (1991) 'Respekt vor dem Meister', in R. Fischer (ed.) *Sanftmut und Gewalt: Der Regisseur und Schauspieler Bernhard Wicki*. Essen: Filmwerkstatt, 6.

Kael, P. (1991) *5001 Nights at the Movies*, rev. ed. New York: Owl. CD-Rom. Available in Microsoft Corp. (ed.) *Cinemania 97*. Redmond: Microsoft.

Patalas, E. (1959) '*Die Brücke*', *Filmkritik*, 12. Reprinted in E. Wicki-Endriss and A. Schneider (eds) *Die Brücke: Filmbegleitheft*. On-line. Available HTTP: http://www.bernhardwickigedaechtnisfonds.de/docs/ger/Bruecke.pdf (accessed 28 February 2005).

Roos, H.-D. (1959) '*Die Brücke*', *Süddeutsche Zeitung*, 25 October. Reprinted in E. Wicki-Endriss and A. Schneider (eds) *Die Brücke. Filmbegleitheft*. On-line. Available HTTP: http://www.bernhardwickigedaechtnisfonds.de/docs/ger/Bruecke.pdf (accessed 28 February 2005).

Straub, L. (1991) 'Der standhafte Querkopf', in R. Fischer (ed.) *Sanftmut und Gewalt: Der Regisseur und Schauspieler Bernhard Wicki*. Essen: Filmwerkstatt, 7.

DER SCHATZ IM SILBERSEE THE TREASURE OF SILVER LAKE
DIE SÖHNE DER GROSSEN BÄRIN THE SONS OF GREAT BEAR

HARALD REINL, WEST GERMANY, 1962 & JOSEF MACH, EAST GERMANY, 1966

The West German film *Der Schatz im Silbersee* (*The Treasure of Silver Lake*, 1962) and the East German film *Die Söhne der großen Bärin* (*The Sons of Great Bear*, 1966) initiated two similar, yet different series of 'kraut westerns', which became the most popular franchises in the history of German cinema (eight films between 1962 and 1968 in the West, twelve films between 1966 and 1983 in the East, not counting spin-offs). Understanding the cultural significance of these films requires an analysis not only of the films themselves, but also of their audiences. Thus, the aim is to examine with whom, when, where and why they were popular. This will reveal that these films can be understood as complex cultural hybrids of national, European and US traditions emerging from a process of global cultural convergence.

The US western is commonly regarded as the dominant genre of the world's dominant cinema. If this were taken at face value, the story would end here: we would interpret both films as imitations of a successful Hollywood formula, based on the simple fact that they are set in the Wild West. However, Hollywood's dominance in Germany has already been refuted in general by Joseph Garncarz. As a specific instance of this, the definition of a genre and its popularity is dependent on the historical and cultural context, i.e. a specific audience's frames of reference and preferences. Even in the USA the western, though obviously based on national myths, has changed over time, and its reception was not determined by genre alone. *Variety's* hit lists do not contain a majority of westerns, and those that were successful were not always typical of their genre. The biggest hits had exceptional production values (for example, *How the West Was Won*, 1962) and elements which made them not only appealing to their core male audience, but a female one as well, such as a romantic line of action (such as *Cimarron*, 1931) or at least attractive male stars (for example, *Butch Cassidy and the Sundance Kid*, 1969 – the most successful western). Outside the USA, westerns lose their special significance as national myths – thus, they were not always as popular as has been assumed, or they were popular for different reasons, because they took on new meanings.

Long before 'Germany's subconscious was colonised by the yanks' (as Wim Wenders once put it) following World War II, the Old World was fascinated by the New World and vice versa. Germans were among the colonisers of America even before a German national identity existed, and this contributed to both nations' identities. An important facet of the German fascination is the special interest in 'Indians', ranging from leisure activities (for example, children's play, clubs) to ideological identifications, sometimes in contradictory ways, which had less to do with real Native Americans than with projected German concerns. Romanticism introduced the idea of an affinity between Indians and Teutons, on which Nazism capitalised, for instance in an (unsuccessful) campaign to recruit Native American support. The 1960s' counterculture also metaphorically appropriated Indians (examples include filmmaker Herbert Achternbusch, urban rebels called *Stadtindianer*, groups propagating green lifestyles, critics of the Vietnam War, and so on). From a common cultural basis of this phenomenon, differences developed in West and East Germany with the division after World War II.

James Fenimore Cooper's (1789–1851) tales were popular and influential in Germany, but their success was surpassed by German variants, first and foremost those by Karl May (1842–1912). May's most successful *Reiseromane* ('travel novels') relate the spectacular adventures of German hero Karl in foreign lands. Karl is peace-loving and has almost super-human powers, including an intellect to match Sherlock Holmes and extraordinary physical skills. In the Wild West he is nicknamed Old Shatterhand because he can knock down an adversary with a single blow. His closest friend and 'blood brother' is Winnetou, a noble Apache chief. Together they protect good people (usually farmers) from villains (usually greedy Yankees and the Indians they have manipulated into allegiance or attacked, so that they are on the war path to take revenge). Karl's frontiersmen friends are often Germans as well, most notably Sam Hawkens, who provides comic relief. There are few female characters and hardly any romantic involvements; Winnetou's sister Nscho-tschi falls in love with Karl, but she is killed.

May did not only write Wild West novels, but he is best known for them. He claimed that the stories were authentic, i.e. that he was the hero 'Karl' of his novels. When (not long before his death) this was revealed to be a lie (along with some other 'sins' of his past), it caused a major scandal and disappointment among contemporaries, but it did not diminish his popularity with new generations of readers. In contrast to some of his colleagues, he had not even travelled to the USA before writing his stories, but his imagination and the way he infused his tales with German characters and concerns made him all the more popular. Not all of his adventure novels were originally intended as juvenile literature, but in time they came to be mainly regarded as such. Not only is the ideology of his works mostly implicit, it is also highly contradictory and thus amenable to diverse readings. The disparate list of May fans vividly illustrates this – it includes Adolf Hitler, Albert Einstein and Ernst Bloch. May shaped Germany's idea of the Wild West for generations, to such an extent that it was regarded as the definitive version. After World War II, US government officials were even advised to read May to better understand the Germans. Thus, it is no surprise that May never became popular in the USA. Ironically, Fred Zinneman (director of *High Noon*, 1952) was also an avid May-reader and even attributed his emigration to the USA to this fascination. The Nazi regime had a paradoxical relationship with May: his enormous popularity and the fact that Hitler himself admired him made it impossible to ban him, but his texts were edited (for example, religious comments were eliminated) and more 'politically correct' imitators were promoted, albeit with little success. The later situation in East Germany was similar: his great popularity prevented May from being strictly forbidden, but 'Hitler's literary mentor' (as Klaus Mann once called him) could not be officially promoted (hence his works were not widely available before the mid-1980s), and socialist variants did not achieve the same popularity. Independent of the cultural context, even though some female readers attest to cherishing May – most famously, perhaps, Thea von Harbou, who called Winnetou her 'first love' – he is more popular with male readers.

Despite May's literary popularity, filming his novels was not a sure bet for Horst Wendlandt, a successful producer of German popular cinema, who came up with the idea (some of the later films were produced by Artur Brauner, in competition). Legend has it that his young son suggested it, but this was surely not Wendlandt's only source of inspiration or advice. Earlier attempts had not been very successful: the first was Fritz Lang's *Halbblut* (*The Half-Caste*, 1919), closely followed by some of the Orient-tales, co-produced by the publisher of the May novels (for example, *Die Teufelsanbeter*, 1920). The most popular adaptation was the annual May festival, an open-air Wild West show, which was also shown on television, but it did not require a mass audience to be economically viable. The fact that the copyright on May's novels ran out in 1962 was certainly one of the incentives.

Neither did the western genre as such have much potential for success in Germany at the time. Before the 1960s, no US western succeeded in becoming a top-ten hit in German cinemas. 'Boy westerns' were programmed as matinees for young audiences, and TV shows such as *Laramie* and *Bonanza* were popular children's entertainment on Sunday afternoons – amongst the few families who already owned a television set or had friends who did. 'Adult westerns' had a similarly marginal, but even less homogenous, audience. Despite US attempts at 're-education' and Adenauer's politics of 'westernisation', the older German generation remained resolutely uninterested in and even dismissive of US popular culture. The younger generation held a more favourable attitude, because the US led the way in the creation of youth culture, and also due to a global (or at least western) cultural convergence towards individualism and consumerism. Thus, younger cineastes discovered the artistic highlights of the western, whereas less intellectually inclined youths enjoyed the action-oriented type. The only US westerns that were successful in Germany in the 1960s (as the box-office listings published in *Film-Echo* show) were *Sergeants 3* (1962) and *The Professionals* (1966), which was probably due to their military themes (war films were popular). In the 1970s, German audiences took an interest in critical US westerns, such as Ralph Nelson's *Soldier Blue* (1970), as well as the Italian 'spaghetti westerns' (violent homages and/or comical parodies of the genre), but this was based on prior acquaintance with the genre and a favourable attitude towards it. The trend was also reflected on television: whereas the first evening showing of a western, *Rio Grande* (1950) in 1963, was almost completely ignored, and the showing of *Red River* (1948) in 1968 was still accompanied by apologetic remarks, more and more westerns appeared in the 1970s among the top-ten film hits on television. But despite this shift in the genre's reception in Germany, the enormous success of the May films not only predates it, it may even have contributed to it, and it also surpasses the success of US westerns to this day (reflected in box office listings, recycling in various formats ranging from television reruns to DVDs, and the proliferation of merchandise, such as the film's soundtrack).

Thus, *The Treasure of Silver Lake* was not advertised in Germany as a western, but as a *deutscher Monumentalfilm*. A magazine photo serial was published prior to the premiere, and a young May fan wrote a worried letter to the *Film-Revue* that the film might be too much like a US western. However, such concern proved to be unfounded. Most reviewers agreed that it was much better than a US western – even though it is evident from their comments that some of them had hardly ever seen one. One reviewer did criticise the film for ignoring the accomplishments of the best US westerns, but what seemed parochial to him was exactly what gave the film its special charm for German audiences at large. The film series targeted a family audience and May was the central selling point. The films preserved May's main characters, but cut minor ones, combined them or invented new ones, and the later films increasingly depart from the stories of the novels. The episodic structure of dialogue, comical interludes and action scenes, which proved well suited for a series format, was retained, but streamlined.

Compared to Hollywood films, the structure was not as consistently linear and driven by the protagonists' motivations, and the narrative pace remained fairly slow (which can be said of most German films). The films often added a love interest, at least for secondary characters, but depictions were very chaste, just as the violence was very moderate (different versions allowed for different age-groups were made). Thus, the main target was a young audience, but advertisements also stressed that the films would appeal to adults who had read May in their youth. The films were 'boy westerns' with the production values of 'adult westerns'. Thus, the May films reflected the general trend of German cinema to increasingly cater to a younger audience, but were also uniquely positioned to interest older generations as well.

The film series is a typical example of what Joseph Garncarz referred to as the 'European phase' of German cinema. The films are European co-productions: the main creative input is German, but to finance the lavish production values, foreign money and co-operation was needed, as well as foreign audiences' favourable response, which influenced production decisions. The director of the first film (and several others) was Harald Reinl, a specialist for filming dramatic stories in striking mountain scenery throughout German genres and historical periods (such as the *Bergfilm* and the *Heimatfilm*). Filming in the US was too expensive, and German locations were not credible enough, so Yugoslavia was chosen, which also provided personnel and could even be used as a further marketing angle, because it was a popular tourist country. Thus, some of the more 'Teutonic' elements of May's novels were eliminated. For instance, in the first film it is not mentioned at all – and in a later film only in passing – that one of the main characters, Old Shatterhand, is German. Throughout the series, actors from many different countries were cast (Götz George – Germany; Lex Barker – USA; Pierre Brice – France; Terence Hill – Italy; Anthony Steel – UK). However, the actors in comedic roles are mostly German, as is the humour itself (for instance, Eddie Arendt as Lord Castlepool, who represents a specifically German stereotype of an Englishman), which may not have travelled well. A special local strategy was the recruitment of German 'Indian clubs' to produce props and participate in promotion. An American, Charles Wakefield, was hired as assistant director for the first film, to ensure 'authenticity', and Artur Brauner even hired a US director, Hugo Fregonese, for one of his May films, presumably with the view to selling the films in Anglo-American markets. The films were shown in the UK and the USA, but in heavily cut versions as B-pictures for double features. German critics like to refer to some favourable foreign reviews, but *Variety* described their potential audience as 'young and undemanding', and in contrast to some of the 'spaghetti westerns', they were not hits. Thus, the film series addressed national, European and international audiences, but in different ways and with varying success.

The most decisive factor for the success of the May films in Germany was probably the casting. Popular stars were cast as well as new ones created through their roles in the series, as contemporary polls and fan magazines show. Glamorous actresses such as Karin Dor were well known and admired, particularly by male cinemagoers. Sweet newcomer Marie Versini became enormously popular with both male and female cinemagoers through her role as Winnetou's sister; she remained a favourite after her work in the series had ended and even though she was unable to find other equally successful roles. Lex Barker as Old Shatterhand was one of the few US stars popular in Germany at the time – a reviewer in the *Frankfurter Allgemeine Zeitung* quipped that he looked more 'Aryan' than any member of the SS. But his popularity, especially with female cinemagoers, was surpassed by Götz George, whose acting style introduced a youthful, energetic physicality. However, the real phenomenon was Wendlandt's discovery Pierre Brice as Winnetou; his androgynous good looks captured adolescent female fantasies for years. Since the films themselves did not provide much romance, the popular teen magazine *Bravo* regularly reported on the friendship between Brice and Versini, thus making them a couple of sorts. Old Shatterhand and Winnetou were often called 'the dream couple of German cinema' – more or less innocently. Literary critics (most prominently Arno Schmidt) have frequently commented on the homoerotic subtext, or at least homosocial quality of May's texts. Responses to this meaning-potential were as varied as it usually is: some found it comical, others took erotic pleasure in it, a few reacted with 'moral panic', and most seemed completely oblivious to it.

The phenomenon of *The Sons of Great Bear* in East Germany is similar in many respects, but also different in some. The socialist government, who controlled the media, had an ambivalent attitude to entertainment: on the one hand it was considered a 'Western evil', on the other a 'necessary evil', because the public enjoyed it. Apart from ideological reservations, imports were expensive, because they had to be bought with foreign currency; nevertheless, more films from Western countries were shown in cinemas and on television than is commonly thought, mostly popular entertainment, and this trend increased over the years. Many East Germans were also able to watch West German television (even when it was forbidden), but since sets were expensive, the medium spread even more slowly than in West Germany. Furthermore, a heated debate exists whether a similar change in values towards individualism and consumerism developed in East Germany as it did in the West. *The Sons of Great Bear* provides a unique opportunity to analyse these complex cultural processes in an exemplary manner.

In 1962, shortly after the Berlin Wall was built (in August 1961) and at a time when West Germany still predominantly rejected US films and produced its own version of the Wild West, *The Magnificent Seven* (1960) made a deep impact in East German cinemas. Within only four weeks, it became the most successful film of the year, and riots even occurred in connection with it, so it was quickly taken out of release. The critical, banned film *Spur der Steine* (*The Traces of Stones*, 1966) later alluded to it. It obviously touched a nerve in a manner that most DEFA films did not and that was unforeseen. After that, very few westerns were shown, but the ones that were would usually go on to achieve significant box-office success (as the listings published by the journal *Film und Fernsehen in der DDR* show). One of the first western series on East German television was *Daniel Boone* (in 1971, seven years after it was made). Importing the May films was out of the question as long as the official attitude towards May was negative, but many East Germans reportedly travelled to Prague to see them. (They were first shown in East Germany on television, in 1984. As legend has it, it was on Erich Honecker's personal request, after he had seen a rerun on West German television. A contemporary review ambivalently voiced that the 'seductive characteristics' of westerns were freedom, adventure and individualism.) Even though East German media were not mainly interested in economic profit, it seemed almost inevitable to react to audience demand for westerns and have DEFA produce its own 'politically correct' versions.

DEFA had produced popular entertainment for children, the fairy tale films, which were also exported with some success. However, the adolescent audience was more problematic. In the 1960s, the socialist regime had high hopes for the new generation of young people, but there was also great concern that they were particularly susceptible to Western values. Young people protesting for Beat music (the 'British invasion') were arrested, their hair was cut, and some were sent to labour camps. Young runaways looking for 'freedom and adventure' were regularly caught on trains at the border. *Bravo* was avidly read by the teenagers who could get hold of copies. Thus, even though the 1960s youth rebellion in East Germany was hardly visible from the outside, a cultural gap existed. Whereas young West Germans could cultivate their own identity by subtly distancing themselves from other Western countries, because they enjoyed a similar freedom, East Germans had an underground fascination for Western culture, because they were not given the same opportunity for producing/consuming their local versions of popular culture. DEFA's 'western' film series partly filled this gap.

The first film was based on novels by Liselotte Welskopf-Henrich (1901–1979), an East German professor of history. Her early novels interpreted the genocide of Native Americans according to Marxist-Leninist doctrine. The later novels tried to overcome the Eurocentrism that came with it, just as in Western representations. Great emphasis was laid on 'historical authenticity', and the films were promoted accordingly as well, in differentiation from both US westerns and the May films. Like the May films, they were not called westerns, but *Indianerfilme*. For the first film, Josef Mach, a director of popular cinema, was imported from Prague. The author was called upon as advisor, but she was dissatisfied, because in her view the film was just sensationalist entertainment. The second film was based on none other than US author Cooper. The other films also had original scripts, so that the series proved to be less homogenous than the May films. Nonetheless, the films are similar to the May films in many respects: they are adventure stories set in spectacular scenery, even partly filmed in the same Yugoslavian locations. They were usually shown in the *Sommerkino*, i.e. cinemas in summer holiday locations – also a connection with tourism, albeit in a more limited and local form. However, there are also significant differences: the central theme is the Indians' fight for survival, so the tone is more serious; the Indians are even more central; and even fewer sympathetic characters are Yankees. This parallels the fact that western clubs were only allowed in East Germany when they were concerned with Indians, not cowboys. *The Sons of Great Bear* was not successful in West Germany, but in other socialist countries, and it was only recently released in English-speaking countries (on video/DVD).

Similar to the May films, the actor playing the Indian protagonist, the Yugoslavian Gojko Mitic (who had played small roles in the May films, and after German reunification played Winnetou in open-air festivals), became a phenomenally popular star. This is all the more significant because East German cinema had not promoted stars before, but propagated 'collective work in ensembles'. Mitic's popularity was even exploited as a socialist role model: for example, a short publicity film (included on the DVD) shows him singing with FDJ children, he is characterised as down-to-earth and as a team-worker, he keeps physically fit, does not gossip about his private life, and so on. However, such didacticism was probably not read by all youths in the manner intended, but rather 'against the grain' and as ambivalently as the regime had produced it. When the Indians in the film are deported to reservations by government officials with the comment 'Education is everything!', it is not far-fetched to imagine how passionately many East German youths could identify with them.

Long after reunification in 1990, even though cultural exchange is now possible without restrictions, the similar, yet different traditions are still cultivated: in West Germany, a parody of the May films, *Der Schuh des Manitu* (2001), was a spectacular success, whereas in East Germany, DEFA's Indian films have become part of the recent wave of *Ostalgie*.

Annemone Ligensa

REFERENCES

Anon. (1961) 'Der Filmbesuch in der Bundesrepublik', *Film-Echo*, 22 July, 839–40.

____ (1963a) 'Der Schatz im Silbersee', *Variety*, 23 January, 6.

____ (1963b) 'Winnetou I: Die Karl-May-Erfolgsfilm-Serie läuft', *Frankfurter Allgemeine Zeitung*, 17 December.

Garncarz, J. (1994) 'Hollywood in Germany: The Role of American Films in Germany, 1925–1990', in D. W. Ellwood and R. Kroes (eds) *Hollywood in Europe*. Amsterdam: VU University Press, 94–135.

Hansen, B. (1966) 'Die Söhne der großen Bärin', *Film-Wissenschaftliche Mitteilungen*, 2, 503–9.

DER GETEILTE HIMMEL **THE DIVIDED HEAVEN** 15

KONRAD WOLF, EAST GERMANY, 1964

The DEFA-production *Der geteilte Himmel* (*The Divided Heaven*, 1964) is based on Christa Wolf's novel of the same title, published in 1963. It was one of the first literary texts to broach the issue of the building of the Berlin Wall on 13 August 1961. The novel's central theme is the political climate in East Germany that led to the building of the wall as a 'protective barrier', thereby setting the seal on the division of Germany. Wolf's novel was prompted by the *Bitterfelder Weg*, which was initiated by East Germany's former head of state and party leader Walter Ulbricht. In 1959, the collective leadership of the Party (SED) assembled for a conference on culture in Bitterfeld, an industrial centre in central East Germany. From there the call went out to East Germany's artists and authors to tackle the contemporary problems of industrial workers and to overcome their alleged *Weltfremdheit*, i.e. their aloofness from ordinary life. The party's slogan 'Poets to the production!' was addressed to authors, and 'Pick up the pen, comrade!' was an appeal to workers to enter the literary field themselves. In retrospect, such a politico-cultural directive turned out to be a boomerang for the Party. Confronted with the everyday life of factory work, many artists lost their idealism regarding socialism. Thus, they increasingly focused on the conflicts and contradictions of their newly developing society.

Wolf's novel *Der geteilte Himmel*, which combined the structural principles of the *Bildungsroman* with the theme of educating a young woman to become a 'socialist personality', met with wide appreciation, but also sharp attacks. For example, the Party's main publication *Neues Deutschland* accused the author of 'regarding the fact of a divided Germany as a national calamity rather than West Germany's imperialism regaining strength'. The criticism targeted the allegedly distorted portrayal of socialist life, especially that Party members were rendered as figures lacking in amendatory power. Yet, despite the critical voices, the novel established Wolf as a major author; *Der geteilte Himmel* received the prestigious Heinrich Mann Prize.

Only one year after its publication, Wolf and her husband Gerhard, together with Konrad Wolf, Kurt Bartel and Willy Brückner (as dramatic adviser) turned the novel into a screenplay, a project regarded as 'one of DEFA's most important works about the present'. It is part of a cycle of productions undertaken by the studio in the early 1960s, also in response to the

Bitterfelder Weg, which triggered films with contemporary themes set in changeable realities. The director, Konrad Wolf, was not only well known in his home country, but also in the West, since his prestigious Holocaust film *Sterne* (*Stars*, 1959) won the Grand Jury Prize at Cannes. However, *The Divided Heaven* far surpasses the director's former aesthetic achievements.

Ulrich Gregor notes, however, that the film's narration was very difficult to grasp for its contemporary audience. The film mostly follows the novel's original story. At the end of August 1961, nineteen-year-old Rita Seidel, after a physical and psychological breakdown, recalls the two preceding years of her life. Originally an office worker in a small village in the region of Thüringen, she is able to escape her dreary existence when she meets the analytical chemist Manfred Herrfurth and is admitted to teacher training. She moves in with Manfred, who lives in the house belonging to his parents, in Halle. Rita's training programme requires an internship in Halle's collectively owned train-carriage works, where she, as a member of the fitter brigade, witnesses typical struggles, such as everyday shortcomings, quarrels about the plan quota and intrigues. She particularly sympathises with Meternagel, the demoted former leader of her brigade. He suffers from his group's lackadaisical and undisciplined attitude towards work and the fact that everyone pursues only their own interests.

The flight to the West of the works' director unsettles the employees. Rita, drawn into the conflict about the socialist work ethos, finds no sympathy in her talks with Manfred. Immediately after finishing his PhD in chemistry, an opportunity opens up at a chemical factory interested in adopting his newly developed process of reducing emissions. Ultimately, however, the procedure is rejected. Manfred is deeply disappointed and becomes increasingly cynical. The relationship with Rita, up to that point characterised by tenderness and a feeling of unity, experiences its first cracks. Moreover, Manfred is jealous of Wendland, the works' new director, with whom Rita gets along very well. In addition, Rita suffers under Manfred's conflict with his father; Manfred accuses him of political opportunism for switching over from the Nazi regime to the SED without so much as a flinch. In her studies to become a teacher, Rita has to put up with Mangold, a fellow student who keeps ranting Stalinist set phrases. When the parents of another student, Sigrid, also flee to the West, Rita defends her against Mangold, who demands that she be expelled. Thanks to the efforts of Rita's mentor, Schwarzenbach, the expulsion is not enforced. In the carriage works, Meternagel succeeds in motivating his brigade, and they surpass the plan quota when everybody works effectively and in solidarity. During a test drive of the new carriages, to which Rita takes Manfred along, they receive the news that the Russians sent their first cosmonaut, Yuri Gagarin, a farmer's son, into outer space. The quarrels between Rita and Manfred become fiercer. Some time later, Manfred uses his participation at a conference in West Berlin as an opportunity to stay there. He begs Rita for a visit. Their meeting, however, is a disappointment. She returns to Halle, where she breaks down, but eventually manages to come to terms with the end of their relationship.

The reservations concerning the content of the story were insignificant by the time of the film's premiere on 3 September 1964, because by then the borders were firmly closed. With the construction of the Wall, the regime had robbed the people of East Germany of the option to leave the country as a means to express their resentment about the social and political conditions. 'This was', as Peter Hoff remarked, 'a mistake, as one could soon tell; under the pressure of a "closed society", the inherent conflicts boiled up even faster.' In the GDR's film culture, the boiling point was reached in December 1965: at the party's 11th central committee meeting, the SED banned several of that year's productions dealing critically with the contemporary living and working circumstances in East Germany. *Spur der Steine* (*The Trace of Stones*) addressed and exposed intolerance and moral double standards; *Das Kaninchen bin ich* (*I Am the Rabbit*) and *Der Frühling braucht Zeit* focused on the alienation of the individual under high political pressure. In *Denk bloß nicht, ich heule*, the conflict between father and son is articulated much more sharply than in *The Divided Heaven*. There, in accordance with the overall melodramatic tone, gender-specific options of solving the conflict are still possible: on the one hand, Manfred's impetuous 'irrational act' (as Konrad Wolf interprets his migration), on the other, the readjustment of the heroine's consciousness and the hinted integration into socialist society. By contrast, the films banned at the 11th plenum displayed a consistent working through of unsolvable and overwhelming conflicts.

While *The Divided Heaven* develops at length Manfred's motivation for quitting the GDR – he aspires to professional recognition, but fails to obtain it, and is troubled by existential philosophical questions – the film's main perspective and potential for identification is represented by Rita. Her decision to return to Halle after her visit to West Berlin is more an emotional choice than a rational one, founded on her solidarity with Schwarzenbach and Meternagel. The two elderly men represent ethos for her (one as a 'worker with the mind', the other as a 'worker with the body'). They sustain her belief in the order of the socialist world – which will succeed despite all challenges and daily obstacles (for example, the attacks by the Stalinist Mangold, Meternagel's demotion). As Erika Richter notes, there is much serious dialogue in this film, 'with a strong, naïve belief that talking is useful and can cause change in people and in society as a whole'. Thus, Schwarzenbach wins against Mangold in their exchange of verbal blows with his moral argument on Sigrid's expulsion: 'You should make sure that someone like Sigrid realises that the Party is there for her!' Although the film does not openly state Rita's reason for returning, it is implied that it is based on her commitment and accords with the values of her guiding figures. By contrast, Manfred's departure seems selfish: he puts his ambition before his love.

The film does not present Rita's return as the climax of a simple, chronological narrative but interweaves it into a complex flashback structure. Its fragmented and jumbled narrative form is the film's specific aesthetic characteristic. The numerous flashbacks represent a series of memories. In the narrative's present, Rita undergoes a process of mourning and convalescence after the traumatic break-up with Manfred. Its stages are announced by short, intermittent shots. These inserts are accompanied by a female voice-over commentary instead of their own body of sound. Rita has withdrawn to her mother's house; it is set below a high motorway viaduct, a metaphor for the 'life' passing Rita by, contrasted with the quietness of her childhood home, which enables her memory-work. Her recovery process is expressed in the broadening of her radius, her gradual approaching and final 'conquering' of the viaduct and thus the growing distance from her motherly space. Rita's last movements are acts of parting and solving: she pins up her hair (symbolising feminine adulthood) and tidies up the attic (the last thing connecting her with Manfred), before picking up her suitcase and heading to Meternagel's flat. At the end, we see her walking in the street among other people.

The Divided Heaven does not aim for goal-oriented suspense or immediacy of experience, but legitimises Rita's decision to stay in the GDR by presenting it as a given from the very beginning. The film directs the audience's interest onto the self-reflective living with that decision by way of 'remembering and working through it'. The film's complexity regarding narrative framing and intricate inner structure is indebted to formal principles of art cinema, especially that of the *nouvelle vague*. Already at the time of its first release, the close resemblance of *The Divided Heaven* to Alain Resnais' *Hiroshima, mon amour* (1959) or *L'année dernière à Marienbad* (1960), and therefore to West European *auteur* cinema, was pointed out in an interview with Konrad Wolf. Yet at the same time, Wolf, talking to Ulrich Gregor, emphasised his distance from Resnais: 'I find the subjectivist-formal aspect of his films interesting and attractive … yet often downright depressing in relation to their themes, because I had expected so much … of Resnais.'

The voice-over narrator of the film is female, which functions as Rita's inner and grown-up counterpart – a mature version of the girl. It is not an interior monologue, because it speaks in the third person and from a point of view that is clearly distinct from the psychological dispo-sition of the protagonist (for example, 'a trite story, which, by the way, lies behind her'). The voice functions as an agent who indicates through flashforwards that it is possible to overcome the self; the voice flanks and supports Rita during her recovery. It is difficult to tell whether the female narrator represents an authority apart from Rita, or whether she is meant to be her inner 'superego'. The ambivalent positioning of the voice-over corresponds, according to Gregor, to the film's alleged 'contradictions between an advanced formal method and dragged-along psychological or ideological "contents"'. The function of the omniscient point of view is to separate Rita's future from her former life and first love; it points to the insurmountability of the beach and stresses the finality of the cut. This mode of speech could be interpreted as the resulting effect of the traumatic sealing-off from love. Perhaps it was the tone of this stern and sincere voice suggestively laid over Rita's anguished face that provoked the critic Helmut Färber to rebuff the film so strongly at the 1966 premiere in Munich: 'The film does not want to represent, but to discipline. Who then is to be disciplined? The film educates or, to put it bluntly, subjects.' It is the pre-set closure to Rita's story of crisis on the plot level that deter-mines the relationship between the female voice-over and the images on screen. For the voice-over to be separated in attitude and tone, i.e. for the splitting of the female voice into diegetic and extradiegetic positions, an irreversible distance to the past events is a precondition. Such distance as precondition for female narration is also depicted within the story: Rita, again in a flashback narration, tells Schwarzenbach about her visit to Manfred, and thereby gives living proof for Schwarzenbach's thesis that trust is an essential prerequisite for living together.

The exterior world is divided into territories of military blocs and separate countries, and thus, eventually, so is the 'heaven' of Rita and Manfred. Moreover, even Rita herself is divided – a split that literally almost tears her apart. Her breakdown and fall onto the rails at the works is depicted as imminently life threatening. From the right-hand side, a train approaches, heading towards another one in the background; Rita falls between them, putting her at risk of being crushed. This shot was devised for maximum dramatic 'impact' by director Konrad Wolf and cameraman Werner Bergmann – its diagonal composition (the vanishing point is the frame's lower left corner) is highly dynamic. The low-angle perspective with slanted framing visualises Rita's sliding away from the world and her perception of an order falling apart. Thus, the narrative and visuals reflect the two levels to which the title (of novel and film) points: the political crisis as well as the psychosomatic crisis of the heroine. Furthermore, the topographical lines of division are extended into the timeline. When Manfred, shortly before their final parting, says, 'At least they can't divide heaven', Rita replies, 'Of course, heaven is the first to divide itself.' Here, the term 'heaven' metaphorically stands for their different expectations, aspirations and concepts of happiness. Rita's retort expresses a defiant and disillusioned insistence on their differing views and values. Gagarin's space flight had inscribed division into the sky. His space travel assigns the sky a history by semantically dividing it into a space of the past and of the future. Moreover, it marks the sky as a new territorial domain of the Soviet Union. Rita's fall onto the rails signifies not only the climax of her crisis, but also the segmentation of the film. It is both closure and new opening at the same time, dividing the narrative's past from its present. The event presents an earthbound counter-image to the technological overcoming of gravity in Gagarin's flight.

The semantics of parting and divide give the film its thematic as well as aesthetic structure. Hence, the film's formalism is not an end in itself, but is employed consistently in support of the main theme. As outlined by Wolf in a storyboard beforehand, Bergmann's black and white camera captures the compositions in highest precision. Division manifests itself in the choice of focusing plane, i.e. via close shots and close-ups the protagonists are set against blurred surroundings, providing negligible background. Furthermore, the consistent decentring of the protagonists in the *mise-en-scène*, filmed with wide-angle optics and in Totalvision (equivalent to the Cinemascope format), creates the impression that they almost protrude from the frame. Such a composition either leaves much empty space when there is only one character on screen (receiving its dynamics from diagonals into unfocused areas), or, when two characters are on screen, each of them receives half the frame's space. Wolf creates graphic divisions in the frames whenever disputes take place, for example, when Manfred and Wendland exchange their differing attitudes concerning the jubilee party of the works. The loving couple receives more action space; for instance, their dancing is filmed in a parallel tracking shot, in contrast to the usually rather static camera. Furthermore, rack focus is used to underline a protagonist's isolation; for example, the device guides the audience's gaze to the effects that remarks by one protagonist have on another.

Division also characterises the film's montage; only a few sequences follow the principles of continuity editing. Typically, closure is achieved by dialogue, often combined with a violation of the '180 degree rule'. This is especially prominent in the coffee-bar sequence, during the cutting between the bar and the table at the window. Manfred and Martin sit at the bar, and Manfred is mocking utopian expectations that technology and science work wonders: 'So, what do all these average people expect from us? A house that runs as smoothly as a well-oiled machine. Cities that regenerate themselves. Life-sustaining measures to achieve biblical age!' Martin adds: 'Automated upbringing of children!' Meanwhile, Sigrid and Rita are talking about Sigrid's parents' flight to the West. The cutting across the line of vision highlights the difference between male and female discourse. While the women exchange confidentialities and confessions, the men outperform each other with irony and coolness. When, at the end of the scene, all four of them sit together, the travelling camera circles the fragile community.

Manfred's workroom in the attic is one of the few studio sets of the film. It is a space created to indicate its inhabitants' social integration/disintegration by means of interior decoration and the room's relationship with the artificially modelled background of the city. Furthermore, it is a 'breathing space', into which the vibrations of the loving couple engrave themselves, a space for their fantasies, and a space where their estrangement from each other and from the outside world is increasingly expressed. Through the spacious window, the attic is connected to the sky and the city; it is exposed to the weather and the seasons and makes them visible. The attic is a bohemian, poetic place of dreams, enclosing the couple's visions and wishes. At one point it is called a floating 'ship'; another time it is regarded as a 'lighthouse' providing orientation. Throughout the film, the attic loses more and more of its relation to the outside; the outline of the city in the window vanishes like a fading 'picture'. The attic visibly empties, at first of things, later of people. The deterioration of the attic represents the equivalent to the disillusionment and later abandonment of the couple's 'symbiotic being', giving the attic a provisional, transitory character.

Thanks to the shooting on location, Halle not only receives a portrait of its landmarks (for example, the Marktkirche, the river Saale, the historical alleyways), but through a *mise-en-scène* of diagonals and vanishing points in numerous symmetrically composed shots, it also acquires a sensual presence, represented in full 'depth'. The city of Halle appears atmospherically rich, with its canyon-like lanes, streetcars and chimneys and frame-filling backgrounds of architectural landmarks. By contrast, West Berlin's foreignness is emphasised through a 'flat' relationship between space and characters. Here, sterility reigns, expressed by standardised interior decoration and objects without any traces of usage (particularly striking is the scene set in the coffee house Kranzler on Kurfürstendamm). The staging of Western consumer goods is similarly fetishised; for example, Manfred's mother carefully arranges gifts from relatives in the West on a table. In accordance with the film's underlying consumer criticism, Western goods are presented as a quasi-abstract brand, their material existence is reduced to their packaging. The contrast between East and West is exemplified in the sensual presence/

absence of food: specific goods consumed vs. items treated only as ciphers. Consumption is related to immediacy. This is illustrated in the elliptic Christmas dinner at Rita's home: the camera concludes the scene by showing the gnawed-off bones of the goose.

Before this 'flattened' background of Berlin, Konrad Wolf places the estranged couple Manfred and Rita. In one scene, they talk in front of a skyscraper, while in the middle plane a woman is pushing a pram to and fro, all the while staying exactly in the same space – a contrasting counterpart to a similar scene in Halle. In the 'Eastern' variant of the motif, several nurses pushing prams walk up from the depth of an alley towards the camera. In these two condensed 'background' actions, more than one hint is packed in. A female audience will register that East Germany is represented as the society offering women a broader variety of options than the West. The West, with its modernist aestheticism, pretends progressiveness through its architecture of public space and the luxurious ambiance of the almost empty coffee house Kranzler. Nevertheless, this cannot hide the fact that the capitalistic West remained rather conservative regarding gender relations, holding on to the old-fashioned view of women as mothers and housewives, whereas the East promoted division of labour, offering professional (and not, as Martin put it, 'automatic') upbringing of children. Thus, *The Divided Heaven*, with just a few strokes, plausibly presents the differences of the two German social orders concerning gender: as Joshua Feinstein has noted, the East offers women career chances that the West does not provide. Thus, Rita's emancipation, her rejection of Manfred's pet name, 'the brown maiden', stands for the progressive notions of GDR society. Her gender, freed from the symbiotic relationship with a man, stands for a unity that was lost in modern life and that socialism promises to resurrect.

Ursula von Keitz

Translated by Daniela Casanova

REFERENCES

Feinstein, J. (2002) 'Straddling the Wall: Socialist Realism Meets the Nouvelle Vague in *Der geteilte Himmel*', in *The Triumph of the Ordinary: Depictions of Daily Life in East German Cinema 1949-1989*. Chapel Hill, NC and London: University of North Carolina Press, 110–36.

Gregor, U. (1977) 'Konrad Wolf. Auf der Suche nach Heimat', in H. R. Blum (ed.) *Film in der DDR*. München und Wien: Hanser, 77–98.

Hoff, P. (1995) '"Der Himmel teilt sich zuerst": *Der geteilte Himmel* (1964), ein Film von Konrad Wolf nach dem Buch von Christa Wolf', in K. F. Reimers, C. Hackl and B. Scherer (eds) *Unser Jahrhundert in Film und Fernsehen*. München: Ölschläger, 134–58.

Richter, E. (1994) 'Zwischen Mauerbau und Kahlschlag 1961–1965', in R. Schenk (ed.) *Das zweite Leben der Filmstadt Babelsberg: DEFA-Spielfilme 1946–1992*. Filmmuseum Potsdam: Berlin, 159–211.

ABSCHIED VON GESTERN YESTERDAY GIRL

16

ALEXANDER KLUGE, WEST GERMANY, 1967

Seldom is the title of a film as programmatic for the movement it (re)presents as *Abschied von gestern* (*Yesterday Girl*, 1967). It symbolises the pronounced 'farewell to yesterday' that was proclaimed by 26 young German filmmakers in the *Oberhausener Manifest* in 1962. Furthermore, the film won many important awards, such as the Special Jury Prize and an OCIC Award – Honourable Mention at the Venice Film Festival in 1966, as well as four Film Awards in Gold at the German *Bundesfilmpreis* in 1967. Revolutions in art have their own standards: the protest against a purely commercial system can be regarded as effective without economic success of its products. In the case of the *Neue Deutsche Film* (New German Cinema) the nimbus of success was created at festivals and by cineastes, but not at the box office, and it only became possible through incisive changes in the production system.

The German film industry, which the young directors criticised, was commercially efficient and popular with German audiences. The German cinema of the 1950s produced many of the top box-office successes of German film history, but was rejected by many film critics and filmmakers for its commercialism. Its producers followed an artisan's instead of an artist's concept of filmmaking, which was highly professional in production, exhibition and distribution, and consistently oriented towards market concerns. But in 1961, two polemical books were published: Walter Schmieding's *Kunst oder Kasse: Der Ärger mit dem deutschen Film* and Joe Hembus's *Der deutsche Film kann gar nicht besser sein*. One year later the *Oberhausener Manifest* was proclaimed, in which a 'sceptical generation' demanded art instead of entertainment.

'The old film is dead. We believe in the new one.' This statement sums up the manifesto signed in Oberhausen on 28 February 1962. The declaration represented the new generation's claim to create a New German Cinema. Its aesthetics and production practices were similar to (German) experimental short films, which met with international critical success, but were ignored by the mainstream of the German film industry, and which the young German filmmakers wanted to realise on a larger, feature-film scale. It is symbolic that a lost and fatherless person like Kasper Hauser was chosen as the hero in one of the new films, Werner Herzog's

Jeder für sich und Gott gegen alle (*The Enigma of Kaspar Hauser*, 1974). At stake was a conflict between generations, and seventeen years after World War II also a political one. The young directors, among them Alexander Kluge, Wim Wenders and Volker Schlöndorff, criticised their 'fathers' role during the Third Reich by postulating personal responsibility for collective actions. This also included an overall rejection of traditional film culture, which was regarded as 'Nazi culture', even though the German films of the 1940s – except for propaganda films, of course – had followed an international narrative tradition that was established in the 1920s. It was overlooked that even many successful European art films, such as those by Roberto Rossellini or François Truffaut, also used principles of classical narrative. Be that as it may, the defining characteristic of the German avant-garde was the effort to deal with the trauma of the recent past in content as well as form.

The directors of the New German Cinema regarded themselves as *auteurs* ('*Filme-macher*'), demanded total control of their films, and resolutely rejected both the economic demands of the film industry and the preferences of the general audience. The directors became stars, promoting their films with their names as the main 'selling point' – at least at festivals. The economic basis for their films was secured by major changes in the production system, for example, state subsidies and television co-production. Retrospectively, the institutional context, such as the important role of the *Film- und Fernsehabkommen* ('film- and television agreement'), is often underestimated, as Joseph Garncarz has pointed out. The usual accounts claim that a widespread dissatisfaction with mainstream film was the basis of the New German Cinema. At the beginning of the 1960s, the German film industry was still very successful, despite the fact that older cinemagoers were increasingly turning to television. Several older directors began working for television, adapting their traditional style to the constraints of the small screen. Even though the young German filmmakers preferred the aesthetics of cinema, they took advantage of the support they found in the German public television system, due to its educational aims. Furthermore, Alexander Kluge, who studied law, lobbied for government subsidising of art films. Thus, the films of the New German Cinema were mostly funded by the filmmakers' own production companies, television and/or public subsidies; they were first exhibited in cinemas and shown on television two years later. Thus, the young filmmakers were free of market concerns, but dependent on government support, which was later romanticised as artistic freedom enthusiastically received by audiences.

On the basis of this institutional framework, the filmmakers of the *Oberhausener Manifest* initiated a paradigm shift in German cinema. The new generation of filmmakers regarded contemporary mainstream films as escapism, political reactionism and aesthetic ossification. The aim was to overcome this 'cinematic crisis' through a radical break with the past in form and an explicit excavation of history in content. Film was to function as a means for understanding and criticising reality. The audience's role was to actively co-construct the film while viewing and to re-construct it afterwards in reflection and discussions. In this concept, the 'author' holds a key position. As a figure of integration and distanciation, often present within his own work and further elaborating it in paratexts, he replaces the star actress/actor, whose appeal is based on identification, and thus transforms the spectator's relationship to a film.

Alexander Kluge is one of the leading figures in this movement of filmmaking. He was especially dedicated in promoting public awareness of film culture in theory as well as practice. Only one year after Oberhausen, Kluge founded a production company called 'Kairos' (Greek for 'opportune moment'). In an interview in 1998 he explained what this concept means to him:

> I would explain it with the example of the time problem. We all know the mechanical time of a television program, which is basically derived from peoples' working hours and the petty mercantile uses they make of their leisure time. For the Greeks, Chronos stood for time that leads to death, time that consumes itself. Chronos is a gigantic god who devours his own children. His antipode in the Greek pantheon is Kairos, 'the fortunate moment'. Kairos is a very small, dwarf-like god with a bald head. But on his forehead he has a tuft (of dense hair). If you catch the tuft, you're lucky. If you are just a moment too late, your grip on his bald head will slip and you won't be able to hold on to him. This character, Kairos, is the 'happy time' that is hidden in the time of people's lives, in their working time, in everything they might do. He is an object of aesthetic activity. With Chronos on the other hand, you can only become a watchmaker.

This production company was involved in the shooting of *Yesterday Girl* (together with Independent-Film). The film marks the actual programmatic beginning of the New German Cinema. Kluge was committed to the aesthetics of 'fragmented sensuousness' favoured by the Frankfurt School. However, in contrast to the avant-garde of high culture, Kluge also valued and used non-canonical sources and everyday material. Furthermore, he regarded mass media as a potential for enlightenment, rather than re-feudalisation of the public sphere, as Jürgen Habermas saw it. The most significant characteristic of Kluge's method is the contextualising combination and interplay of disparate elements. Thematically, Kluge's texts and films were dominated by questions dealing with *Lebenslauf* ('personal history'). With his film *Yesterday Girl*, he established these questions as the main theme of West German art cinema after 1962.

As an allusive analysis of West Germany during its 'economic miracle era', *Yesterday Girl* has become one of the most renowned examples of the New German Cinema. Kluge confronted the country with a look at the lives of the outcast 'elements' of society and their struggle with the system during a period of general economic upturn. After fleeing from East Germany to West Germany in 1957, the main protagonist of his film, a young woman named Anita G., must face the fact that the German Democratic Republic may be east of the Federal Republic of Germany, but is certainly not east of Eden. The audience accompanies her on her journey, which is not a sentimental one, but rather a stranger's in a strange land. The film opens with the statement: 'It is not a precipice that separates us from yesterday, but a changed situation.' The two German countries share an unwillingness to deal with the past. The film's English title, *Yesterday Girl*, describes Anita's role even more accurately. The protagonist is not only a Jewish woman from the other side of the Berlin Wall, but also stands for a past era no one wants to remember. On her journey, she lifts veils – not just white curtains in a West German television commercial for a detergent, but shrouds spread over a repressed past. The film contains several sequences composed of a montage of personal photographs from the past. Photographs of people in uniforms indicate that almost no one is spared of having not only a war victim, but also a killer in the family. 'Does yesterday come tomorrow?' is the anxious question of one of the intertitles.

The story is simple, but it is presented from different viewpoints. Kluge uses 'literary' devices; for example, he divides the film into segments similar to the chapters of a book, most of them introduced by a written or spoken motto. Anita G., having grown up near Leipzig, tries to make a living in West Germany in 1959. Very soon she must learn that the system only works in favour of those who possess the necessary prerequisites. Homeless and without a job, Anita soon gets into trouble with the law: she steals and is imprisoned for it. The conviction makes the building of a new life even more difficult: she cannot get or keep jobs. Several love affairs with married men seem to offer her a new beginning, but she is repeatedly confronted with her past. This vicious circle, along with her lovers' indecision or refusal to accept her as their official partner, prove that all her efforts were doomed from the outset. Her relationships are variations of a quotation from Bertolt Brecht's *Stories of Mr. Keuner*, which one of her lovers summarises as: 'In a love affair you tend to create an ideal of how the other person is supposed to be. Again and again, people make the disastrous mistake of trying to form their partner after this ideal instead of adjusting the picture to their beloved.' Finally, when Anita finds out that she is pregnant, she turns herself over to the police in order to give birth in the only surroundings that offer her at least some sort of shelter – prison. By quoting Dostoevsky's *Crime and Punishment*, the final intertitle sums up Kluge's credo: 'Everyone is responsible for everything. But only if everyone knew that, we would have heaven on earth.'

The story of Anita G. was inspired by an authentic case. Kluge wanted to portray a real individual person, the life of a woman that could be used as a probe for society. The film is based on a story Kluge published in his book *Lebensläufe*. The challenge of turning a text into a film, Kluge once said, lies in using the same amount of intelligence for a different medium. To help the actors reflect the proper mood, Kluge shot scenes in chronological order. There was no re-shooting; if a scene did not work, it was cut. However, documentary methods do not automatically create documentaries. What Kluge had in mind was a work of fiction, a film resembling a novel. The documentary style was created by the actors, not the director. As reviews noted, Alexandra Kluge (Kluge's sister) 'was' or even 'embodied' rather than 'played' the part of Anita G. Kluge often said that Alexandra contributed a large part of text to the final film version: 'She's a co-author of sorts. Not only because she improvised some of her lines, but also because I can feed off of her. One can develop a lot from an actor.' There was an original script of about 200 pages, in which many things were changed before the scenes were actually filmed. Before shooting their scenes, the director discussed them with the actors and accepted suggestions and changes. However, Kluge does not use the real woman's story or Alexandra's contribution to voice an explicit critique of patriarchy.

Films like *Yesterday Girl* broke with narrative conventions and, inspired by foreign examples, used an eclectic mixture of styles, including fiction, documentary, literature and even opera. Kluge's filmic montage is comparable to a rhizome (as conceptualised by Gilles Deleuze and Félix Guattari), which reflects his use of sources and his concept of history. By creating a collage of various materials and counterposing documentary and fiction, Kluge's work bears resemblance to an archaeological excavation of repressed recollection. He propagates the necessity of analysing recent history by thematic reference to past events, and by formal reference to Walter Benjamin's philosophy of history. This becomes particularly clear from one passage that is – according to Kluge – central to Benjamin's theses on the philosophy of history:

> A Klee painting named 'Angelus Novus' shows an angel looking as though he is about to move away from something he is fixedly contemplating. His eyes are staring, his mouth is open, his wings are spread. This is how one pictures the angel of history. His face is turned toward the past. Where *we* perceive a chain of events, *he* sees one single catastrophe, which keeps piling wreckage upon wreckage and hurls it in front of his feet. The angel would like to stay, awaken the dead, and make whole what has been smashed. But a storm is blowing from Paradise; it has got caught in his wings with such violence that the angel can no longer close them. This storm irresistibly propels him into the future to which his back is turned, while the pile of debris before him grows skyward. *This* storm is what we call progress.

Kluge's application of this philosophy of history, in his texts as well as films, relies on the active participation of the audience. The aim of his disparate collages is to lead the audience through a history marked by traumatic breaks to new insights. In Kluge's view, the social value of film extends beyond the cinema. By presenting history as significant events and the present as a position from which these events must be interpreted, film can further the understanding of history – the present must always be the point of attack.

Critics feared that Kluge's films would alienate spectators who were too conventional to follow such a style. He countered that the human brain's capacity for selection, association and interpretation allows that kind of montage. Everyday life demands constant choices from a mosaic of impressions, to separate the important from the dispensable. 'I believe that we may expect much more of the audience in this respect. Because in traffic, or when a person goes through life, he picks up many more mosaic-like things, which he selects. He absorbs the important things and ignores the unimportant, and he constructs the important things for himself, doesn't he?' If an individual's memory could be directly turned into a film, *Yesterday Girl* is a perfect example of Kluge's idea of what it would look like.

Cinematographically, *Yesterday Girl* consists of a disharmonious interplay of close-ups and different types of pans – a composition combining traditional and innovative means of narration. Some sequences bear resemblance to *nouvelle vague* aesthetics, others are characterised by documentary style. Legal phrases are quoted extensively, alternating with scenes of bizarre dreams (a nocturnal ballet of policemen and cars) and nightmares (Anita chased by Nazi myrmidons). The most characteristic stylistic device is the frequent use of photographs, illustrations from children's books, paintings, drawings and intertitles. Some constructions, such as the alternation of diegetic and non-diegetic elements, conceal rather than reveal the director's intentions. For example, one sequence shows Anita and her lover singing the German national anthem along with a radio broadcast; in the following sequence, this soundtrack continues while we are shown images of an old Jewish cemetery. The film refrains from any spoken comment, but we are confronted with hares on the reliefs of the tombstones – the hare is a flight animal. The story progresses mainly through voice-over narration, which is spoken by Kluge himself. To several elements of the story only hints are given, either in subordinate clauses of the voice-over or in silent intertitles. In the end, the story completes itself only in the spectator's subjective interpretation, which is exactly what Kluge wants. His intention is to create films in the imagination and interpretation of the audience. He regards montage as a concept to be executed – or completed – in the eye of the beholder.

'It is impossible to learn not to learn' one of the intertitles states. Kluge's interest in history lies not in the abstract contemplation of events; his interest lies in the way events affect people in their everyday lives. The grotesquery he often creates functions as a mirror that distorts the so-called 'reality'. This distorted view enables us to question our perception of common experiences and subsequently makes us look at them more closely. In the ideal case, the spectator takes the view of a naïve child. Looking through a child's eyes facilitates re-evaluation – which is what Kluge aims to achieve, and he wants the audience to join him. In *Yesterday Girl*, we are confronted with scenes seen through Anita's bewildered eyes. The resulting lack of understanding brings us closer to Anita and her view of the world, since we gain our impression of the various people and situations based on Anita's way of perceiving them. The mixture of subjective and objective storytelling hinders a full understanding of the director's intention – an invitation to take a second look at the film.

'Quis custodiet ipsos custodes?' ('Who watches the watchers?'), the Roman poet Juvenal asked in his *Satires*. Anita's final stare at the spectator has been compared to the freeze-frame of Antoine Doinel in François Truffaut's *Les quatre cents coups* (*The Four Hundred Blows*, 1959). The original film poster for *Yesterday Girl* depicts Kluge's concept in a single image: painted in watercolours of blue and grey, it shows a close-up of Anita G. looking at us with expressive eyes and a 'Mona Lisa' smile. In contemplating her, the eyes of the mutual beholders meet. We are watching the watcher. But Anita has little power to act on what she sees – the motivation to act is expected of the audience.

Thomas Ballhausen and Günter Krenn

AUTHORS' NOTE: We would like to thank Annemone Ligensa for numerous valuable suggestions and for translating the text.

REFERENCES

Benjamin, W. (2003 [1940]) 'On the Concept of History', in *Selected Writings, Volume IV: 1938–1940*, eds H. Eiland and M. W. Jennings. Trans. E. Jephcott *et al.* Cambridge, MA: Harvard University Press, 389–400.

Deleuze, G. and F. Guattari (1987) *A Thousand Plateaus: Capitalism and Schizophrenia*. Trans. B. Massumi. Minneapolis; MN: University of Minnesota Press.

Garncarz, J. (1999) 'Drei Generationen: Wandlungen der Institution Kino in der Bundesrepublik Deutschland', in E. Buck (ed.) *Männer und Frauen*. Köln: Theaterwissenschaftliche Sammlung/Universität zu Köln, 138–53.

Habermas, J. (1962) *Strukturwandel der Öffentlichkeit: Untersuchungen zu einer Kategorie der bürgerlichen Gesellschaft*. Neuwied: Luchterhand.

Hembus, J. (1961) *Der deutsche Film kann gar nicht besser sein*. Bremen: Schünemann.

Kluge, A. (1962) 'Anita G.', in *Lebensläufe*. Stuttgart: Goverts, 85–102.

____ (1966) *Abschied von gestern: Protokoll*. Frankfurt am Main: Filmkritik.

____ (1975) *Gelegenheitsarbeit einer Sklavin: Zur realistischen Methode*. Frankfurt am Main: Suhrkamp.

Obrist, H. U. (1998) 'Interview with Alexander Kluge'. On-line. Available HTTP: http://www.nettime.org/Lists-Archives/nettime-l-9802/msg00000.html (2 May 2012).

Schmieding, W. (1961) *Kunst und Kasse: Der Ärger mit dem deutschen Film*. Hamburg: Rütten & Loening.

DIE LEGENDE VON PAUL UND PAULA

THE LEGEND OF PAUL AND PAULA

17

HEINER CAROW, EAST GERMANY, 1973

In *Die Legende von Paul und Paula* (*The Legend of Paul and Paula*, 1973), Paula (Angelica Domröse) is a young woman living with her illegitimate daughter in an old Berlin tenement block. She works in the bottle-returns section of a supermarket and dreams of self-realisation through a great love. Paul (Winfried Glatzeder), who grew up in the same quarter as Paula and knows her by sight, is reaching the end of his studies. He falls in love with Ines (Heidemarie Wenzel), whose father owns a shooting gallery, and whom he marries when she becomes pregnant. In the same night, on the same fairground, Paula meets the man who will father her second child. She barely survives a complicated birth and is warned by the clinic's doctor not to become pregnant a third time. During her absence, the father of her child amuses himself with other women. Paula throws him out of the flat.

On completing his degree, Paul is called up to serve his time in the National People's Army for three years, and his wife and son bid him farewell. On one of his leaves, he finds his wife in bed with a stranger, but he does not want a divorce. After his discharge, Paul swiftly climbs the career ladder in the state apparatus. This is signified by the move from the tenement block to a newly built apartment and by the company car, a Wolga, which he has to share with a colleague. His relationship with his wife is clearly deteriorating, indicated by the bored look in her eyes when they have sex, by the separate beds in the new apartment and by the family row that erupts on the child's birthday. As emphasised by the latter scene in particular, everyone in Paul's world appears dubious und distorted, like characters of a satire. In contrast to this, Paula's world is human. Her children are growing up normally; the colleagues in the supermarket look after her, the doctor stops to speak to her on the street and enquires how she is. And then there is Saft, the tyre dealer (Fred Delmare): he makes her an offer of a carefree and elevated standard of life, one which he himself, overtaxed by work, has up to that point been unable to enjoy.

Paul, who is disappointed by his marriage, and Paula, who feels too young to spend every evening drinking alone in bed, properly meet for the first time in a dance bar. At first they dance with other partners, but then the inevitable happens. A relationship develops between

THE CINEMA OF GERMANY   169

these two very different temperaments. Paula enjoys the affair as if in a state of euphoria, to which she yields with complete abandon. Paul, by contrast, is confused. The difference in their nature is visually underlined by their two apartments. The furniture in Paul's flat – a large and, for the standards of the GDR, comfortable new apartment near Berlin's Ostbahnhof station – is more or less identical with that found in all apartments of this type. Paula lives in a shabby Berlin tenement block on the other side of the street. The difference becomes particularly apparent when Paula, coming home from work one day, is faced with having to carry the coal, which was unloaded in front of the building, in buckets into her cellar at the rear of the building. Despite its outward dreariness and the effort that has to be made to heat it, the interior of the apartment affords possibilities for individual creativity. The layout defies any standardised furnishing, and Paula has used this to her advantage, despite her low income.

Paul does not want to lose his son or risk damaging his career, so he is avoiding a divorce. Paula fights for her new happiness; she wants this new man to be hers exclusively. The stories she relates about her past are elaborately visualised in the form of bizarre dream sequences. They are a reflection of Paula's unbridled desire to marry Paul. These sequences, together with Paula's idea of decorating her bed with flowers in the style of the hippy movement and to drink champagne with Paul, are among the most beautiful images of the film. Up to this point, Paula, with her courage, vitality, hunger for love and unconventionality, is fighting an all-or-nothing battle. Paul, by contrast, is a careerist who is willing to subordinate his happiness to social convention. Their different characters and situations correspond to their fundamentally different attitudes to life. There is no real contact to bridge this gulf.

The peripety begins at a reception with international guests. (About one year before the film was released, international recognition of the GDR had begun. The State and Party leadership strove to shine on the international stage. This fact should be borne in mind as a background to the scene.) Paul is responsible for the success of the reception. His wife is dancing with one of the foreign guests, when Paula appears, wearing a wig and sunglasses. When Paul recognises her, he reproaches her for not being satisfied with compromises and wants to end the affair. At this, she slaps him in the face, kisses him and leaves, unhappy and desperate. The following weekend, she catches herself screaming at her children unjustifiably, so she sends them both to the local cinema. After the film, her son is fatally injured in a car accident. Paula blames herself, Paul and their relationship for this tragedy.

Paul, who did not want to commit to Paula, becomes aware of the great loss that he is suffering from her absence and tries to regain contact with her. But Paula does not want to let him into her flat or exchange a single word with him. Paula now turns to the considerably older and not particularly attractive Saft. He is not the great love she sought, but will provide security instead. He, in turn, is very glad that his fondness for Paula, which he has felt for years, finally seems to be reciprocated. The prevailing scarcity of goods has worked in his favour, because his tyres have become a precious commodity, which can be acquired not only in exchange for money, but also for a range of products not officially available for purchase. Thus, Saft has managed to become conspicuously wealthy, and he uses this wealth to finally entice Paula to his side.

The more important Saft apparently becomes in Paula's life, the more effort Paul invests in his struggle to win her back. He paints a huge heart with both their names on Paula's door, and he sleeps and eats in the stairwell outside her flat. He neglects his work, thereby breaking the social barriers between them and becoming her equal. However, on receiving a warning from his workplace, he undertakes a half-hearted attempt to rescue his marriage (a delaying factor, as it were). But his wife has long been with another man. Paul leaves their apartment without uttering a word, goes to Paula's flat, asks her neighbours for an axe, and breaks open the door. At first, Paula stays withdrawn in the rearmost corner of her bed. Only when Paul energetically embraces her does she give in to her feelings, tearing his white shirt – an image that counts among the most memorable images in the history of DEFA films. One of the neighbours, who has followed the events right into the bedroom, has brought a camera along and photographs the scene.

Paul and Paula finally become the ideal loving couple, as in a fairy tale. Paula considers it her greatest fortune when she once again becomes pregnant – but, indeed, she does not survive this pregnancy. In the film's final shot, Paul is seen lying in bed together with the three children. It is a very sad scene, but at the same time full of life. It is accompanied in the background by the song 'Geh zu ihr', written for the film by the GDR's most famous rock group, the Puhdys.

The Legend of Paul and Paula is a simple love story. It initiated the dominant theme of Heiner Carow's work, continued with *Ikarus* (*Icarus*, 1975) and *Bis daß der Tod Euch scheidet* (*Until Death Do Us Part*, 1979). In all these films, the plot focuses on the relationship between the sexes. *Coming Out* (1989), the fourth film in this loose series, which premiered on 9 November 1989 – the day the Berlin Wall fell – was the first GDR feature film to have as its central topic same-sex couples living together. Among the cast of partly tragicomic, partly grotesquely exaggerated characters, Paula, enchantingly portrayed by Angelica Domröse, is the psychologically most complex role of the film. Her temperament, sensuousness and ability to cope successfully with everyday life point to a strong, differentiated personality, which embodied the longing for independence, inner freedom and self-determination like no other character in a DEFA film up to that time. Paula as a character was a provocation, just as much as the representation of the world which Paul inhabited, heightened even more by the film's music.

What is most striking about the narrative of *The Legend of Paul and Paula* is the way the protagonists' behaviours cross each other. At first, Paula is a high-spirited and almost carefree young woman, but her attitude to life changes abruptly after the death of her child. The occasional comments about her children she made to Paul, which suggest how loving a mother she is, are emphatically confirmed at this point. Paul realises much too late what it is that he really loves in Paula. From this moment on, he fights for her in a comic and also somewhat over-excited manner, and thus, in line with the basic tenor of the whole film, for romantic love. The final scene – Paul with the children in bed – underlines the fact that it was not only for career reasons that he did not wish to risk a divorce. The scene emphasises Paul's love for his son from his first marriage – the only character from Paul's old life, and no longer depicted as a caricature.

Death and the destruction of old tenement houses both mark and symbolise turning points in the film. The opening credits consist of a series of images. They begin with the blasting of a housing block. In the background, new houses can be seen. It is clear that the old is making way for the new, or as was believed at the time, for 'the improved'. The scene is accompanied by the Puhdys singing 'Wenn ein Mensch lebt' ('If a Person Lives'), which became a classic of GDR rock music. Paul is seen throwing out household items he no longer needs. As he steps into the street, builders can be seen. In the next shot, Paul is holding a framed photo of himself and Paula. This is the photo that was taken by the neighbour after the breaking down of the door. This picture frame appears twice more in the course of the film. While Paula is living alone, the frame is shown containing a photo of her grandparents, which fades over to the dream sequences with Paul and Paula in a boat. The second time the picture frame is hanging from a window handle, displaying the picture of Paul and Paula, and the camera swings over to it after it has captured Paul with the three children. Thus, the picture frame literally functions as the 'frame' for the whole film. Paula's son lying in the bed next to Paul, the Puhdys' song and the photograph allow Paula, too, to 'go on living'. The plot is framed in the beginning by the house demolitions and at the end by images of new housing blocks. During the course of the film, the ongoing work on the housing blocks is shown again at the beginning of Paul's career.

The audience is only indirectly confronted with death. The last images of the two characters who die – first her son and then Paula herself – convey pure zest for life: the boy is seen radiantly joyful, running out of the cinema into the street. The next shot shows Paula in her flat, running to the window at the sound of screeching car brakes. Then we see a silently assembled group of people, and following a pan of the camera, the chalk marks on the street surface. Directly afterwards, we learn from conversations of Paula's colleagues that she is working again, obviously to distract herself from the accident. Paula's death is announced to the viewer via voice-over, while she is shown descending into an underground station. These pictures and sounds, along with the integration of death into the action of the film, have the effect that death does not come across in Carow's work as a final farewell without hope for the future. Rather, death marks transitions in the storyline, which signify not an end, but a continued life of desire. Death does not destroy anyone nor throw them off track; rather, like the demolition of the houses, it stands for a new beginning.

In 1965, the 11th Plenary of the Central Committee of the SED had banned beat music. All ensembles or groups that had appeared were dissolved. Shortly after this, the movement founded itself anew, but performers had to sing their texts in German. Before the 1970s, none of these groups managed to record songs that were accepted by young people as genuine GDR rock music. With *The Legend of Paul and Paula*, the Puhdys succeeded in filling this gap. In 1972, the young group had just recently presented the first three of their own songs on the radio. In the GDR, the radio was decisive for promoting young musicians. While he was looking for suitable music, the soundtrack composer Peter Gotthardt heard the Puhdys for the first time. Two of their earlier songs can be heard when Paul and Paula meet in the dance bar. The other songs were composed by Gotthardt. The lyrics were written by the screenwriter Ulrich Plenzdorf. With these songs the essential characteristics of GDR rock music were established. The Puhdys' entire repertoire, which up to that point was mostly made up of international hits, was lastingly influenced by the songs for the film. It was with these compositions that the provocative voice of Dieter Birr (stage name: Maschine) and the bluesy voice of Dieter Hertrampf (stage name: Quaster) first made their mark so strikingly. Plenzdorf's lyrics contained clearly recognisable borrowings from the Psalms and the Song of Songs. For technical reasons, the music had to be recorded at the radio station in Berlin's Nalepastraße, since it had the only studio with multi-tracking equipment for synthetic sound production. However, since rock music was not yet socially accepted, the studio management in Babelsberg required Carow also to include conventional orchestral music. The director and composer decided to include a violin concerto that was played open air on Mont Klamotte in Friedrichshain park. In the film, it is at Paul's urging that he and Paula attend the concert, to 'educate' her. This scene is an example of how the film positions itself towards everyday GDR life, which, especially in this period, constantly encouraged its citizens to sign up for further education even in their leisure time.

One year before the premiere of *The Legend of Paul and Paula*, on 16 May 1972, Plenzdorf's play *Die neuen Leiden des jungen W.* (*The New Sufferings of Young W.* – a modern version of Goethe's *Die Leiden des jungen Werther* [*The Sorrows of Young Werther*, 1774]) premiered in Halle. This play, which was also published as a novel, was intended to be made into a film, but this was not taken up by DEFA nor by television. The stage version broke all records, as *The Legend of Paul and Paula* did one year later in the cinema. Both works share the rejection of the main characters' social panorama, which many feature films up to then had treated as obligatory. In the film, the characterisation of individuals is no longer approached by way of society; rather, the individuals survey their surroundings and arrive at a 'modern' and individually inflected view of society. Socialist society is no longer presented as the outcome of class struggle, but as given – in this, too, *The New Sufferings of Young W.* and *The Legend of Paul and Paula* are alike. In this respect, both works link up with attitudes that began to form in the GDR at the end of the 1960s. Further examples of this trend are the films *Dr. med. Sommer II* (*Medical Doctor Sommer the Second*, 1970) and *Männer ohne Bart* (1971).

Concerning the issue of women, too, substantial changes emerge at the beginning of the 1970s. Of particular note were the five protocols recorded on tape that Sarah Kirsch published in *Die Pantherfrau* (*The Panther Woman*). They present women giving candid accounts of their everyday life under socialism. The mid-1970s saw the appearance of *Guten Morgen, du Schöne* by Maxie Wander. She also interviewed women about their relationships with men, their struggle for social recognition and the price for independence. Probably best known is the work of Christa Wolf; for instance, *Nachdenken über Christa T.* (*The Quest for Christa T.*), *Kein Ort. Nirgends* (*No Place On Earth*) and *Kassandra* (*Cassandra*) all involve stories of women's emancipation in their social environment. In this cultural context of increased attention to women's problems, DEFA's output included such films as *Der Dritte* (*The Third*, 1972), *Die Schlüssel* (1972), *Bis dass der Tod Euch scheidet* (*Until Death Do Us Part*, 1979) and *Solo Sunny* (1980). These films point to conflicts in society at large as well as contradictions between aspirations and reality, the costs of which are mostly borne by women. At the same time, women are presented as being the stronger sex, they have and evoke more sympathy, and they are spiritually richer and physically more sensual. Men pale by comparison: they are indirect representatives of the state, achievement-oriented, conformist, less passionate, uncritical and selfish. There are few exceptions: in *Until Death Do Us Part*, unlike in *The Legend of Paul and Paula*, Carow presents a tragic love story with a completely anachronistic relationship between the sexes.

The Legend of Paul and Paula was shot between 2 May and 18 August 1972. The first cut was approved on 27 September; the studio version was approved on 15 November and the *Staatliche Abnahmekommission* ('state approval board') granted final approval on 27 November. Between 14 March and 4 April 1973, the director and other members of the team travelled to various places in the GDR to present their film to audiences at special previews. At these screenings, there were discussions with the audiences. A report summarising the results stated: 'All sides welcomed the fact that for once there was a film that told of "the productive power of love". The film allows and encourages people to talk about what love really is, or about what, from time to time, people think it is. There are viewers who miss a spiritual level in this love story. Such opinions are to be found above all among young intellectuals … It is surprising how strongly women of widely differing age groups identify with Paula. It often happens that, prompted by discussions about this character, they come to speak about their own lives and their own problems.'

These statements about how the film was received poignantly illustrate the deficits of standard DEFA films' depictions of individual love and good fortune. At the same time, Carow's contribution to partially overcoming these deficits was set against a backdrop of GDR reality that felt genuine to contemporary audiences. Despite granting approval, the love scenes, which were relatively permissive for their time, the film's perspective on GDR society, and the characterisation of the two protagonists remained topics of continued debate at the highest levels. On the morning of 29 April 1973, the day of the film's official premiere, it was not quite certain whether it would actually take place. Erich Honecker personally reserved for himself the final decision. Only after he had seen it on that morning was the film finally released, without further cuts.

Among cinemagoers, the film met with an extremely favourable response. By 31 December 1973, *The Legend of Paul and Paula* had been seen by 1,749,145 viewers, ranking second in the GDR box-office listings for the year (the top film was *Apachen*, one of DEFA's 'Red Indian films'). By 31 December 1985, the film had accumulated an audience of 3.1 million people. It was re-released in 1993 and achieved cult status. In one Berlin cinema, the film played in late night showings for years without interruption. It was the blend of exceptional acting, memorable music and the penetrating interpretation of early 1970s reality that made it the most popular DEFA film of all time.

Wolfgang Mühl-Benninghaus

Translated by Christine Maaßen-Wilder

JEDER FÜR SICH UND GOTT GEGEN ALLE
THE ENIGMA OF KASPAR HAUSER

WERNER HERZOG, WEST GERMANY, 1974

18

The story of Kaspar Hauser is quintessentially German. In the nineteenth-century, the reputed aristocratic descendant is captured while still a small child and imprisoned in a dungeon due to shifts in the dynastic power base. He is unexpectedly released as he reaches adulthood. Unable to talk and barely able to walk, he lacks any social skills and is entirely uncultured. The public is intrigued by the 'Hauser case' and speculation about the boy's origins runs wild. The Baden house of princes is suspected of familial ties and thrown into a deep crisis. Only a few years later, Hauser was brutally murdered. Even today speculation surrounding the boy has preoccupied criminologists. The story throws into relief the particularism of Germany's small states, which is still palpable today; the 'ennoblement' by blood relation, which was the criterion for German nationality until recently, and the romantic longing for knowing one's origins, which motivates the search for mysteries hidden in the dungeons, castles and waste-lands of Germany's countryside. The news magazine *Spiegel* even ran a title about Hauser in 1996, when it was hoped that a DNA-analysis would clear up the mystery of his lineage once and for all. But the investigation was in vain. This is a German story because, apart from the historical intrigue against a child, lineage is still a high-profile topic and the mystery of noble (and superior) ancestry forms part of the national mythology. But 'Kaspar Hauser' is more than this. It is a story of how we become human through culture, socialisation and education. It is an idea of human character that enjoyed particular favour in the eighteenth and early nineteenth century; it is a story of the late Romantic period, and as such it was interesting to Werner Herzog as a filmmaker.

Herzog's film *Jeder für sich und Gott gegen alle* (*The Enigma of Kaspar Hauser*, 1974) is a typical example of the New German Cinema of the 1960s and 1970s. It was produced under the *Film-Fernseh-Abkommen* ('film and television agreement') by the director's own company (Werner Herzog Films) in co-operation with a television station (ZDF), and it is character-ised by the intensive teamwork of friends and colleagues (the cast included film critic Enno Patalas, writer Elis Pilgrim and filmmaker Herbert Achternbusch, amongst others). Klaus

Wyborny, who can be counted amongst experimental German filmmakers, was involved in the project as cameraman. Nonetheless, concerning themes and style, Herzog is one of the most idiosyncratic of the New German filmmakers. Herzog likes to write, stage and direct stories about the normal and the abnormal, of outsiders who are emotionally driven, often act on impulse, and, prone to fits of violent rage, try to have things their own way. His films are characterised by the desire to explore human nature, to point to the reality behind the smooth surface of what is considered 'normal'. He tells stories of boundaries and of those who cross them, looking for the forces that motivate human behaviour. 'Can you not hear the scream of terror that we like to call silence' is the introductory motto to his film *The Enigma of Kaspar Hauser*.

Herzog begins his film with the blurred outline of a man taking Kaspar Hauser from the tower where he was imprisoned. Before that, there are a few brief shots of the chained Kaspar eating, playing with a toy horse (he wants to make it write), being beaten and, finally, being tied up and dragged away by the man. From torture and extreme confinement, Kaspar is forced into a strange and hostile world. After the man, who remains unrecognisable, has (somewhat violently) taught Kaspar to walk, he is abandoned in a square in Nuremberg. An increasing number of people gather round to marvel at him, until he is taken to a house belonging to the captain of the cavalry, for whom he is thought to carry a letter. There he is seen lying, almost as if dead, in the straw of the stable; he becomes the object of curiosity of the servants of the house. There is a persistent atmosphere of claustrophobia. Most characters are shown only in part, their faces in close-ups, and they are dressed in brightly coloured uniforms and strange costumes. The multitude of faces intimidates both Kaspar and the viewer. This examination, during which a clerk scribbles down everything that is shouted to him, conveys the nineteenth-century mania for transcription: the peculiarities of life are recorded encyclopaedically. The film seems to imply that the documented version of the facts, which was to form the base for the bourgeois legends surrounding Kaspar Hauser, may very well be accurate. But Herzog, by making the documenting process the focus of the scene, is aiming to tell a different story – the story of how a basic natural element of the human spirit will prove immune to all the disciplinary forces of civilisation and stubbornly prevail against cultural norms.

Kaspar is eventually taken into police custody. The tower in which he is placed has similarities to the tower we saw at the beginning of the film. But this time he manages to make friends with the warder and his family. Kaspar learns how to sit at a table, eat from a plate and drink from a cup. The warder's son proves to be a patient instructor. The towns people visit to make fun of Kaspar or just to gape at him; local boys taunt him with a drunken chicken, and he retreats frightened into a window niche; a little girl recites children's poetry to him, but he does not understand it; the citizens regard him as an exotic phenomenon; the servants, ordinary farmhands and maids speechlessly stare at him, mirroring his own lack of communication skills; the civic dignitaries discuss how to proceed with him. Kaspar is on the receiving end of other people's actions, which he, like the audience witnessing his plight, passively endures.

Because he is felt to be a public burden, Kaspar is handed over to a circus, where he is exhibited as a freak, alongside dwarfs, the incurably depressed and 'Red Indians'. When Kaspar cannot stand the circus life, he flees with an 'Indian' and a small man called Mozart, who is said to be a depressive. He is found in an apiary, shaken down from the trees and sent to Herr Daumer, who introduces him to culture, science and religion. Daumer wants to educate Kaspar and turn him into an exhibit of Enlightenment theories of human culture. Kaspar tries his hand at the piano, is questioned by priests about God, and is examined in logic by a learned gentleman (Alfred Edel). His observations of nature are characterised by strange associations, and he repeatedly impresses his mentors with surprising insights.

Eventually an English aristocrat (based on the historical figure of Philip Henry, the fourth Lord Stanhope) shows an interest in him and displays him before an amused and disconcerted court society at the nearby town of Ansbach. Hauser thus passes through all social levels and remains strange to each. The more cultured people are, and the more conventionally they behave, the more difficult it is for him to get along with them. Kaspar is haunted by strange visions of the Caucasus and the Sahara, which have no specific reference, but stand for foreign, exotic lands in general; they are represented in the form of magic lantern projections and inserts of sepia-tinted silent film. Here, Herzog transformed Hauser's historically documented dreams of castle facades and coats of arms, which would have alluded to the theory of the unjustly disinherited prince. Herzog is more interested in images that are indecipherable and can at the most be given a mythical interpretation, because they bear reference to Kaspar's inner life.

While bourgeois society maintains its interest in him, Kaspar also feels himself watched by mysterious men; a dark figure breaks into Kaspar's house and brutally assaults him. After his recovery, Kaspar begins to investigate the mystery of his birth, but to no avail. Another assault follows, after which Kaspar dies. In dying, he has visions again – of a caravan with a blind leader who knows the way by tasting the sand. A post-mortem examination of Kaspar's body declares his brain as abnormal; this is regarded as the reason for his strange behaviour. The reason for his murder is left in the dark; the film gives only a few hints. Kaspar had begun to write down his story as far as he remembered it. He had hoped to find his own identity this way, and also to come to terms with the enigmatic world that surrounded him. Herzog here alludes to the Romantic idea(l) of knowing the world through writing, by making a personal transcript of it. Kaspar's mystery might eventually have been uncovered by writing, but the murder prevented this.

Which story is being told here? The historically documented one of the strange, 16-year-old boy who suddenly appeared on the Unschlittplatz in Nuremberg on 26 May 1828, and was killed on 14 December 1833 in Ansbach? It seems to be a different story, one that is also linked to the times in which the film was made. Although Herzog uses many historical details, he simplifies them into a well-crafted plot. Thus, Kaspar's several 'fathers' are amalgamated into the single character of Daumer. Other details are changed in accordance with the director's intention of telling the story of a failed attempt at education.

The film begins with soft-focus landscape shots, a woman's portrait, gossamer images of a boat trip over a small lake, a woman who pauses while washing clothes in the river. A voice-over sings 'Dies Bildnis ist bezaubernd schön' (from Mozart's *Zauberflöte*), and we are left to wonder whether the song refers to the portrait of the woman or the image of humanity that Kasper Hauser embodies. Other shots show a green cornfield undulating in the wind to wistful music. This is where the film's motto is inserted. The 'scream of terror that we like to call silence' is thus revealed to be the agony of nature tormented and abused. The fate of Kaspar Hauser becomes representative for that of the outsider in general. Kaspar and the tall dark man are shown taking a rest along the long road that appears to have no end. Then there is a view of a plain, where villages and towns might be. The landscape becomes a contrast to an as yet uncertain civilisation, to the local estate communities of the nineteenth century, a society that in its *Biedermeier* eccentricities and punitive philanthropy has distinctly obsessive traits. Landscape here does not mean freedom, as it does in the American western, but the silenced and sinister forces secretly at work in human relations. Just as the site of Hauser's imprisonment, the tower, stands in plain sight in the middle of the landscape, it has nevertheless served to conceal his whereabouts from society.

In later sequences, the long shots of vast, silent landscapes, which counterpoint the constriction of human habitations, tend to be replaced by images of Daumer and Hauser moving through a garden it represents fenced-in nature, a space that is enclosed, tamed and seemingly carefree. Ideas of paradise come into play here, and the *Biedermeier* version of the *locus amoenus*, which includes the idea of the gardener who cultivates a young plant, aiming for straight growth, and carefully separating the weeds from the flowers. Daumer also sees himself as a gardener who has set himself the task of cutting down the wilderness inside Kaspar, and of straightening the untamed growth. In the garden, everything is subject to human will – in this case the will of the human being as cultivator/educator. But the example by which Daumer seeks to demonstrate this fails: when he aims to kick an apple that has fallen off a tree towards a visitor's foot, the apple bounces over the foot. This leaves Kaspar jubilant: for him at least, the apple has a life of its own.

However, like a bourgeois childhood, the garden is not really enclosed, and outside influences keep intruding. At the end of the film, a fatally wounded Kaspar collapses on a bench, after having reeled into the garden, which had seemed like paradise in its cultivated and protected character. Nature appears to be idyllic, and human relations destructive, but always half-concealed by the bright green of the leafy trees and the beautiful flowers, so that this security has, after all, turned out to be deceptive. Thus, Kaspar's journey leads him from extreme confinement to vast uninhabited landscapes to the city and small town, and finally, via the garden, into an enclosed space again – Daumer's apartment, which is where Kaspar dies. His venture into the world has been brief and futile. Kaspar at one point calls it, 'having crashed into the world'.

Speechlessness is one of the main themes in the stories surrounding Kaspar Hauser. He is placed in the world as a creature without language. When he first stands on the market square, he finds himself unable to answer a citizen's questions about where he comes from and where he is headed. It is only when the man mentions a number of local towns at random that Kaspar repeats the word 'Regensburg', which establishes the general idea that he is in some way connected to that place. He is also very quick at writing the name 'Kaspar Hauser'. But communication is impossible, so he and the ordinary citizens are worlds apart. Only the children appear to establish a limited connection with him, and thus he retains a childish aura about him for the adult viewer. It is the warder's little son who helps Kaspar learn how to speak. But this is fraught with difficulties. It begins with naming what is physically knowable – nose, chin, mouth, arm, hand. The ear already proves somewhat more complicated, because it cannot be seen. When the little boy holds up a mirror, Kaspar looks into it uncomprehendingly. Recognising his mirrored reflection is a cultural accomplishment he is not yet able to perform.

Herzog expresses his understanding of Kaspar's culturalisation by continually referring back to the animal world. Between scenes of Kaspar's learning to speak, we see him at the window, feeding a young bird with a pipette. Or, he leads a cat through the room by its front paws, to which the warder's son protests that cats do not walk upright. Since this is how Kaspar himself learned how to eat and walk, he tries to pass it on to animals. It is with them, not with human beings, that he feels an affinity. When he is exhibited at the circus freak show, he is framed by shots of horses, camels and monkeys – domesticated animals with which he is put on the same level. The film emphatically demonstrates that closeness to natural creatures is different to being degraded by becoming a living exhibit. Daumer, who has seen Kaspar at the freak show, finds him after his escape in an apiary. He takes him home, planning to educate him and make him human. He is patient and solicitous – but also full of high expectations.

After two years of living in the Daumer household, Kaspar begins to form strikingly unconventional thoughts and phrases. He speaks his own brand of German regarding grammar, word formation and pronunciation. Just as Kaspar's life in civilised society always seems forced, his manner of speaking is characterised by effort and bodily tension. Bruno S., who plays Kaspar, was discovered by Herzog while he was working on a documentary about street musicians (*Bruno, der Schwarze* [*Bruno the Black*, 1970]). An outsider who was regarded as mentally retarded, he also appeared in Herzog's *Stroszek* (1977), this time presenting a personal interpretation of speech problems. In the role of Kaspar, he expresses the animal vigour of the young man with an extraordinary intensity virtually unattainable for a professional actor. His phrasing has poetic qualities, often allowing for deep insights that appear to be unintentional. Kaspar, for instance, talks about his 'painful crash' into the world, or when he describes his emotions when listening to music, he says, 'music moves deeply in my breast'.

Kaspar breaks social rules, because he does not realise they are rules. This applies to conversational as well as scientific rules. When the university professor confronts him with the riddle of what question one should ask a man to see whether he always tells the truth or is a pathological liar, Kaspar does not come up with the logical solution of double negation. His startling question is: 'Is the man a frog?' – to which the truth-telling man would have to say no, and the liar yes. The professor, of course, does not accept this answer, because it is outside his logical system. The point Herzog is making is that it is not Kaspar who harbours abnormal tendencies, but bourgeois society.

Under Daumer's tutelage, Kaspar familiarises himself with the cultural practice of writing, to the point of exploring himself as a newly developed identity with it. He wants to write an essay about himself, but he keeps it secret even from Daumer. Herzog explores Romantic theories of how full humanity can only be attained through writing, or rather literature. But when Kaspar sits down to write his *Bildungsroman*, he gets stuck at the very beginning. This is made apparent not by textual, but by visual means. Herzog uses the film sequences of the Caucasus and the Sahara desert, which never get further than the beginning, as a narrative tool. On the one hand, the images depict a utopian landscape as it might have been constructed by the contemporary revolutionary architect Claude-Nicolas Ledoux (1736–1806) or a visionary master builder like Etienne-Louis Boullée (1728–1799) – enigmatically closed and uninhabited spaces, dotted with small, pyramid-like houses. On the other, images such as the sepia-shots of a Saharan caravan, led, as Kaspar says, by a blind Bedouin, are taken from Kaspar's innermost thoughts and feelings, and like the Bedouin who leads his caravan through the empty desert, Kaspar is left alone with his mental images, which display how little he feels at home in the civilised world. The dreams and visions of the Caucasus and the Sahara tell of a distant, prehistoric life; it is, as Klaus Nothnagel describes, 'a vision of a different existence, a trembling premonition of the unattainable and unglimpsed in his (and our) experience of reality'.

Kaspar is accomodated by Daumer, an educated, respectable citizen with a well-tended garden, a well-kept house and an orderly life. Georg Friedrich Daumer is also a historically documented figure: a former schoolmaster at a Pietistic grammar school, who had retired early and was only 28 years old in 1828. The real Kaspar Hauser lived with him until two years before his death in 1831. Herzog simplifies the history here because he has other things to say. Daumer turns Kaspar into an educational experiment; while other people only show a passing interest in him, Daumer makes Kaspar's education his life's work. The film smoothly passes over two years, and we see Kaspar prosper under Daumer's instruction. It seems to have been successful, and Kaspar appears to have been won over to culture, the result of Daumer humanising him. But Herzog wants to show that this 'progress' is only skin-deep; Kaspar refuses to let anybody see his soul. He continues to utter quirky thoughts and inscrutable ideas. Bourgeois education has, at most, reached him partially.

This leads to Herzog's critique of contemporary philanthropy. Daumer is basically a philanthropist, whose motivation is the desire to help Kaspar and mankind. What constitutes a human being was a controversial subject of pedagogy, for instance, of Jean-Jacques Rousseau or Joachim Heinrich Campe, and yet, unlike the radical model that Daniel Gottlob

Moritz Schreber was to expound a few decades later, which was to feature in the critical literature of 1970s as 'black pedagogy' – a method of terrorising children whose development was regarded as unsatisfactory. Herzog paints a more moderate picture. It is theologians and professors who tend to inflict their insensitivity on Kaspar. They think of themselves as the guardians of what is true and good by virtue of their profession, and they are characterised as narrow-minded personalities. Herzog makes Kaspar respond to Daumer's educational offerings, but the effects are idiosyncratic. Kaspar's education is all his own, lies outside the cultural canon and is impervious to rules. He manages to construct his own identity, which remains incompatible with his surroundings.

The Romantic interest in the formation of a complete human being via culture, for which the historical Hauser provided a debatable model, becomes in Herzog's version a conflict between civilisation and the natural forces buried deep inside human beings. Kaspar, by having been excluded from civilisation for a long time, albeit by barbaric means, is somehow still in touch with his natural origins and with irrational worlds. There is something unruly and intractable about him. Thus, Hauser's isolated early childhood is not seen as a flaw in need of quick repair but as the source of a spiritual richness, which should not be spoiled hastily. All attempts to socialise Hauser therefore seem strange and often comical. Ultimately, civilisation is represented as an obscure and very eccentric community based on compulsion; socialisation becomes a form of violation.

What, then, makes this a German story? The historical events surrounding the foundling created a stir amongst German contemporaries. Most of them would probably not have believed too deeply in the humanising effects of culture. Literature enthusiastically took up the Hauser story as a motif, often in the form of a girl of noble origins who grows up in humble circumstances and remains high-minded against all odds until, mostly with the aid of a hero, the mystery of her aristocratic birth is lifted and she is re-installed to her original place. For example, in the much-read sentimental novels of Eugenie Marlitt, this motif recurs several times, and it was a popular light fiction theme in general. In these novels, the raw human material does not have to be shaped to make a noble being. Human beings are noble by nature, and it is society that attempts to suppress their true character. The veneration due to their dynastic descent becomes the characters' human right. The mystery of noble birth has inspired a large number of Kaspar Hauser novels, plays and stories, for example, from Karl Gutzkow to Jakob Wassermann and Klaus Mann up to Rainer Maria Rilke and Peter Handke, as well as other films, for example, by Robert A. Stemmle and Peter Sehr.

Herzog is ultimately interested here in the unformed and intractable elements of humanity that can prevail against all cultural influences. His version of the story is distinctly German, emphatically different from François Truffaut's *L'Enfant Sauvage* (*The Wild Child*, 1970), which amounts to a plea for a sensitive pedagogy. In Herzog's film, the ungovernable is seen as 'depth', as something that can be neither interpreted nor overcome. Herzog is not interested in solving the Hauser 'case'. He leaves the inscrutable to itself and trusts in the force of the visual instead – asking the viewer to find his own meaning in it.

Knut Hickethier

REFERENCE

Nothnagel, K. (1992) 'Werner Herzog', in H.-M. Bock (ed.) *Cinegraph: Lexikon zum deutschsprachigen Film*, installment 4. München: edition text + kritik, E1–E11.

DEUTSCHLAND IM HERBST GERMANY IN AUTUMN

Alexander Kluge, Volker Schlöndorff, Rainer Werner Fassbinder, Edgar Reitz et al., West Germany, 1978

Deutschland im Herbst (*Germany in Autumn*, 1978) is unique. It is an omnibus film, to which several German directors of international renown contributed, such as Alexander Kluge, Volker Schlöndorff, Rainer Werner Fassbinder and Edgar Reitz. Directors who regarded themselves as maverick *auteurs* of the New German Cinema came together for a collective effort with the intention of breaking the silence in the aftermath of a wave of terrorist acts that deeply shocked Germany.

The eponymous 'Autumn' was the one in 1977. On 5 September, the commando unit of the terrorist group RAF ('Rote Armee Fraktion') kidnapped Hanns-Martin Schleyer, the president of the German federation of employers, murdering his chauffeur and three police escorts. The kidnappers demanded the release of eleven comrades, among them the founders of the RAF: Andreas Baader, Gudrun Ensslin and Jan Carl Raspe. The German government refused and, under a near-total information embargo, initiated a manhunt for the kidnappers and their hostage. On 13 October, a Palestine commando hijacked a Lufthansa airplane with German tourists and joined in with the RAF's demands. After flying over Africa, the terrorists landed in Mogadishu, Somalia, where a German anti-terrorism team stormed the airplane, killing three of the kidnappers but rescuing the passengers unharmed. The next morning, the three RAF leaders were discovered dead in their prison cells. On 19 October, the RAF communicated that Schleyer had been shot. The government under Chancellor Helmut Schmidt, a coalition of the Social-Democratic and Liberal parties, refused to comply with the terrorists. This line of action was supported by the conservative opposition and its party leader Helmut Kohl – even though this meant certain death for Schleyer, who was a personal friend of Kohl's. The imprisoned terrorists staged their suicides as murders, to make the German government look like 'Nazis', just as they repeatedly called attention to Schleyer having been an SS officer. Among the German (and West European) Left, many believed that the prisoners were murdered until the RAF disbanded in 1997, when many new details came to light.

The Left had preferred to ignore the fact that the RAF had murdered their helpless victim with shots in the neck, a common SS 'execution' method. On the other hand, the spectacular success of the anti-terrorist team in Mogadishu diverted attention from the serious mistakes made during the search for Schleyer.

These events, of course, were not only deeply shocking, but also rich in psychological drama, crises and violence, and cast with real and pseudo-heroes. No wonder, then, that the story of the RAF and their crimes were eagerly taken up in fiction and non-fiction films. Conversely, the protagonists of the RAF were more than fleetingly attracted to cinema: Holger Meins had studied at the German Film and Television Academy in Berlin, Christoph Wackernagel had worked as an actor and Andreas Baader styled himself as a film hero.

In mid-October 1977, the directors Kluge and Schlöndorff as well as Theo Hinz, executive director of the production company and distributor Filmverlag der Autoren, decided to examine the past events and to document the funeral services. As Kluge later wrote in an article that was signed by many of the contributing directors, the project was to be a 'cooperative' one. By the end of October, while Kluge and Schlöndorf were filming the funerals of Schleyer and the RAF prisoners, Fassbinder, who was known for his remarkable speed, filmed his episode in a single weekend. Peter Steinbach, author of radio plays, wrote an episode for Edgar Reitz; the Nobel-prize winning author Heinrich Böll wrote one for Schlöndorff. Katja Rupé and Hans Peter Cloos were members of a political theatre group in Munich. Maximiliane Mainka, Peter Schubert, Alf Brustellin and Bernhard Sinkel contributed documentary and semi-documentary episodes. Some parts of *Germany in Autumn* are by-products of projects on which the directors and authors were working at the time. Kluge, together with Hannelore Hoger, was preparing *Die Patriotin* (*The Patriot*, 1979), and preliminary studies for this film can be seen in his episode. Steinbach and Reitz were working on a film cycle with the working title 'Made in Germany', later to become the highly successful and acclaimed mini-series *Heimat* (1984), a panorama of Germany between 1919 and 1982, and set in a small village.

Germany in Autumn was financed by Filmverlag der Autoren. Since February 1977, this distributor, also a collaborative creation of the filmmakers of the New German Cinema, mostly belonged to Rudolf Augstein, the founder and editor of the critical news magazine *Der Spiegel*. Thus, it is likely that most of the money for the film was put up by Augstein. In contrast to most other films of the New German Cinema, the film did not receive a government grant, nor was it co-produced with a television station. Nevertheless, the film was a success. After a much-noted premiere at the Berlinale in March 1978 and the release in German cinemas in Autumn, the film soon not only recovered its production costs of around 300,000 Euros, but also made a sizable profit. Thus, in Germany alone, around one million cinemagoers saw *Germany in Autumn.*

Kluge had initiated a number of such cooperative projects, ranging from the establishment of public grants for films to media legislation. Nevertheless, he was more of a theoretician of cooperation than a practitioner. Thus, it is no surprise that *Germany in Autumn* is mostly a Kluge film. The exposition, the transitions, the 'miniatures' (as Kluge calls short non-narrative inserts), the discoveries of the simultaneity of unusual events, the historical references, the literary intertitles (in white on light-blue ground), the use of music by Joseph Haydn, Franz Schubert ('Winterreise'), Pyotr Ilyich Tchaikovsky and Ennio Morricone, are all typical of Kluge, who also speaks the commentary with his instantly recognisable, whispering voice. But according to Peter C. Lutze, Kluge's voice and the intertitles 'provided the cohesion necessary to bind these extremely heterogeneous elements together'. Kluge regarded the editor, Beate Mainka-Jellinghaus, as the most important team member because she brought structure to the episodes and the disparate material. Presumably, it was she who, together with Kluge, considerably reduced the film's length after the first showing. Schlöndorff, in an interview for the Kinowelt DVD edition of the film, conceded that in art nothing but 'dictatorship' is feasible, so Kluge edited the film with Mainka-Jellinghaus. As can be imagined, the cuts especially caused much ill-feeling among the participants.

The film begins with images of the funeral service for Hanns-Martin Schleyer. They are shot with a 35mm camera set on a stand. Medium-long shots and close-ups provide the opportunity to study the people attending the funeral. For instance, the politicians Kurt Georg Kiesinger and Hans Filbinger are easily recognised. They were both former members of the National Socialist German Workers Party (NSDAP); Kiesinger worked for the Nazi administration and Filbinger was a military judge. After the war, both had tried to deny their Nazi past and rose through the ranks of the Conservative Party. Finally, they were both confronted with their Nazi past – Filbinger as premier of Baden-Würtemberg and Kiesinger as Chancellor. Thus, the film's beginning alludes to the problem of continuity in Germany's history. In 1950s and 1960s Germany, there were many politicians and functionaries with a Nazi past, including Schleyer. *Germany in Autumn* does not deny this connection, but relativises it. In the voiceover, Kluge reads excerpts from a letter that Schleyer wrote to his family during his captivity. Thus the hostage, who had been made a symbol of the continuity in German history, is individualised as a human being trying to articulate himself in terrible circumstances. The RAF had denied him this right – just as the government did with their refusal to negotiate. The opening sequence ends with an intertitle: 'Having arrived at a certain point of cruelty, it does not matter anymore who committed it, as long as it stops.' These words are attributed to 'Frau Wilde, mother of five children', and the date '8 April 1945' is added. In the context of the film, these words mark the wish to break free from the logic of terrorism as well as of government politics in order to escape from the vicious circle of violence. The date and the German name suggest someone who desperately tried to survive during the bombings of the final days of World War II. Nevertheless, the 'quotation' is probably fictional – as author, Kluge regularly spoke in many voices. In a collection of stories published in 1978 under the title *Unheimlichkeit der Zeit*, the same words appear in the report of an anonymous woman who relates her experiences to a British officer after the war.

The film's longest episode is Fassbinder's. The director appears in it as himself, working on his TV miniseries *Berlin Alexanderplatz* (broadcast in 1980). Fassbinder's longtime companion Armin Meier (misspelled as 'Amin' in the credits) as well as his mother Liselotte Eder are also part of the cast. Thus, during the public political upheaval, the private Fassbinder is shown working, drinking, quarrelling, addicted to drugs and depressed. The episode comprises two parts, which are interwoven, and both deal with the question what the events of autumn 1977 mean to people in Germany. In the first part, Fassbinder talks to Armin and in several telephone conversations to different people about the situation after the hijacking of the airplane. In the second part, he talks to his mother about how to deal with the terrorists. The first sequence seems to strictly follow Fassbinder's script, but the second part develops a life of its own. The staged situation develops into a real dispute between mother and son, as the director probably intended. Both Armin and Lieselotte demand an end to the kidnappings by force. Armin suggests that the airplane should be blown up in Mogadishu, and the imprisoned RAF leaders should also be killed. Lieselotte wants one terrorist to be publicly executed for every dead hostage. Fassbinder objects to both positions, which reflect common contemporary attitudes, but he is unable to convince Armin and Lieselotte. When his arguments fail, he becomes so enraged that he strikes Armin and screams at his mother. In one of the telephone conversations, Fassbinder complains that the police demand of the public to act as informants. Addressing a potential eavesdropper, he shouts: 'I don't care if you're listening!' Later, he says that he cannot go on working – he sniffs cocaine, then continues work on the script. When a police siren is heard nearby, he reacts hysterically: he grabs the cocaine and flushes it down the toilet. When Armin returns from a night of bar-hopping with a young man who has no place to sleep, Fassbinder is beside himself with rage. He demands that Armin throw the man out. The young man leaves; a long shot shows him crossing the street with a suitcase in his hand. It is the only shot after the interview sequence at the beginning that shows something other than Fassbinder's flat.

The other episodes of the film are shorter and less intense. The first episode shows how a young woman is assaulted and struck down in an underground car park. A woman helps her, brings her to her flat, dresses her wounds and makes tea for her. In the second episode, the bell rings at the door of a young pianist (Katja Rupé). When she opens, a man with a bleeding head wound is standing on the doorstep. She lets him in without many questions, but eyes him nervously. A newspaper with wanted photos of RAF members is lying on the table. The man places a bowl of fruit – which contains a dagger – over it. The dagger falls to the floor in slow motion. A shot of a woman's mouth screaming follows. But the stranger only wanted to ask a question about the dagger, which turns out to be a holiday souvenir. In the third episode a couple is searched at the border between Germany and France. While their papers are being examined, the couple talks to one of the customs officers. With a machine gun slung around him, he bends down to their car window and boasts about the manhunt for the terrorists, in Hunsrücker dialect: 'We'll catch every last one of them!' The fourth episode shows a meeting of the advisory board of a public television station. They are debating the question whether in times of terrorist attacks Sophocles' drama *Antigone* should be shown. Whereas the members of the advisory board are sarcastically criticising the drama, the director has prepared an apologetic prologue for the production, which is read by two of the actresses (Angela Winkler and Franziska Walser) in unison.

These fictional episodes differ widely in form and quality. The first two episodes attempt to create tense and fearful situations with exaggerated theatrics and crude effects. The episode at the border by Edgar Reitz is, like Fassbinder's, well staged and structured. In the fourth episode, directed by Schlöndorff and based on a text by Böll, Mario Adorf's acting stands out and Dieter Laser's performance is reminiscent of his role as a tabloid reporter in *Die verlorene Ehre der Katharina Blum* (*The Lost Honour of Katharina Blum*, 1975), also based on a text by Böll and directed by Schlöndorff. A common feature of the episodes is the fact that the protagonists, who become involved in violence or suffer from the national state of emergency, are mostly artists and intellectuals. At the end, they all withdraw – literally into interior spaces (for example, flats, the car) or psychologically through cynicism. The represented world is manichaic: public space is associated with coldness, danger and violence (evil), and private space with warmth, solidarity and help (good). Only Fassbinder's ecstatic and self-critical performance deconstructs this simple dualism: interior and exterior are not separate. The danger is external, but also evoked from within. The violence that Fassbinder fears, he also acts out. He advocates democratic values, but does not adhere to them himself. His fear is not simply the consequence of violence and political repression, but also self-produced paranoia.

Apart from the prologue and the epilogue, the film contains further documentary episodes. The first one is introduced by Kluge with a miniature on acts of state. It begins with images of Field Marshall Rommel, who was forced to commit suicide by the Nazi regime in 1944. Afterwards, the regime organised a public funeral service in his honour, which was attended by Rommel's son Manfred. The film inserts an image of Manfred Rommel from newsreels of that event. (Manfred Rommel reappears in the epilogue, explaining why in 1977 as mayor of Stuttgart he allowed the terrorists' burial in the Domhalden cemetary.) Shots of the funeral service for Schleyer follow this miniature. Then, abruptly, completely different historical material is inserted, showing a man who was shot in a car. The police find the murder weapon at the site. Kluge comments: the King of Serbia was murdered by the Germans in Marseille in 1938. (This is incorrect: The assassination was committed in 1934 and by a right-wing Croatian.) The film returns to Schleyer's funeral: a Turk with a rifle is arrested in front of the church – he says he wanted to shoot a pigeon for lunch. Schlöndorff shot his material on the day of the funeral at Daimler-Benz. The funeral is broadcast in the car museum. The camera pans over the luxurious limousines. The factory observes a three-minute silence; afterwards, work is resumed. President Walter Scheel makes a speech at the funeral; he slips up when he comes to the subject of freedom and protecting democracy. Thus, the montage of material from different places and times, together with the voice-over comments, opens up multiple associations and allows for diverse interpretations regarding difficult subjects such as state violence, historical continuity and public commemoration.

The next documentary episode has a fictional frame. A television journalist (Helmut Griem) interviews RAF member Horst Mahler, jailed for numerous crimes, on the origins of terrorism. Mahler had left he RAF three years before. His analysis sounds so detached that one almost forgets that he co-founded the RAF. He states that in 1945, the anti-fascist revolution was not fully achieved, so the generation of 1968 tried to complete it. The RAF failed to convince the public at large that fascism was still very much alive in West Germany and the USA. (In 2007, Mahler joined the right-wing radicals who deny the Holocaust, praise the German 'Volk' and denounce the USA as a criminal state.) Then Wolf Biermann is shown reciting a poem on the death of the imprisoned RAF terrorists, whom he calls the 'alchemists of revolution'.

The third documentary episode contains 16mm colour material of a NATO manoeuvre, shot by Maximilane Mainka and Peter Schubert. It deals with topics such as the costs and effort involved, the surveillance of the enemy and military obedience. In the context of a dispute about the duty to wear a camouflage net, an officer rhetorically asks, 'What use are my orders if they aren't observed?' Elegiac images of autumn accompanied by the music of Tchaikovsky follow, until Kluge quotes another letter by Schleyer. It expresses mortal fear and likens his situation to the war. It even states: 'It is never sweet and pleasant to die for your fatherland.' The montage of this episode implies a connection between military logic and Schleyer's predicament. Contemporaries felt that Helmut Schmidt was able to make decisions in situations of crisis because he had front experience as a Lieutenant in World War II, and the anti-terror task force was led by ex-Wehrmacht soldiers. For them, no other course of action than rejecting the terrorists' demands was imaginable. This sealed Schleyer's fate, who did not 'heroically' regard it as 'sweet and pleasant'.

The prologue before Schleyer's funeral corresponds to the epilogue with images of the RAF members' funeral at the end, dealing with the difficulties and debates surrounding the event. An image of Gudrun Ensslin's corpse in the coffin is inserted. Manfred Rommel explains why he allowed the burials. The funeral is attended by thousands of people, most of them young. Many have concealed their faces with hoods, and some carry posters accusing the state of murdering Baader, Ensslin and Raspe. The crowd is accompanied by numerous film and photo-cameras. One of the demonstrators shouts at the reporters: 'Photo vultures!' The police have secured the area and record the attendants of the funeral on video. The demonstrators shout 'The SA marches' and 'Sieg Heil!', as if in support of the RAF's claims that West Germany is still a fascist state. After the funeral, violent brawls between some of the demonstrators and the police occur. The crowd is represented partly on video, partly on 35mm colour film. Whereas the video images make the crowd a grey amorphous mass, on film the colourful costumes of green parkas and Palestinian scarves gives it the appearance of an audience at a pop festival. This impression is emphasised by the music Kluge selected: the song 'Here's to You' was composed by Ennio Morricone for the film *Sacco and Vanzetti* (1979), which was about the two anarchists who were put on trial and executed in the USA in 1927. The melo-dramatic song is performed by folk singer Joan Baez, who also wrote the lyrics of the song. At the end, a woman in a wool skirt and colourful poncho is shown. She is holding a little girl by the hand, who is also dressed in autumn colours. The woman is walking along the road, trying to hitch a ride. Now and then, the little girl beats the fallen leaves on the pavement with a stick. This montage of Kluge's was criticised for using the stereotype of motherhood as remedy for socio-political violence and/or as emotional closure. Kluge stated that the funeral crowd had intended to sing the Baez song, but was too overwhelmed, so he let the soundtrack give voice to their emotions. In retrospect, the Baez song is emotionally precise, but intellectually superficial. Everything becomes one: the suicide of the RAF leaders and the death sentence of the Italian immigrants in the USA, the Stalinism of the RAF and the Anarcho-Syndicalism of Sacco and Vanzetti. One could call this emotionalised conflation kitsch.

The heterogeneous parts of the film are only rarely joined by hard cuts. For example, two fictional female characters supply soft transitions. The first is the history teacher Gabi Teichert (Hannelore Hoger), who is trying to excavate 'the basis of German history'. Two of Kluge's discoveries are attributed to her, and she attends an SPD party meeting, where she listens to the speeches of politician Herbert Wehner and the author Max Frisch. The second is a young woman who is a member of a political group and – according to Kluge's ironic voice-over comment – 'is privately owned by an important television journalist', namely the man who interviews Mahler. The journalist shows her the interview and lets her attend Wolf Biermann's reading. Furthermore, she is the woman who helps the victim of assault in the underground car park. Continuity is also created with music: it is used to bridge sequences, to signify the continuation of an interrupted sequence, or to announce a new episode. Not least, the commentary mostly spoken by Kluge explains sequences, giving background information and creates an ironic distance to some of the images.

The montage of heterogeneous elements (miniatures as well as episodes) gives the film a playful tenor, despite its serious subject matter. Many textual and visual elements do not seem to have a fixed meaning. The audience is invited to interact with the film, choose which associations to follow and to form their own interpretation. The subjects touched upon are multiple: military logic, the death wish of the RAF prisoners, the German continuity of state violence, the commemoration of the dead, the melancholia of the 'German Autumn' and Schubert's 'Winterreise'.

Klaus Theweleit did not have anything positive to say about *Germany in Autumn* as a whole (he only commended Fassbinder's episode): 'on seeing the film again it gives the impression of being utterly deranged'. However, the question is, whether a 'deranged' representation is not more suitable to the absurd events, as tragic as they may be, than any straightforward and 'sane' analysis. Klaus Kreimeier praised the 'rejection of coherence, the renunciation of a non-contradictory, consumable production of sense, the insistence on the non-evident'. On the other hand, Kreimeier does criticise the 'left-wing melancholia' of the film, which later ossified into a 'cult of concern among the alternative grass-roots movements'.

Germany in Autumn is a highly unusual film in German film history, especially when viewed today. In this wild mixture of fictional and non-fictional elements, the real events often appear surreal and the best of the staged scenes feel authentic. It is an aesthetic conglomeration that threatens to fall apart at any moment, but is somehow held together by montage and Kluge's comments. Seen from a distance of over thirty years and with a 'postmodern sensibility', the film comes across as political in scenes that were regarded as merely playful by contemporaries (the narcissism of Fassbinder's performanc, for instance), whereas much of the intended political impact was lost in light of later developments (such as the interview with Mahler). Thus, *Germany in Autumn* was produced for a specific historical moment, or as Kluge put it: 'The threads in my films are not apparent to everybody. These films are made for certain situations. Everybody in these situations knows the context.' However, in its best moments, it is a film that remains touching today.

Dietrich Leder

Translated by Annemone Ligensa

REFERENCES

Kluge, A. (1977) *Neue Geschichten. Hefte 1–18: Unheimlichkeit der Zeit*. Frankfurt am Main: Suhrkamp.

Kreimeier, K. (2006) 'Die RAF und der deutsche Film', in W. Kraushaar (ed.) *Die RAF und der linke Terrorismus, vol. 2*. Hamburg: Hamburger Edition, 1155–70.

Liebmann, S. (1988) 'On New German Cinema, Art, Enlightenment, and the Public Sphere: An Interview with Alexander Kluge', *October*, 46, 23–59.

Lutze, P. C. (1998) *Alexander Kluge: The Last Modernist*. Detroit, MI: Wayne State University Press.

Theweleit, K. (1998) 'Bemerkungen zum RAF-Gespenst – "Abstrakter Realismus" und Kunst', in *Ghosts: Drei leicht inkorrekte Vorträge*. Frankfurt am Main: Stroemfeld, 13–100.

DAS BOOT THE BOAT

WOLFGANG PETERSEN, WEST GERMANY, 1981

Das Boot (aka *The Boat*, 1981), a film about the final mission and ironic fate of a German submarine in World War II, based on the semi-autobiographical 1973 bestseller of the same title by Lothar-Günther Buchheim, is a milestone in the career of its director Wolfgang Petersen and also in the development of German popular cinema. The film's success at the West German box office and its surprisingly strong commercial and critical impact in the US launched Petersen on a career as one of Hollywood's – and thus the world's – most popular filmmakers, whose trademark is the creation of intense – and frequently claustrophobic – suspense in films such as *In the Line of Fire* (1993), *Outbreak* (1995), *Air Force One* (1997) and *The Perfect Storm* (2000). *Das Boot* also marks the transition from the politically charged and aesthetically complex films of the New German Cinema, several of them about the World War II era, which achieved considerable critical and, to a much lesser extent, commercial success domestically and internationally, to the revival of German genre cinema (adventure films, thrillers and, especially, comedies), which, after a dramatic decline in the 1970s, returned to the West German box-office charts in the 1980s.

Compared to the New German Cinema, the film's depoliticisation as well as its aesthetic mainstreaming and spectacularisation stand out. However, in comparison to the generic traditions of the World War II combat film in Germany and the US (as discussed by Jeanine Basinger), *Das Boot* is characterised by the relative aimlessness of the submarine's mission, a strong emphasis on the boredom and passivity of its crew (hence on reaction rather than action), a general lack of character development and the notable absence of the typical transformation of the combat unit (for example, from initial disunity to final cohesion). Thus one could argue that, regarding its narration, the film retains key aspects of European art cinema (as described by David Bordwell). What is more, the film's apolitical approach to its subject provoked an all the more politicised response from film critics, both in West Germany and abroad. At home, the source novel's author and other commentators went so far as to accuse Petersen of turning an anti-war novel into a celebration of German soldiers (which the director vehemently denied). US critics expressed their ambivalence towards what they perceived as a highly effective genre picture that forced them to adopt the perspective of the former enemy. The complex form and contested status of *Das Boot* are closely connected to its production history, situated at the intersection of the German and US film industries, German television and German literature. Within a few years of its publication in 1973, Buchheim's *Das Boot*, whose introductory note describes it as 'a novel, but not a work of fiction', had become a modern classic of German war literature. Based on the author's own experiences, the 600-page volume tells the story of a German submarine's mission during the autumn and winter of 1941 through the first-person narrative of a young war correspondent who joins the crew. The novel begins with the drunken revelry on the night before the submarine's departure, proceeds with alternating episodes of long waiting and dramatic enemy encounters, and ends with the submarine's destruction in harbour during an air raid. In simple, yet vivid language, the narrator describes activities on the submarine in minute detail, focusing both on technical procedures and on characters, especially the charismatic captain, but also including long passages on his own past and his current state of mind.

The film rights to Buchheim's novel were initially acquired by US producers. Throughout the 1970s, American companies and filmmakers, with greater or lesser input from Germans, were heavily involved in a number of films on the Third Reich and World War II. These included *Cabaret* (1972), a substantial commercial and critical success (including winning an Academy Award for art director Rolf Zehetbauer, who later worked on *Das Boot*), the war epic *A Bridge Too Far* (1976), also a big hit, Sam Peckinpah's controversial combat film *Cross of Iron* (1977, a German/British co-production with the German title *Steiner – Das eiserne Kreuz*), and the hugely successful and influential television mini-series *Holocaust* (1978). The initial American attempt to film *Das Boot* involved, at different times, the veteran action directors John Sturges and Don Siegel, and the stars Robert Redford and Paul Newman.

Like many Hollywood productions of the late 1970s, the adaptation of *Das Boot* was financed by a West German tax shelter company. However, in 1979 this company decided to sell the project to the West German film studio Bavaria, which had just appointed the former television executive Günter Rohrbach as its head of production. Rohrbach secured financing from two West German public service broadcasters (WDR and Süddeutscher Rundfunk) and conceived of *Das Boot* as a six-hour television mini-series. He also made certain that, before the television broadcast, which was scheduled for 1985, a shorter version would be released in cinemas through the leading West German film distributor Neue Constantin. The prospects

for this theatrical release seemed good, because, since the late 1970s, films set in World War II had been very successful at the German box office, for example, the documentary *Hitler – Eine Karriere* (*Hitler, a Career*, 1977), Ingmar Bergman's German/American co-production *Das Schlangenei* (*The Serpent's Egg*, 1977) and Volker Schlöndorff's *Die Blechtrommel* (*The Tin Drum*, 1979).

Widely regarded as not only the most costly (its final budget was DM 25 million), but also the most ambitious production in German film and television history, *Das Boot* received a lot of press attention, both in Germany and the US, much of it focused on the film's director Wolfgang Petersen. Born in 1941, and trained both in the theatre and at the Berlin film school, Petersen was one of Germany's leading television directors. Since the beginning of the 1970s, he had made several feature-length episodes of the highly popular German police series *Tatort* and a range of made-for-television films, including the hit *Smog* (1972) and the controversial homosexual drama *Die Konsequenz* (*The Consequence*, 1977). He had also made an award-winning theatrical film, *Einer von uns beiden* (*One or the Other*, 1973), and, in the late 1970s, two of his made-for-television films received theatrical releases. A 1978 promotional text for the US theatrical premiere of *The Consequence* declared presciently: 'A sensitive and original director with a good commercial sense of making films for larger audiences, Petersen is likely to be the first German director to score an American and international box-office success.'

Initially, Petersen's hopes for his international breakthrough had been attached to an adaptation of Richard Neeley's thriller *The Plastic Nightmare* (which he did eventually make in 1991, under the title *Shattered*). For this project, Petersen had set up his own company, Radiant Film, with financing from Hollywood, Neue Constantin and German television. However, in June 1979, instead of proceeding with *The Plastic Nightmare*, he took over *Das Boot*. Up to that point, Petersen had usually worked with established scriptwriters, but he had also received writing credits for some of his productions, most notably *The Consequence*. Now he faced the challenging task of transforming Buchheim's book into a script. According to Ulrich Greiwe (in turn quoting Rohrbach), an earlier US script had transformed the novel into 'an anti-German underwater western', while Buchheim's script had been much too long. In writing his own script, Petersen had to balance the different demands of the theatrical and television versions, especially their varying lengths; when finished, the film released in German cinemas in September 1981 ran 149 minutes, while the six-part mini-series broadcast on German television in 1985 was almost twice as long (yet another version – a three-and-a-half hour 'director's cut' – was released in 1997).

The original theatrical release version of *Das Boot* follows the story of Buchheim's book quite closely. However, due to the enormous length of the novel, the film has to leave out many details as well as some key events. Perhaps most importantly, the submarine's encounter with a passenger ship towards the end of the novel is omitted. As a consequence of a series of misunderstandings, the captain, to the horror of his subordinates, orders a torpedo attack on what he believes to be an enemy vessel. Only after the torpedo fails to launch is the ship revealed to be exactly what it claimed all along – a civilian ocean-liner from neutral Spain. The captain dryly declares that, had the attack succeeded, it would have been necessary to destroy all evidence of their mistake by killing the survivors.

The film also amplifies certain aspects of Buchheim's story. More emphasis is placed, through dialogue and photographs, on crew members' loved ones (except for the women in the narrator's life, who are completely absent from the film). A subplot involves a young crew member and his French girlfriend, who is pregnant with his child; he is constantly writing letters to her, but never gets a chance to post them. Furthermore, the film foregrounds the chief machinist's fall and redemption. He loses his mind under combat stress and refuses to obey orders (as he does in the novel), yet later redeems himself, when the submarine needs urgent repairs after a battle, by working beyond the call of duty (which is barely mentioned in the novel). The film also highlights the fact that, while the crew on the whole seem unconcerned about politics, one of the officers is a clean-cut Nazi, who is ridiculed by the other officers.

Another important change concerns the novel's focus on what the narrator can personally perceive. While the film generally adheres to the limited perspectives and experiences of the submarine crew – never switching, for example, to scenes showing the enemy or the German high command – it is by no means restricted to the war correspondent's perceptions. There are numerous exterior underwater views of the submarine and of exploding water bombs. And while the novel's narrator constantly reminds readers of his lack of involvement in most of the activities on the ship, the film features extensive Steadicam sequences, the camera racing through the submarine's narrow corridors to capture the frantic movements of the crew. In this way, the novel's emphasis on the narrator's observations, reflections, memories, dreams and fantasies is replaced by the film's foregrounding of action.

However, *Das Boot* is a curious kind of action film. To begin with, judging by the standards of classical narration (as described by Bordwell), the goals of the protagonists are not as clearly articulated and forcefully acted upon as one would expect. While it is obvious that the captain wants to do his duty and sink enemy ships, and the war correspondent wants to obtain an interesting story and exciting pictures, the precise mission of the submarine is somewhat ill-defined and open-ended.

Cruising the North Atlantic, the crew waits seemingly without end for radio commands that will direct them to where the action is, or for chance encounters with the enemy. The first battle with an enemy destroyer almost leads to the destruction of the German submarine, which spends a long time underwater under constant bombardment. This also happens during the second encounter, with the difference that the German submarine gets the chance to launch torpedoes, which do in fact sink several enemy ships. However, after the submarine escapes the attack of two enemy destroyers, its crew has to confront the pitiful death of enemy sailors. Then, instead of being rewarded for their achievement with a much-needed return to their harbour in France, the crew is sent to Spain and from there to Italy, which is the equivalent of a suicide mission, because the submarine has to pass the narrow and heavily guarded Straits of Gibraltar. The motivation for the order is only vaguely explained, but the difficulty of carrying it out is made very clear. After an aerial attack, the submarine is badly damaged and sinks to the bottom of the sea, from where it returns to the surface only after a long and desperate period of waiting. It is a great 'success' for the crew to have survived, but they have failed to carry out their mission, and they are not ordered to continue. Instead, they return home. They receive a hero's welcome in their French harbour, but are bombed in an aerial attack. Many of the crew members are killed, including the captain, who, in his final moments, sees his ship sinking, while the war correspondent looks on in horror.

Even though the story is more episodic than goal-directed, one would at least expect that the protagonists and/or the whole crew undergo a substantial transformation. Indeed, there is plenty of material for constructing dramatic arcs: the outsider status of the war correspondent and of the young Nazi officer, the social diversity of the crew members and the occasional eruption of conflicts between them. However, the film disappoints generic expectations by refusing to show how hierarchical divisions and personal conflicts can be overcome through shared experiences, and none of the characters undergoes much change. Instead of exploring the psychology or social relations of the crew, the film emphasises the alternation of boring routine and stressful battle action. If the boredom and frustration of having to wait for battle are depicted as increasingly unbearable for the crew, the actual battle is shown to be much worse. A key element in the crew's misery is their utter helplessness during most phases of battle, their passive dependence on the technological resilience of the ship and the wisdom of their captain's decisions as well as blind luck.

When there is progression in the narrative, it consists mainly of the gradual physical deterioration of everyone and everything, with beards growing longer, faces becoming paler and clothes shabbier while disarray and filth are spreading on an increasingly damaged boat. Thus, the film depicts a process of gradual physical destruction, which culminates in the climactic bombardment destroying the submarine and killing most of its crew. Indeed, this final destruction is hinted at by a title at the very beginning of the film, which, quoting from the introductory note of the novel, states: '40,000 German sailors served on U-boats during World War II. 30,000 never returned.' Rather than being prompted to focus on the particular mission of this particular submarine, viewers are invited to contemplate the terrible odds of its crew. The primary narrative question is not whether the mission's goal – whatever it may be – will be accomplished, but when the crew will encounter death, and who might survive.

Politics play an even smaller role in the film than in the novel. The young Nazi officer is merely a harmless figure of fun. When the captain and his officers complain about Nazi propaganda (on the occasion of radio broadcasts) or about orders they receive from the German high command, it is because of the latter's stupidity and military ineffectiveness rather than ideology and warmongering. As military professionals, the captain and his officers are only interested in doing their job. While the successful torpedo attack on British ships confronts the crew with the lethal consequences of their actions, the film avoids the more difficult questions raised in the novel by the captain's behaviour during the encounter with the Spanish passenger ship, which thoroughly undermines the previously not only paternalistic, but almost super-human stature of the captain, revealing him as a ruthless killer. By omitting this episode, the film opts for a simpler and more positive view of the German military, at least as exemplified by this particular submarine and its crew.

Neue Constantin released *Das Boot* in over two hundred German cinemas on 17 September 1979. The distributor's press book declared: '*Das Boot* is a film about war, a film about people at war. *Das Boot* tells the story of young men, still almost children, eager for adventure, seduced by fascist propaganda, enthusiastic about marvellous technology.' The reference to 'fascist propaganda', which does not in fact play much of a role in the film, shows that the distributor was anxious about the possibility that the film would be criticised for ignoring politics and glorifying German soldiers. Along similar lines, Petersen was quoted as saying: 'Obviously, I did not approach this subject matter without hesitation, but after reading the book I hesitated no longer. I felt that here I was able to experience most directly what war is really like.' Petersen stated that he aimed both to entertain and to educate.

The distributor's fears turned out to be justified. Buchheim, who had already been highly critical during the film's production, publicly attacked the film after its release (but later supported the television version as a more adequate adaptation). Journalists joined his attack, for example, Hans Dieter Müller with an article in the *Frankfurter Rundschau* headlined 'About War at Sea: Why Lothar-Günther Buchheim's *Das Boot* is a good anti-war novel and Wolfgang Petersen's adaptation a bad war film.' In his review for the *Tagespiegel* Volker Baer summed up the critics' main concerns: *Das Boot* 'is a war film like many others, neither stimulating reflection nor helping viewers to form their own opinions. Much of the film is simply too pretty, too smooth, even when dealing with destruction, too sentimental in the face of death.' Journalists compared *Das Boot* to big Hollywood productions, sometimes positively – for example, when celebrating its technical virtuosity and suspenseful action – but also negatively, when they noted that the film was merely generic rather than the work of an *auteur* (an *Autorenfilm*), only superficially realistic and ultimately a melodramatic and perhaps even ideologically dangerous distortion of history.

While the critical response was divided, West German audiences responded positively to the film, judging by the fact that *Das Boot* became the sixth highest-grossing film of 1981. Perhaps somewhat surprisingly, this tragic tale of courageous German soldiers was also a success outside Germany, especially in the US where, upon its release by Columbia's arthouse division Triumph Films in February 1982, it quickly became the highest-grossing German import ever. In an interview for the trade paper *Variety*, Petersen emphasised the thoroughly German nature of this production as the very basis of its international potential: 'In using an all-German cast and crew, our thinking was that perhaps the best commercial way to make a real, original film that can break through in international markets is to produce an authentic, realistically German picture.' At the same time, in an interview for the *New York Post*, Petersen tried to assure prospective viewers that he had not made another German art film: 'This isn't an intellectual movie. ... It's a movie about people made for people [showing them] how war feels, how horrible and claustrophobic it is.' In response to the criticisms the film had received in Germany, Petersen also tried to defend the apolitical approach he took in *Das Boot*. He told the *New York Times*: 'This is the first time anybody's tried to make a film about normal young soldiers without discussing all the time our guilt. ... A lot of people say you can't show a film like this without speaking about the Nazis. But I wanted to make a small human story'.

By and large, US reviews initially went along with the marketing strategy adopted by Triumph Films and Petersen, describing the film as a 'rough-and-tumble action picture' (*Christian Science Monitor*) and one of 'the great war films' (*New York Post*), on a par with Hollywood classics from the 1940s and 1950s, the 'first unsanitized portrait' of life on a World War II submarine (*Newsweek*), 'rich in physical detail' (*Village Voice*). What made the film stand out from the 'great US tradition' to which it was frequently compared was, of course, its German perspective: 'the novelty here is getting the inside German view' (*Time*), 'war from the reverse angle' (*Los Angeles Times*). Almost invariably, however, this 'novelty' eventually caused even the most enthusiastic reviewers to qualify their positive comments with reflections on the film's politics: 'the film's problem for some may be an inability to empathize utterly with a German crew during the last clear-cut war' (*Los Angeles Times*); 'you never forget that men like these sank hundreds of ships and killed thousands of men' (*New York*); 'there's a suspicion of narrative whitewash at work, exonerating its characters from Nazihood. … Petersen encourages us to root for Nazi survival, to effect a suspension of nationalistic sympathy which I'm unprepared to muster' (*Village Voice*). Yet, for most commentators, the film's action remained compelling, and its efforts to show 'disillusioned' German soldiers (*Newsday*), while avoiding their 'glorification' (*New York Post*), and also 'to honor the enemy' (*New York*) were regarded as genuine and honest. Perhaps the surest sign of the film's acceptance in the US as a classic war film in the tradition of Hollywood's own great achievements in this genre were the six Academy Award nominations *Das Boot* received, including Best Director and Best Film (rather than Best Foreign-Language Film).

In conclusion, *Das Boot* is one of the most expensive productions and one of the biggest hits of German cinema. It is also a complex hybrid: a German production made with the international, especially the US, market in mind; the outcome of a collaboration between the film and television industries so typical of Germany since the 1970s; a two-faced event, both action film and television mini-series, simultaneously generic and 'arty'; perhaps the most 'personal' film of its writer-director Wolfgang Petersen, yet launching him on a career as one of the world's leading action specialists; a political conundrum, politicised precisely due to its refusal to address politics. *Das Boot* is also one of the most important precedents for bestseller adaptations, such as *The Name of the Rose* (1986) – made in English and with an international cast – which, mostly produced by Bernd Eichinger for Neue Constantin, have since become the most consistently successful products of the German film industry in international markets. As a World War II combat film, however, *Das Boot* has failed to spark a major production trend in Germany. In his overview of the long and, until the 1950s, hugely successful history of German war films, Knut Hickethier notes that, following the genre's commercial and critical decline in the 1960s, no sustained output has re-emerged. High-profile productions such as *Das Boot* and, much later, *Stalingrad* (1993) and *Der Untergang* (*Downfall*, 2004) have so far remained isolated reminders of one of the richest, and most problematic, generic traditions of German popular cinema.

Peter Krämer

REFERENCES

Basinger, J. (1986) *The World War II Combat Film: Anatomy of a Genre*. New York: Columbia University Press.

Bordwell, D. (1985) *Narration in the Fiction Film*. Madison, WI: University of Wisconsin Press.

Buchheim, L.-G. (1973) *Das Boot*. München: Piper.

Greiwe, U. and W. Petersen (1997) *Ich liebe die großen Geschichten: Vom 'Tatort' bis nach Hollywood*. Köln: Kiepenheuer & Witsch.

Hickethier, K. (2007) 'Der Krieg als Initiation einer neuen Zeit – Zum deutschen Kriegs-filmgenre', in H.-B. Heller, B. Röwekamp and M. Steinle (eds) *All Quiet on the Genre Front? Zur Praxis und Theorie des Kriegsfilms*. Marburg: Schüren, 41–63.

Der eine kann's. Der andere auch.

MÄNNER

Ein Film von Doris Dörrie

FILMVERLAG
DER AUTOREN

MÄNNER MEN

DORIS DÖRRIE, WEST GERMANY, 1985

When in October 1985 Doris Dörrie's *Männer* (*Men*) premiered at the Hof International Film Festival, the leading annual showcase for German cinema, the film was received as a sign of hope for the country's film industry. According to the film-magazine *EPD Film*, 'the viewers were overjoyed, occasionally clapped their hands, stomped their feet and shouted bravo, seemingly in unison, as if wanting to give voice to their unhoped-for wish that German cinema might not be dead after all'. Similarly, the bleak state of contemporary German cinema served as a contrasting foil in the critical discourse on this film, once it had become a sensational commercial and solid critical success. Co-financed on a modest budget by the public television station ZDF, *Men* was not primarily intended for theatrical release. When the film was picked up by a distributor in January 1986, it opened on only twenty screens. Dörrie, born in 1955, already had a few productions (mainly for television) under her belt, which had been favourably received, above all *Mitten ins Herz* (*Straight Through the Heart*, 1983) and *Im Innern des Wals* (*In the Belly of the Whale*, 1984). But nothing prepared her or anybody else for the success of *Men*, which sold 5.1 million tickets in Germany.

During the mid-1980s, the few other German films that were commercially successful were mostly vehicles for comedians who were not film stars, but had become household names through regular TV appearances. There is a reference to one of those contemporary German box-office hits in *Men*: in the end credits, one can glimpse a cartoon image of an elephant scribbled on an elevator wall. This so-called 'Ottifant' is the signature logo of Otto Waalkes, who starred in, co-authored and co-directed the nonsense comedy *Otto – Der Film* (1985), which became the top-grossing German film of the decade, drawing 8.7 million viewers. Reviewers repeatedly and favourably compared Dörrie's comedy of male manners to the coarse humour of films such as *Otto – Der Film*, as well as to the rather serious tone of the New German Cinema, which by then had run its course. The critical discourse on *Men* reflected a desire to connect with any tradition of sophisticated comedy that German film history might muster. Critics and interviewers frequently referred to Ernst Lubitsch and Billy Wilder – without ever specifying why *Men* reminded them of those masters.

As soon as the film had become a modest hit on the US art-house circuit, Hollywood was invoked as another frame of reference. The director and screenwriter of *Men* had studied in California and New York before graduating from the Munich Academy for Film and Television. Dörrie repeatedly attributed her sense of humour to her two-year US experience, but emphasised that she was especially interested in German subjects and regarded *Men* as specifically German in tone and detail. She took pride in having beaten Hollywood blockbusters at the German box office, and although she acknowledged being tempted to work independently in the USA, she regarded her relaxed working style as incompatible with Hollywood's mode of production. Indeed, her only Hollywood production, her fifth feature-film, *Ich und Er* (*Me and Him*, 1988), turned out to be a devastating experience.

The filmmaker's gender was regularly remarked upon in the critical discourse on this 'post-feminist' film, which occasionally was contrasted with the explicitly feminist strand of the New German Cinema. Dörrie described her perspective as 'unavoidably feminine', and indeed, the beginning of *Men* might be read as suggesting feminine authorship, because the opening shot is located in a professional space traditionally associated with women, namely, in an outer office, where a group of typists are at work. The credits create the impression of being themselves typewritten, since the letters appear in rhythm with a typing sound. However, after that, the narration is restricted to the male characters' point of view, whereas female characters get little screen time. Only in the last sequence does the plot's perspective slightly shift, when the main female character appears and the two male leads are in for a final surprise.

The protagonist, Julius Armbrust, is introduced as a 'creative director' who, at work, dallies with a female subordinate, with whom he is having one of his recurring affairs. Yet he is furious when, on the morning of his twelfth wedding anniversary, he finds out that his wife Paula is having an affair of her own. Once their two children have departed to a summer camp, Julius cancels the holiday trip that he and Paula were about to go on. He moves to a hotel and spies on his wife and her lover, Stefan. He observes Stefan throwing his former girlfriend, under her loud protests, out of their flat, which they had shared with another man, Lothar. When Stefan, who turns out to be a leftover hippie, posts a wanted ad for a new roommate, Julius applies. Calling himself Daniel and pretending to have just broken with a bourgeois lifestyle, he moves in with Stefan and Lothar, presumably with the intent of investigating what Paula sees in her lover. It is the juxtaposition of the two male protagonists that gives structure to the narration. At first, Julius and Stefan appear to be each other's opposites with regard to socio-economic status, lifestyle, habits and worldview. One is a competitive careerist, breadwinner-husband and father, living comfortably in suburbia, whereas the other ostentatiously takes an anti-establishment stance and barely makes ends meet by freelancing as a graphic designer and serving fast food. However, it gradually turns out that the men are not so different after all. Julius tries to win back his wife by turning his rival into a mirror image of himself. He recommends and coaches Stefan for a job as an art director, which actually makes Paula lose interest in her lover, because he suddenly seems quite similar to her husband.

Given the fact that the film juxtaposes two different milieus and that its plot hinges on the protagonist's investigation of his rival's private sphere, it is surprising that Dörrie mostly forgoes establishing shots and long shots. Moreover, cameraman Helge Weindler, who seems to have mainly used mobile cameras, only moves his camera (almost without exception) when reacting to the characters' actions. The Armbrusts' spacious home and the bohemian chaos of the shared flat in downtown Munich are only fleetingly registered by the camera. This discretion is most astonishing when Julius gets his first look at how Stefan lives. Up to that point, when Julius spied on Stefan, the camera aligned itself with Julius's gaze, even though there are few point-of-view shots in the film. In the sequence showing the flat for the first time, however, no shot implies Julius's point of view, nor does the camera investigate the space on its own. The predominance of medium shots, medium close-ups and medium-long shots, combined with modest frame mobility, might be attributed to the fact that *Men* was an 'amphibic film'. In the German film industry this term designated films that were (co-)produced by a television network and aimed to fit both the small and big screen. Combined with a relatively long average shot-length – some two-dozen takes last for approximately one minute – the film's style allows for an impression of casual intimacy with the characters and thus contributes to the unforced naturalness that critics praised about the dialogue scenes. At the same time, Dörrie does not emphasise the statements and habits of Stefan that – as we can only infer in retrospect – provoke Julius to come up with the plan of transforming his rival. Moreover, the objectivity of the narration keeps the spectator mostly at a distance. Such contradictory effects of a simple but subtle style may be the reason why some critics regarded Dörrie's perspective on her subjects as 'sympathetic', whereas others felt it was 'detached'.

Time and again the filmmaker ironically referred to her film as being based on 'anthropological field work'. She claimed to have modelled her dialogues on various conversations between men that she had intentionally overheard. In connection with this publicity discourse, which was frequently repeated in the press coverage of the film, the matter-of-factness of the title suggested a (mock) general definition of men and masculinity. With this theme, the film was in tune with other elements of contemporary German pop culture; for example, Herbert Grönemeyer had a hit in 1984 with a pop song of the same title. While the verses of his 'Männer' made general claims about how men are, the chorus called into question 'when a man is truly a man'.

By involving her men in a series of masquerades, Dörrie foregrounds the performativity of their masculinity and their identities in general. Julius is obviously playing a role when he presents himself to his rival as 'Daniel'. Consequently, as soon as he has moved in with Stefan and Lothar, we see Julius changed into jeans and t-shirt, in contrast to his usual business attire. But, significantly, when Stefan tells his new roommate that he wonders which outfit is more of a disguise – the suit or the jeans – Julius answers: 'Both.' Later Julius likens his job (which, fittingly, is packaging design) to a game and confesses that his main professional competence is being good at talking. Furthermore, Stefan's bohemian lifestyle turns out to be just as much of a masquerade. He makes a secret of his sideline job at a fast food restaurant; and it is tellingly easy for Julius to make Stefan adopt the trappings of a careerist. Both men refer to business attire as a disguise, and Dörrie's *mise-en-scène* creates a parallelism between the scene in which Stefan tries on Julius's suit and the one in which Julius checks his new 'disguise' of casual clothes in the mirror.

Somewhat simplistically, Stefan reflects on masculinity as performative when he remarks, 'men are what they do, and women are what they are'. Surprisingly, the filmmaker subscribed to that view, as she repeatedly made clear in interviews. 'It sounds sexist, but maybe it's not. Men fall apart … when they can't define themselves through the social framework. … There's something inside that prevents us [women] from becoming too dependent on social recognition.' Dörrie's men, however, obviously feel uneasy about the performativity of their identities. When in the last sequence Julius taunts Stefan for thinking he was 'the only original', both begin to strip to their underwear. Whereas the narration implied that clothes make the man, the protagonists seem intent to prove some corporeal essence at the last minute. Similarly, it might be read as a paradoxical defense against the apparent social construction of their gendered identities that both men literally put on a mask, namely an ape-mask, when they check their respective new masquerades in the mirror. That recurring ape-mask-motif is reminiscent of the beastlike 'hairy man' or 'wild man', which figured as the symbol of an essential 'deep masculinity' in a new discourse that emerged in the USA in the early 1980s and achieved wide notoriety in 1990 with Robert Bly's bestseller *Iron John*. In accord with the ideas of this 'men's movement' a certain 'wildness' seems to be lacking in Julius's marriage. When

Julius finds out about Paula's affair by discovering a love bite on her neck, he furiously tells her that he can be just as much of a wild man as her lover seems to be. It is in the disguise of the ape-mask and resorting to apish noises that Julius charms Paula during her surprise visit to the shared flat, as he hides behind that mask to keep her and Stefan from seeing through his charade. After finally returning home, he jokingly defends his snoring by telling Paula that it was a man's job to ensure his wife's safety and deter wild beasts with snoring.

In accord with a long tradition of representations of erotic triangles, the two male rivals begin to bond and thereby marginalise the female object of their desire (as well as women in general). Stefan and Julius are repeatedly engaged in unmotivated conversations that have women and their purported difference from men as their subject. The first of these dialogues is especially denigrating to women, since both men jokingly ask themselves what they need women for – and they come up with sex as the only answer, likening it to sports. The homosocial bonding calls for a queer reading, as suggested by Susan Kassouf. The men playfully refer to falling in love with and marrying each other. In one sequence they embrace while exuberantly jumping around, until they fall onto a bed, and Stefan, lying on top of Julius, feigns a kiss. This pivotal scene begins with a moment of relaxed intimacy, as both men lie scantily clad on Stefan's bed while Julius feeds Stefan, who cannot use his bandaged hands. His hands are bandaged, because Julius has earlier intentionally poured boiling water over them. Significantly, moments of homosocial bonding are preceded by acts of violence (on Julius's part).

Dörrie's narrative turned out to serve as a blueprint for the *Beziehungskomödien* ('relationship comedies') that would dominate German cinema in the first half of the 1990s and often thematically focused on men and masculinity. Like *Men*, two of the most successful films of that cycle have protagonists who move in with another man, while their heterosexual relationships are in crisis. However, in Sönke Wortmann's *Der bewegte Mann* (*The Most Desired Man*, 1994) as well as in Rolf Silber's *Echte Kerle* (*Regular Guys*, 1996), the man with whom those protagonists cohabitate turns out to be gay. Hence, the homoerotic tension that is not explicit in Dörrie's *Men* becomes a central element of those two films. While the protagonists end up committed to heterosexual relationships, the narration explicitly poses the question whether they were sexually aroused by or, respectively, had sex with their gay hosts.

The conversion narratives of *Der bewegte Mann* and *Echte Kerle* result in the modernisation of a masculinity that is – to use the categories of the New Men's Studies, which emerged in the late 1980s – 'hegemonic' within or at least 'complicit' with a patriarchal gender order, which subordinates women as well as some groups of men. Homosexual masculinity is the most conspicuous of such 'subordinated' masculinities, and in the films mentioned it serves as a catalyst for the reform of the protagonists into less chauvinistic and, in general, more likeable persons. This liberalisation accounts for the light tone of those 'feel-good-movies', whereas the melancholia of *Men* might be attributed, in part, to the different course of its conversion narrative. At the outset, Stefan combines traits that were regarded as typical of the purported 'new man', who was the recurring subject of popular discourse in the early 1980s. At first, Stefan is not competitive, shuns violence, gives priority to romance over work, does his own housework and claims to want 'a strong woman'. Yet over the course of the story this new man is groomed for hegemonic (or at least complicit) masculinity.

In accord with the constant theme of masquerade, costume is the most significant element of Dörrie's *mise-en-scène*. From the outset, she calls our attention to Julius's business attire, which we see being brushed, ironed, washed and delivered from the cleaners. When we first get a glimpse of the protagonist, he is straightening his tie. As we learn later on, Stefan met Paula when she brought her husband a tie for the office (and she does so again in the final sequence). Apart from costume, Dörrie employs various motifs to convey similarities between the two men as well as gradual changes. Among the most conspicuous motifs are watches and alarm clocks. Having ostentatiously given away his Rolex at their first meeting, Julius (during his holidays) subjects Stefan to a rigid time discipline while coaching him for the job interview. Whereas Stefan used an alarm clock only to be punctual for a date with Paula, for which he interrupts his work, his transformation is complete when he declines to meet her due to lack of time in his new job as art director. An even more crucial motif is introduced when Julius, erroneously thinking he is alone in the flat, is about to rummage around in his rival's private belongings. The scene opens with a medium close-up of his hands passing along dozens of small toy cars neatly placed in a row, next to which a somewhat larger toy Porsche can be glimpsed. That toy car later takes on special significance in the pivotal scene already mentioned.

The pivotal scene in the bedroom is accentuated by being the only one to seemingly begin with a fade-in. While the dialogue has already set in, the screen remains black, because the camera is placed behind some obstacle in relative darkness, until it pans to the left, framing both men in a long shot, as they lie on Stefan's bed. The camera then tracks in to a medium shot of Stefan and Julius, who are engaged in a conversation, without paying attention to the TV broadcast of an ice hockey match. Since it is not motivated by the movement of a character, this panning and tracking, even though moderate, stands out in the film. But most significant about this scene is the one instance in *Men* where Dörrie cuts away from characters engaged in a dialogue to some seemingly marginal element. Both men are in the middle of another haphazard conversation about the differences between the sexes, when Julius begins to taunt Stefan for lacking ambition and being a failure. Stefan reciprocates by mocking Julius for being 'successful, dynamic, divorced' and reproaches him for basing his notion of freedom on money. When Julius propounds a simplistic liberal philosophy, according to which everybody is fundamentally free, Stefan responds that he would love to move to a lonely island with Paula, if only she did not feel attached to her husband and children, hence being un-free. Precisely at the point when Stefan claims to be willing to leave everything behind, Dörrie cuts to a medium close-up of the remote-controlled toy Porsche, which he has begun to play with. Thus, *mise-en-scène* and editing subtly undercut his anti-materialist stance. And, indeed, Stefan will immediately buy a real version of that very toy car, once he has landed the job that Julius helped him to get. Thus he proves Julius right, who mockingly said that all his rival dreamt of was a Porsche.

Since it turns out that 'Stefan's leftist ideas are all surface', as Dörrie stated, the conversion narrative of *Men* might be read as a renunciation of the utopian ideas of 1968. There was consensus about such an interpretation among the panellists of a round table discussion organised by the feminist film journal *Frauen und Film*. According to Gertrud Koch, the film supported the new belief – itself ideological – that all ideologies had come to an end, while Karsten Witte diagnosed an aggressive turn against difference. In general, the panellists regarded the success of Dörrie's film as reflecting an anti-emancipatory backlash and a conservative *Zeitgeist*. Indeed, Stefan melancholically tells Julius that he has lost his 'utopia', even though we are never given any specifics about those utopian ideals. When his former girlfriend protests about being thrown out of the shared flat, she accuses him of contradicting his '*Sozi-Gequatsche*' ('socialist chatter') with his actions; yet we never get to hear any 'socialist chatter'. Stefan's political stance is reduced to a mere cliché, as we see a sticker and a poster with the portrait of Che Guevara adorn the kitchen cupboard and the bathroom wall, respectively. We even receive some indication that Julius used to subscribe to left-wing ideas as well, since, in response to an ironic remark of Lothar's girlfriend regarding 1968, he brusquely tells the much younger woman that she does not know what she is talking about. Thus, because both protagonists seem to have turned their backs on the political ideas of 1968 at one time or another, the film might indeed be read as implying that there was no feasible or attractive alternative to careerism and bourgeois lifestyles. Dörrie stated as her aim: 'I became interested in opportunism and its connection with the 1968 generation – my peer group. I wanted to know what happened to those people, how they established themselves … It's my experience that if the Stefans of the world dream about Porsches they should go ahead and make money and get them. The Juliuses should learn not to take money so seriously. … If a few people like Julius begin to think about opportunism, I'll have accomplished a lot.' It remains doubtful, however, to what extent Julius lastingly changes, if at all. Once his holidays have ended, he returns to his home in suburbia and puts on business attire again – and Paula once again brings the tie that he forgot to his office.

However, what contributes to the melancholic tone of the film is the fact that it does acknowledge a desire for escaping the constraints of bourgeois lifestyles and hegemonic masculinity. While living in the shared flat, Julius visibly loosens up to an extent for which his strategic adoption of a disguise cannot account. He gradually takes on his rival's (formerly) careless appearance and obviously borrows from his wardrobe. In an early scene, he tricks Stefan into putting on a paper hat and stepping onto a table, telling him that this was part of the manager test he himself had taken – only to finally inform his rival that a manager would never do such a thing. Yet Julius is shown wearing a paper hat and standing on a table while painting the walls. When he leaves the shared flat, we see him in medium close-up, taking a last look at the place, and we hear him sadly sigh. Since the passing of time is another theme of *Men*, expressed by Eric Burdon & The Animals' song 'When I Was Young' played twice as diegetic music, we might read the narrative as implying that experiments in alternative life-styles and masculinities inevitably have to be discarded like other follies of youth.

Yet one last irony seems to have escaped Dörrie as well as critics like Witte. In post-modern capitalism, above all in such fields as advertising and packaging design, opportunism has come to be regarded ambivalently, whereas certain differences are perceived as reposi-tories of flexibility and creativity. Julius hints at this when he tells Stefan, in preparation for the job interview, that he must not defer to others in his graphic design work, because that would be fatal in his profession. Furthermore, Julius learns that his employer has decided to make Stefan his co-worker, because Julius has become 'a bit inflexible' lately. The superior who tells Julius the bad news in a way incorporates the new times: on the surface, his appearance is conservative – but when the camera pans behind him it calls our attention to a pony tail held together by a fancy slide.

Holger Römers

REFERENCES

Kassouf, S. (1997) 'Versteckspiele: Eine *Queer*lektüre von Doris Dörries *Männer*', in W. Erhart and B. Herrmann (eds) *Wann ist der Mann ein Mann? Zur Geschichte der Männlichkeit.* Stuttgart and Weimar: Metzler, 310–19.

Koch, G., D. Kuhlbrodt, K. Witte and H. Schlüpmann (1986) 'Bei neuestem Licht besehen', *Frauen und Film*, 41, December, 84–9.

LOLA RENNT RUN, LOLA, RUN

TOM TYKWER, WEST GERMANY, 1998

Tom Tykwer's third feature film *Lola rennt* (*Run, Lola, Run*) released on 20 August 1998, proved extremely popular with German audiences; it has also become a landmark film for the international standing and market presence of German cinema abroad. Even in the USA, where German films rarely have mass appeal, it was well received by art-house audiences in New York, Los Angeles and other cities, and the film won the Audience Award at the 1999 Sundance Film Festival and was Best Foreign Film at the 2000 Independent Spirit Awards. Interestingly, it gained less public attention in France, Italy and Britain. Nearly two decades after the box-office success of Wolfgang Petersen's *Das Boot* (*The Boat*, 1981), *Run, Lola, Run* seemed to belong to that rare type of film that breaks new ground in the search for alternative principles of narrative construction.

When *Run, Lola, Run* first appeared on screens, the 20-minute-race was immediately noted for its innovation and originality, its use of pulsating music and the time-loop concept, with its particularly comic elements. Its game-like structure and editing style impressed many. Tykwer successfully joined diverse formal devices from film history and blended them into a single production with a 'running time' of only 77 minutes. US film critic Roger Ebert fittingly summarised: 'It's an exercise in kinetic energy, a film of non-stop motion and visual invention.' The film's overall theme formed in Tykwer's mind well before he started working on the shooting script: he visualised the energy of a human body in motion. In an interview, Tykwer stated that 'a film about the possibilities of life clearly had to be a film about the possibilities of cinema as well'. Thus, numerous images of a young woman frantically running – filmed in lateral tracking shots, in varying distances and angles – created a basic pattern for the *mise-en-scène* and mobile framing.

These stylistic devices, at times used excessively, are not subordinated to the narrative throughout, but foreground the experience of time; they direct the audience's attention to the temporal possibilities of editing. The aesthetic quality of the cinematic parameters is at least equal to their function in conveying information; this distinct approach to film form was widely regarded as a 'closed loop of style'. Yet critics also pointed to the 'essentially empty nature of the exercise'. In March 1999, Janet Maslin wrote in the *New York Times*: 'It's a furi-ously kinetic display of pyrotechnics from the director Tom Tykwer, who fuses lightning-fast visual tricks, tirelessly shifting styles and the arbitrary possibilities of interactive storytelling into the best-case scenario for a cinematic video game.'

The post-production of the film took the director and his small team several months. They did not transcend the constraints of television co-productions, but rather demonstrated what is possible within this system. The final form of the film was created in the editing room, including the addition of a soundtrack that reinforces a mostly non-diegetic aural landscape. French editor Mathilde Bonnefoy created a pronounced cinematic rhythm; according to David Bordwell, *Run, Lola, Run* has an average shot-length of 2.7 seconds. Furthermore, he notes a significant change in the film's tempo: 'The first version of the three-part story is extremely fast with an average shot length of 2.2 seconds. In the second version, the shot duration was roughly the same at 2.6 seconds on average. However, in the third part of the film, the shots had an average length of more than 4 seconds. The editing slows down particularly in this last segment.'

A viewer seeking to understand the underlying premise of *Run, Lola, Run* might regard it as a surrealistic film – or as a story determined by the strict rules of a computer game. Lola (Franka Potente) is confronted with the near impossible task of finding 100,000 German Marks within twenty minutes for her boyfriend Manni (Moritz Bleibtreu), but also gets the chance to repeat her attempt twice. Making a storyline that has the protagonist repeatedly cover the same ground and brief stretch of time both understandable and engaging was quite an unlikely and indeed daring approach for a German film. It involves a discontinuous editing style that repeatedly restarts the line of action. After the audience has followed Lola through the streets of central Berlin, there is a series of shots of a red telephone receiver flying through the air and noisily slamming down. The plot of the film is not governed by realism or ration-ality – Lola is killed by a police bullet in the first segment, which is not marked as a flashback – and therefore bears more resemblance to experimental cinema than science-fiction, because no explanation is given.

The mechanics of the plot are organised around the people Lola encounters on the streets. At several points, pedestrians, cyclists and vehicles appear more or less at random, and Lola has to pass them, jump over them or ignore them. Thus, other characters and objects function as obstacles on her racetrack, some intentionally, others not – but in any case: the more spectacular, the better.

Run, Lola, Run is comprised of five parts: the opening credits, an exposition (a phone conversation between Lola and Manni) and the three runs, two of them ending with a sequence of the lovers' pillow talk that simultaneously serves as a well-placed interlude. In the short epilogue, the couple walks away with the money from the casino in a plastic bag. The main purpose of Lola's first run to Manni is to introduce certain places, characters and narrative relations, which reappear in numerous variants until she escapes from the time trap. As Benjamin West notes, 'in fact, an analysis of strictly the outward appearance of [*Run, Lola, Run*] becomes unavoidably redundant, for the film's myriad external features that evoke the sensation of a video game result from a significantly smaller number of internal features'. For Lola, minor details are of existential significance, for example, whether she runs into the woman with the baby stroller and thereby loses precious time, or is able to avoid the collision. Whereas the three versions of the main part appear to consist of contingent events linked to each other, the first four minutes of the film confirm the impression that these functionally equivalent scenarios can be identified as parts of an overarching narrative system with fixed elements. Tom Whalen remarks: 'Each contact effects changes in all that follow (like the "run" of the stacked dominoes falling that we see on Lola's TV when she is talking to Manni on the phone in the narrative's opening), but the points of (present or absent) contact … never change.'

After setting a deadline for the action and with it a sense of narrative drive, the film leads the viewer through three widely different and mutually exclusive narrative timelines. Although Lola's vibrating energy is channelled in a certain direction, the plot with its ordering of details, events and outcomes changes unpredictably. Even the smallest incidents have unusual effects. As Christine Haase states: 'The film thus divests Lola's running of narrative meaning and undermines the classical assumption of "principal causal agency" as resting with the character, because the causal relations between Lola's actions and the outcome of the episodes are tenuous and unverifiable at best.'

As if the film were able to reflect its own construction, the plot returns to the starting point in the apartment on the Albrechtstrasse, restarts Lola's rescue attempt a second time and revises the story of the failed grocery store robbery Manni just committed. The second round is not only the complete opposite of the first one; it is its continuation by other means. Lola, now a bank robber, is not arrested by the police, but instead removed from the danger zone. Manni, the small-time crook, is run over and killed by an ambulance as his girlfriend looks on in horror. In the third section, by contrast, Manni no longer needs help, but takes the initiative himself by chasing down the bum who took the bag of money on the subway.

In spite of its strange plot and spatially discontinuous editing, *Run, Lola, Run* does not completely ignore the cause/effect conventions of classical cinema, but it reworks them. While systematically deconstructing linearity at the level of the film as a whole, the individual strands of the middle section develop in linear temporal progression. It is significant how little control the energetic and agile Lola has over the chain of events and how limited her range of knowledge is. Haase notes that the opportunities she sees to replace the money are defined by genre: 'The extremely tight deadline propels the film forward, and the cutting to clocks and watches happens with such frequency that it is difficult not to see it as an ironic quote of the traditional "measuring of a deadline" in action films.'

Such an overall serial design only works if the principle of similarity and repetition is maintained in spite of the individual cinematographic qualities of the shots. Conversely, in order to heighten the breathless pace of the film and to indicate the passage of time, certain frames are repeated, but with different durations, sound effects, vantage points, and so on. As West comments: 'That is, although the episodes generally share the same story time and space, different points of view allow them to vary dramatically in their trajectories through that space, to dramatic effect.'

One may even assume that the non-narrative, abstract relations between the different narrative units are the actual basis of the film's formal strategy. The mutual correspondences between the three runs are not only plot-driven but based on a much more far-reaching stylistic system. Like Lola, a receptive audience increases its knowledge of the film's diegetic universe after each run, by recognising the constant interplay between the elements of her environment.

The complex opening credits introduce flame-haired Lola as a cartoon version of herself and display a variety of genre conventions, media formats and camera techniques. They establish some of the cinematic codes that compete for the audience's attention in their construction of analogies and contrasts. The opening sequence places the film into the context of pop art. With its multitude of highly disparate elements, it implies a triumph of visual culture over literary culture, which is represented by a quotation from T. S. Eliot's 1942 poem 'Little Gidding': 'We shall not cease from exploration / And the end of all our exploring / Will be to arrive where we started / And know the place for the first time.'

A clock, ticking loudly and with its hands moving forward far too quickly, is presented right at the beginning, outside the spatial and temporal framework of the narrative. Richard Falcon notes that *Run, Lola, Run* 'starts with a stylish sequence picking faces out of a crowd, which later coalesce to form the title. […] The voice-over suggests a copywriter's search for the meaning of life … but also offers us the answer courtesy of a comically gnomic quotation of Sepp Herberger, the legendary football coach who took [West] Germany to victory in the 1954 World Cup: "The ball is round, the game lasts 90 minutes … everything else is theory".

In the section immediately following, the viewer sees 'cartoon Lola' from behind, running along a long blue and black tunnel. She is startled by bats, fights with cobwebs and alarm systems, and sprints through three clock dials. The walls of the tunnel are covered with pointed teeth and clocks. On her way, she shatters the letters of the opening credits that are arranged in a semicircle around her, emphasised by a clanging sound. A pendulum swings menacingly. At the end of the tunnel she is sucked into a vortex. The electronic music keeps time with the rhythm of her steps. The most striking visual aspect is the forward motion through the tunnel, accentuated by the narrow space of the corridor. Next come portraits of the characters, as photographs against a dark backdrop. Like police mug shots, their faces are shown from all sides, accompanied by the clicking of cameras and flickering flashlights. The names of the actors are inserted with a crashing sound effect.

The narrative begins with an aerial shot of Berlin. The slam camera drops from a great height somewhere into the city, lands in the courtyard of an apartment building and speeds into a window on the top floor, along a corridor and into Lola's room. During the phone conversation – Manni's cry for help – memories of past events are condensed into flashbacks in black and white. By means of abrupt cuts and soft-edged wipes, the events leading to the loss of the drug money are strikingly illustrated beyond the words of the dialogue. A clichéd motif appears in the first flash forward: the future life of a minor character is depicted in cinematic shorthand as a series of postcards and photographs speeding past. For the precarious decision Lola has to make after the phone call, the film also uses a visual equivalent: a rapid succession of single-frame shots suggests her thoughts and feelings. As Whalen points out: 'Lola herself, long before we enter the casino, seems to be in the middle of a wheel when she turns round and round as the faces of people she considers asking for the DM 100,000 appear before her, among them her father, who shakes his head "No", and an animated figure (later we'll recognize him as the live-action croupier [Klaus Müller] in the casino), who says, "*Rien ne va plus*".'

The scenes of Lola's father and Jutta Hansen inside the bank office, shot on digital video with a wobbly camera, slow down the visual flow. 'The three versions of the intimate conversation between Lola's father … and his mistress, a colleague of his, could belong to a different film', notes Haase; 'they are shot on grainy video and partly filmed with a handheld camera, which gives them a Super-8 home movie quality. A quiet mood is created by the close-framed, fairly static composition of the scenes and their washed-out colors, intimate close-ups, and halting shots, which appear twice as slow in comparison to the hyperkinetic environment from which these scenarios emerged.' Video images transferred to film are used in sequences where Lola is absent, such as those of her father and his mistress and of the homeless man buying the bike at the take-away.

The scenes of Lola's and Manni's pillow talk, summing up the couple's relationship in a witty 'what-if' dialogue are shot in fairly static takes, but coloured red. They are joined to the following runs by graphic matches. Drawing inspiration from Stanley Kubrick's *2001: A Space Odyssey* (1968), Tykwer combines various levels of space and time through the corresponding motion of falling objects before and after the cut.

Viewers will recognise an artificial construction that does not simply aim to reproduce Lola's run to the bank and the meeting point with Manni, but also produces visual and auditory rhythms for an overall sense of movement. Thus, Hans Schifferle's analogy of a 'clockwork with visible mechanics' is hardly sufficient. Lola's strength and drive is not only displayed in many shots through physical performance; it is intensified in highly rhythmic sequences by means of an extremely mobile camera and various visual effects. Bordwell concludes that 'it seems that this film wants to try out all available cinematic techniques, similar to the French *nouvelle vague* films from the early 1960s'. Tykwer sometimes uses types of framing and editing devices such as the jump cut, which he adopts from directors like Jean-Luc Godard and which were considered radical in their time.

The variety of camera distances, camera angles and levels of framing is striking, and cameraman Frank Griebe was clearly given much freedom; like an active agent, the camera can be everywhere and film Lola from nearly every point in space. Whereas the mobile camera usually adjusts to the protagonist's movement, supervising and anticipating Lola, it can also move independently of her, as Hans-Dieter Seidel observes: 'Even when the camera is not next to the runner, it stays on her heels, lets her run diagonally across the screen, follows her from high above or chases after her.' Tykwer's films often contain camera movements that liberate themselves from the protagonists, travelling in any direction and thus changing their orientation. An example is the distinctive and very smooth single-take that opens Lola's three runs. In the corridor of the apartment, the Steadicam first moves along with Lola, showing her flight from her room to the door. Then it suddenly turns off into the adjoining living room to the right. There it focuses on Lola's mother in an armchair, glides towards her and circles around her, before zooming-in on the image on television. When the camera takes up Lola's running steps outside the building in the front garden, it cranes down from a high view to a lower position, until Lola seems to actually collide with it at the garden gate.

The calculated, colourful appearance designed for Lola combines her unmistakable spiky hairstyle with an outfit that consists of a light blue tank top, green checked trousers and heavy black boots. Viewers catch glimpses of tattoos on her stomach and shoulder. Her look underlines her urban existence and vividly sets her apart from her surroundings. Some commentators, including Roger Ebert, were reminded of a computer game icon: '[the] heroine is like the avatar in a video game – Lara Croft made flesh'. For others, she represents the prototype of an independent girl. Lola is not burdened with doubts and has no desire for introspection. West notes that 'the aspect of realism in Lola's appearance, as well as the multitudinous extreme close-ups of her, emphasise her gestures and facial expressions, and thus lend her distinct emotional identity, in the absence of extensive background character information.' Lola's willingness to act on impulse becomes apparent not only in her running but also in her piercing screams, which, although repeated three times, always sound like an exclamation of surprise. Her voice is also a physical force: when Lola decides to put all her money on the number 20 in the casino, her high-pitched scream not only shatters glass (like Oskar Matzerath's in *Die Blechtrommel* [*The Tin Drum*, 1979]), but also stops the movement of the roulette ball at the right moment.

The playing field of Tykwer's protagonist is Berlin. However, the city is reduced to only a few views, and its historic buildings, squares, bridges, streets and construction sites are transformed into an imaginary, constricting, almost uninhabited urban space. When one calculates the distances Lola has to run, it becomes obvious that her journey is fictitious, as Haase points out: 'Accompanied by the hypnotic sounds of techno, Lola's run leads her through an urban cityscape connected only by editing, since no human being could traverse the vast distances between the depicted (East and West) Berlin locations in twenty minutes.'

How does *Run, Lola, Run* relate to film history? Falcon reminds us that 'Tykwer was a Berlin repertory cinema programmer and made television documentaries on Lars von Trier, Peter Greenaway and Wim Wenders among others', so he clearly approached this project as a well-versed cinephile. The film itself could be classified as describing a form of urban mobility that was first explored in the 1920s by Walter Ruttmann's *Berlin – Die Sinfonie der Großstadt* (*Berlin – Symphony of a Big City*, 1927); *Run, Lola, Run* also invites comparison with Wenders'

short film *Same Player Shoots Again* (1967). Wenders similarly said that he wanted to set up a gangster film like a game of pinball; his film centres on a shot of several minutes in length that shows a man carrying a machine gun, framing him only from the feet up to the chest, thus divesting him of his individuality. This shot is repeated five times, each time coloured differently. The interest of the shot comes from the self-conscious use of technique and style. A link between the two films is especially noticeable in the short opening sequence that shows an abandoned room and an empty phone booth. As Whalen suggests, 'The first shot recalls the television in Lola's mother's room at the beginning of each of the three "rounds" ... though what is playing on the television is an animated Lola running outside the door, and as the camera moves into the television, the frame becomes all animation.' Furthermore, both shots are characterised by a simple yet mysterious composition of objects; 'The second shot of the Wenders film ... is directly referenced by Tykwer whenever we see Manni in or leaving the phone booth.'

Watching Lola run across the Oberbaum Bridge, with its distinctive neo-gothic arches, allows viewers to detect a theme in the seemingly unmotivated editing. Tykwer and Griebe carefully constructed the movement's relation to the camera. They photographed and edited it in distinctly cinematic terms, turning Lola's athleticism and physicality into a spectacle. Parallel shots in real-time are alternated with slow-motion shots from the front, so that a contradictory perception is created. The expressive energy of movement is captured, not just mimetically, but as an abstraction. This sequence of the first run offers moments of pure visual stimulation. Tykwer's film takes up experimental techniques from the history of cinema, but is no longer involved in the practices of the avant-garde movement of the 1960s and 1970s. This is partly due to the mode of production within a commercial system, but what sets *Run, Lola, Run* apart most is its use of non-diegetic music and an acoustic dramaturgy that influences Tykwer's visual language. What makes his approach so interesting is his attempt to bridge the gap between cinematic experiment and mainstream storytelling. Even the closing credits playfully break with convention: they roll from top to bottom in reverse order, while 'The End' moves from right to left across the screen.

Thus, the style of *Run, Lola, Run* cannot be adequately explained as a reference to computer games or as a homage to the Hollywood action film. Instead, it represents a distant echo of a specific paradigm of German cinema – and a gesture of turning away from it. The change in the approach to narrative cinema among young German filmmakers whose careers began after the fall of the Berlin Wall, even though they do not form a unified group with a common critical or theoretical position, can be described as a rejection of the 'cinema of experience' and a (re)turn to the 'experience of cinema', but in a new form. Thus, this generation of filmmakers is actively distancing itself from its predecessors of the New German Cinema, i.e. directors such as Wim Wenders, Rainer Werner Fassbinder and Volker Schlöndorff. *Run, Lola, Run*, as Thomas Elsaesser puts it, is 'experience of cinema' – 'cinema as a refuge from self-consciousness and self-awareness, the search for a kind of post-ideological space, attracting spectators to an experience of "pure being as pure seeing"' – albeit in a modified, positive sense. Tom Tykwer proved that aesthetic innovation *can* be popular.

Sabine Gottgetreu

REFERENCES

Bordwell, D. (2001) *Visual Style in Cinema: Vier Kapitel Filmgeschichte.* Frankfurt am Main: Verlag der Autoren.

Ebert, R. (1999) '*Run Lola Run*', *Chicago Sun-Times* (2 July). On-line. Available HTTP: http://www. rogerebert.suntimes.com.

Elsaesser, T. (1989) *New German Cinema: A History.* London: British Film Institute.

Falcon, R. (1999) '*Run Lola Run / Lola rennt*', *Sight and Sound*, 9, 11, 52.

Haase, C. (2003) 'You Can Run, but You Can't Hide: Transcultural Filmmaking in *Run Lola Run* (1998)', in R. Halle and M. McCarthy (eds) *Light Motives: German Popular Film in Perspective.* Detroit, IL: Wayne State University Press, 395–415.

Maslin, J. (1999) '*Run Lola Run*: A Dangerous Game With Several Endings', *The New York Times* (26 March). On-line. Available HTTP: http://www. nytimes.com/library/film/032699lola-film-review.html.

Schifferle, H. (1998) '*Lola rennt*', *epd Film*, 8, August, 36.

Seidel, H.-D. (1998) 'Die Zeit und der Flimmer', *Frankfurter Allgemeine Zeitung*, 20 August, 31.

Tykwer, T. (1998) '"Ich will Authentizität und Leidenschaft". Ein Gespräch mit Film-Regisseur Tom Tykwer von Rüdiger Suchsland', *Junge Welt*, 24 August. On-line. Available HTTP: http://www.jungewelt.de/archiv.

West, B. (2000) 'The Cinematic Video Game *Lola Rennt*'. On-line. Available HTTP: http://www.students.cec.wustl.edu/~bmw3/thesis/Honors_Thesis_Lola_Rennt-Title.html (3 June 2005).

Whalen, T. (2000) '*Run Lola Run*', *Film Quarterly*, 53, 3, 33–40.

GOOD BYE, LENIN!

23

WOLFGANG BECKER, GERMANY, 2003

In *Good Bye, Lenin!* (2003), on the eve of the celebrations marking the 40th anniversary of the founding of the GDR, Alex Kerner finds himself caught up in an anti-government demonstration. As the protestors are brutally set upon by the state police, Alex's mother, Christiane (an idealistic socialist committed to the GDR) passes by and is so horrified by what she sees that she collapses, falls into a coma and is taken to hospital. Although she recovers, Alex is convinced that she will be unable to stand the shock of finding out that – during the time she was unconscious – the GDR has ceased to exist. Accordingly he hatches an elaborate plan. With the help of his sister, Ariane, his Russian girlfriend, Lara, and his colleague from the West, Denis, he restores the family flat to the way it looked in GDR times in order to deceive his bed-ridden mother into believing that nothing has changed. But whilst creating an illusion of the GDR within the flat itself is one thing, preventing the rapidly changing world outside from intruding on his scheme proves to be quite another. Just as Alex is on the point of coming clean, the tables are turned, when Alex's mother reveals that – contrary to what he and his sister had always believed – it was not their father's philandering that caused their parents to split up, but their mother's reluctance to risk having her children taken away from her by applying for an exit-visa to leave the GDR and join her husband (who was, at the time, attending a conference in West Berlin). With the truth now out in the open, Christiane suffers a relapse. When it becomes clear that she has not long to live, Alex travels to West Berlin and succeeds in persuading his father to visit his mother one last time in hospital. Unwilling to continue with the charade any longer – and unaware that Lara has, in any case, told his mother everything – Alex avails himself of Denis's video-editing skills one last time and produces a 'news bulletin' that celebrates not only the triumph of socialism, but also the removal of the Berlin Wall so as to allow those disillusioned with their lives in the Federal Republic to cross over into the GDR. Three days after the firework display to mark (the real!) German Reunification, Alex's mother passes away, and her ashes are scattered across East and West.

Few films can have caught the public's imagination in Germany quite so powerfully as Wolfgang Becker's *Good Bye, Lenin!* when it was premiered on 9 February 2003 at the Berlin

Film Festival. Produced by X-Filme Creative Pool – the production company best known outside of Germany for Tom Tykwer's hit *Lola rennt* (*Run, Lola, Run*, 1998) – it immediately attracted huge audiences. Just three months after the film's premiere more than 5 million people in Germany had seen the film. Indeed it was regarded as such an important contribution to the public debate on post-unification Germany that a special screening was organised for members of the German parliament, and the German government's *Bundeszentrale für politische Bildung* produced an educational booklet to accompany the film.

Good Bye, Lenin! is perhaps the most successful of a series of comedies focusing on life in the former GDR and the impact of German reunification that began to emerge towards the end of the 1990s and which included Leander Haußmann's *Sonnenallee* (*Sun Alley*, 1999) and Sebastian Peterson's *Helden wie wir* (*Heroes Like Us*, 1999). Prior to this, films addressing such issues had tended to fall into one of two categories. At one end of the spectrum, there were films like Jörg Foth's *Letztes aus der DaDaeR* (1990), Egon Günther's *Stein* (1991) and Herwig Kipping's *Das Land hinter dem Regenbogen* (1992). Although fascinating in their own right, these films – all of them directed by individuals with their roots in DEFA, the GDR's state-owned production studio – made little impact, partly because of the rapid pace of political developments, and partly because of the films' oblique and often highly complex metaphorical language. At the other end, the early 1990s also saw the production of a wave of German comedies based on crude caricatures of *Ossis* (a disparaging term used by citizens from the Federal Republic to refer to those from the former GDR). Whilst these lightweight and unashamedly commercial films – typified by Peter Timm's *Go, Trabi, Go* (1991) and its sequel, *Go, Trabi, Go 2: Das war der wilde Osten* (1992) directed by Reinhard Klooss and Wolfgang Büld – can hardly be regarded as serious contributions to the discourse of post-unification Germany, they nonetheless anticipated the shift towards the use of humour and irony in subsequent approaches to the contentious topic of German/German relations. As the 1990s drew to a close and 3 October 1990 – the date of German Reunification – began to recede into the distance, a new generation of filmmakers and writers emerged who possessed the confidence to adopt an often wickedly ironic approach to the topic of post-unification Germany. However, as the critical reception of *Sonnenallee* – a collaboration involving the (West German) director Leander Haußmann and the (East German) writer Thomas Brussig – the use of humour in dealing with the GDR and its past still touched many raw nerves. Nonetheless, in explaining the basic premise behind *Sonnenallee* – 'I grew up in the GDR. That doesn't make the GDR any better. But I still have fond memories of that childhood' – the film's scriptwriter, Thomas Brussig, was to establish an agenda that Becker would take to its logical conclusion in *Good Bye, Lenin!* some four years later.

Good Bye, Lenin! is, as its title suggests, a film about taking one's leave of the past. But it is also a film about memory and identity – and, in particular, what it means to be East German in a world in which the GDR no longer exists. As such the film represents an important contribution to contemporary debates about *Ostalgie*, a term used to refer to a nostalgic, sentimental view of the GDR past. But in stark contrast to the plethora of programmes on German television focusing on life in the former GDR – typified by RTL's *Die DDR Show* – *Good Bye, Lenin!* strives for a much more differentiated understanding of the concept of *Ostalgie*, whilst at the same time highlighting the importance of memories (both individual and collective) in creating a new sense of German identity.

Far from presenting a conventional critique of life in the GDR, Becker focuses on family relationships – a topic he had explored in his previous film *Das Leben ist eine Baustelle* (*Life Is All You Get*, 1997) – and, in particular, on the bond between Alex, the film's youthful protagonist, and his mother, Christiane. As Bernd Lichtenberg, the Cologne-born author of the screenplay commented: 'I was more concerned with writing a film about a close-knit family where history bursts in like an unexpected guest.' For Alex, the implications of the period leading up to German reunification have less to do with history and the socio-economics of life in a united Germany than with his belief that his mother should be spared the trauma of discovering that the GDR no longer exists. By focusing on the love between mother and son, and showing how each constructs a web of lies to protect the other, the film presents the viewer with a theme that, on the surface at least, would appear to transcend the ideological divide between the two German states. As Lichtenberg continued: 'I'm sure that families where people deceive each other and where lies obscure the truth are things you come across in both East and West.' At the same time, however, by setting this 'universal' story within a specifically GDR context, the film simultaneously offers viewers two distinct modes of spectatorship. On the one hand, for non-GDR viewers it 'corrects' the received picture of the GDR by reminding them that family relationships in the East were not fundamentally different to those in the West; on the other, for viewers from the former GDR, the fact that this 'universal love story' is set in the former East presents them with an opportunity to draw on the insider knowledge necessary to decode the numerous references to a specifically GDR way of life, and thereby affirm a sense of their cultural identity as something unique and distinctive.

One of the most striking aspects of *Good Bye, Lenin!* is the way in which the film offers a corrective to images of the GDR as a bleak and unremittingly inhospitable environment. Although, in the mad dash to unification, the whole history of the GDR seemed to have been swept under the carpet in a spirit of collective amnesia, Becker's film goes out of its way to recreate memories of a past to which citizens of the GDR could look back in pride. In part these memories are made up of moments of private intimacy: the memories of Alex's idyllic child-hood captured on the sequence of amateur Super-8 footage with which the film begins. But, as Nick Hodgin notes, these memories of the past soon assume a collective dimension when the film cuts to a television broadcast about the East German cosmonaut, Sigmund Jähn, and we are reminded that the first German in space was not from the Federal Republic, but from the GDR – a triumph of which Alex is justifiably proud and which prompts him to remark that 'on 26 August 1978 we were world class'. Similarly, when Jähn presides over the 'marriage' between the *Sandmann* and his 'Russian bride', Mascha, the film reminds us that the Sandman – the tiny wooden puppet that conquered the hearts and minds of children in both East and West Germany – was not a West German creation, but one of the most successful 'exports' produced by the GDR. As the film unfolds it becomes increasingly clear just how deeply these childhood memories have imprinted themselves on Alex's psychological make-up; for as the posters on his bedroom wall and his continued fascination with space travel underline, Jähn's visionary achievements remain an inspiration throughout his life, while the 'cosmic marriage' between the Sandman and Mascha constitutes the blueprint for his own relationship with Lara, his Russian girlfriend.

Although *Good Bye, Lenin!* sets out to challenge stereotypical notions of life in the GDR, it does not shy away from criticising some of the more unpleasant aspects of the state. As Alex and his sister watch Jähn's exploits in space, their reactions are overshadowed by the presence of the Stasi-men in the background interrogating their mother about her husband. In a similar vein, the hollowness of the regime's rhetoric is exposed when images of a hung-over Alex sitting in front of a propaganda poster attached to a run-down housing-block bearing the message 'Putting people at the heart of a socialist society' are juxtaposed with larger-than-life images of Erich Honecker and Mikhail Gorbachev sitting on the tribune watching the military parade to mark the 40th anniversary of the founding of the GDR. Nonetheless, the inclusion of Alex's cynical voice-over – 'Change was in the air, while the members of the world's last great shooting club paraded outside our home' – reminds the viewer that GDR citizens were just as capable of seeing through the absurdity of the state's extravagant rhetoric as their Western counterparts.

But Alex's irony is not solely confined to the GDR. As his mother lies in a coma, increasingly he narrates the events of 1990 in terms of her socialist discourse, with the result that the viewer is confronted with a highly amusing account of German unification from a Marxist perspective that exposes the reality behind the West's promise of freedom and opportunity. Here too, the film operates through a juxtaposition of word and image; for like the jar of 'Russian gherkins' he picks up only to be told 'they're from Holland', the promise of 'freedom' extolled by the West turns out to be equally illusory. And when he refers to the 'first free elections' in the GDR's history, the transition from shouts of 'Helmut!' to cries of 'D-Mark!' act as an ironic commentary on events. However, at times the criticism is less muted; each time he visits the local hospital to check on his mother's progress, he finds that yet another GDR-trained doctor has been lured to the West by the prospect of more money. And when he goes to the bank to convert his mother's savings into the new currency only to be told that the deadline has already elapsed, the viewer is treated to an example of German bureaucracy at its worst.

Set against such negative images, however, is the genuine friendship that develops between Alex and Denis, his (Western) colleague at X-TV, the satellite-TV company where they both work. By depicting Denis as a loyal friend who comes to Alex's rescue on numerous occasions, the film challenges stereotypical notions of West Germans as arrogant and exploitative. When Alex's mother wants to watch the news, it is Denis who makes it possible by unearthing a set of old GDR news bulletins recorded on video. And when he assures Alex that she will never notice that the programmes are a year old, his observation that 'it was always the same old crap!' is not intended as an aggressive put-down of his GDR colleague, but is symptomatic of a healthy scepticism that corresponds to Alex's own views on the relationship between truth and politics and his belief that 'the truth was something that was pretty questionable and could easily be adapted to fit the way my mother saw things'.

Much of the comedy in *Good Bye, Lenin!* stems from the way in which – in a manner not dissimilar to Billy Wilder's classic Cold War comedy *One, Two, Three* (1961) – it launches a critique of the ideological systems in both East and West by playing each off against the other. Throughout the film we laugh at the way in which the characters attempt – with varying degrees of success – to adapt to the sudden transformation of the discursive structures underpinning their lives. But, as the film shows time and again, whilst at a superficial level the two ideological systems may appear to be very different, in each case the underlying rhetoric is essentially the same. Indeed it is precisely for this reason that Ariane has no difficulty exchanging one system for the other. For her, embracing the new ideology involves little more than throwing out her old clothes and dressing up in the new fashions of the free market economy: the striped Burger King uniform she wears at work and the (no less ideologically marked) 'America' T-shirt that she wears at home. The same applies at the level of discourse too: out goes the socialist economy's banal slogan 'Quality supplied by all to all' and in comes Burger King's equally hollow mantra: 'Enjoy your meal and thank you for choosing Burger King'.

Whilst much humour in *Good Bye, Lenin!* is derived from the juxtaposition of two mutually hostile ideologies, Becker's film adopts a more serious tone when it addresses questions of memory and identity. In the course of the film we are presented with a range of different attitudes to the phenomenon of *Ostalgie*. At one end of the scale, there is the complete rejection of everything associated with the East – essentially the stance taken by Alex's sister, Ariane. After the collapse of the GDR, she abandons her studies, takes a menial job with Burger King, and plunges into a new relationship with Rainer, her West German boss. It is she who is the driving force behind what Alex terms the 'Westernisation' of the family home; indeed her reluctance to go along with Alex's elaborate scheme (a reluctance which prompts him to accuse her of wishing their mother were dead) together with her rage when she discovers that their mother has concealed the letters sent by their father from West Berlin, hint at a deep-seated desire on her part to distance herself from everything that reminds her of her GDR past, whilst at the same time embracing a new (non-GDR) identity.

Ariane is, of course, still young and her willingness to turn her back on the past is in part due to the fact that she still has the opportunity to carve out a new identity for herself in the future. But if her attitude represents a rejection of *Ostalgie* in any form, the attitude of the elderly residents in the block of flats where Alex lives represents the very opposite, namely a desire to cling to an idealised image of the GDR and to reject everything associated with the Federal Republic. For Herr Mehlert, Frau Schäfer and Herr Ganske, there is no realistic prospect of establishing a new identity within a unified Germany; for them unification means the obliteration of their past identity as GDR citizens. Accordingly when Alex tells them that his mother does not even know that the Berlin Wall is no more, Herr Mehlert remarks 'lucky her'. For him and his co-residents, the opportunity to play a part in Alex's fictional world is, quite literally, an opportunity to be transported back into a past they wish they had never left behind, a past in which their identity as GDR citizens had a legitimate basis; and it is this feeling that is underlined by Frau Schäfer's 'ostalgic' remark: 'It's so nice talking with your mother. It feels like the old days.'

Her remark underlines the pivotal role played by Alex's mother in the film's narrative structure as a whole. Devoted to her children and adored by all who come into contact with her, Christiane's essential warmth and humanity is underlined by the photographs of her posing dressed up as a mermaid for the 'Neptune Festival' with the children from her class. As such she represents a figure with whom all – regardless of their ideological persuasion – can identify. Nonetheless, it is impossible to ignore the fact that not only is she idealistic and utterly committed to the GDR, she actually represents everything that is positive about socialism, most notably the desire for a better and fairer world. No character in the film more fully embodies the utopian vision of socialism that is articulated towards the end of the film when Alex's stand-in GDR premier announces the opening of the border with the words 'Socialism … means not only dreaming about a better world, but making it happen.' But whilst Christiane is portrayed as passionately committed to socialism, it is a crucial part of her characterisation that at no point in the film is she ever explicitly associated with the party apparatus of the SED (Socialist Unity Party) that was in power in the GDR. As a result, her character provides a link for those viewers who wish to identify with the ideals of socialism *per se* but felt that these ideals had been betrayed by the GDR regime. This, of course, was the position adopted by a number of intellectuals in both East and West who argued that the state should not simply embrace Western capitalism, but be reformed along genuinely socialist lines. Even more importantly, however, in both their characterisation of Christiane and the inspired casting of the East German actress, Katrin Saß, in the role, Becker and his team explicitly address the needs of all those unwilling (or perhaps even unable) to accept that their positive memories of the GDR should simply be consigned to oblivion.

Seen from this angle, the significance of the fictional 'GDR' that Alex creates becomes even clearer. Although to begin with he convinces himself that – like Herr Mehlert, Frau Schäfer and Herr Ganske – his mother will be unable to come to terms with the sudden collapse of the state, it is soon obvious that his project is at least as much bound up with his own needs as it is with hers. Following the 'news bulletin' that he and Denis put together to 'explain' the presence of citizens from the Federal Republic on the streets of East Berlin he observes that 'the GDR I created for my mother increasingly became the one I might have wished for'. That is to say, his fantasy assumes a utopian dimension as he seeks to construct an imaginary version of what a genuinely socialist GDR could have been like and, in the process, creates a monument to the hopes and aspirations of those who, like his mother, pursued an ideal only to be betrayed by the regime itself.

One of the great strengths of *Good Bye, Lenin!* is the way in which it prompts the viewer to reflect on the complex relationship between history, memory and fiction. In particular the film reminds us that the past is never simply given, and that engaging with the past is a process almost always conditioned by the needs of the present. At one level, it is tempting to see a parallel between the fictional 'GDR' that Alex constructs for his mother – 'A country', he concedes, 'that never existed in that form' – and the activities of the SED regime's propagandists; for in both cases an attempt is being made to 'make good' some of the more obvious shortcomings of 'real existing socialism' in the GDR. However there is a clear difference between the motives behind Alex's imaginary socialist utopia and the GDR propagandists' more cynical manipulation of the truth. For just as his mother had lied about the past out of love for her children, so too the fictional 'GDR' he creates is rooted in his love for her. And, as the ending of the film underlines, this love is reciprocated. Ultimately, it is Alex – and not Christiane – who remains trapped in an illusion. When he brings his estranged father to visit his mother in hospital, Lara has already told Christiane about the recent political upheaval; and the bemused look Alex receives from his mother makes it clear to the viewer (though not to him) that she now knows the truth. Nonetheless, as her enthusiastic approval of the final broadcast staged by her son underlines, it is she who seeks to preserve the fiction of her 'ignorance' (and with it her son's happiness). Although Alex may tell himself 'I believe it was a good thing she never discovered the truth. She died happy', the fact is (as Lara knows) that she died happy *despite* knowing the truth.

Good Bye, Lenin! is much more than just a comedy about the conflict of ideology; it is a thoughtful reflection on the need to hold on to memories of the past. Just as Christiane's temporary recovery from her coma provides Alex with an extended opportunity to prepare himself for the eventual trauma of losing his mother, so too the extended stay of execution the GDR enjoys in the family home opens up a discursive space in which to reflect on memories – both positive and negative – of the past. At the same time, the film also hints at the possibility of a new concept of German identity (and one that would be of an altogether different order to that exemplified by the shouts of 'Deutschland! Deutschland!' as the East Germans 'unite' behind the West German national soccer team). For when Alex goes to visit his father, he spends some moments sitting together with his half-brother and half-sister watching TV. Yet in this intimate domestic scene – in which the children from the West and the young man from the East are momentarily united by their common passion: space travel and the Sandman – Becker's film offers a glimpse of a future in which ideological differences between East and

West might be transcended. For when Alex's half-brother cries out 'Look! The Sandman's an astronaut today!', Alex's reply – 'Where I come from, we say "cosmonaut"!' – looks forward to a world in which cultural difference might be transcended and yet done so in a way that would preserve a unique sense of one's own identity and origins.

Seán Allan

REFERENCES

Hodgin, N. (2004) 'Berlin Is in Germany and *Good Bye, Lenin!*: Taking Leave of the GDR?', *Debatte*, 12, 1, 25–45.

Maischberger, S. (1999) '*Sonnenallee* – Eine Mauerkomödie: Interview mit Leander Haußmann und Thomas Brussig', in L. Haußmann (ed.) *Sonnenallee: Das Buch zum Farbfilm*. Berlin: Quadriga, 8–24.

DAS WUNDER VON BERN THE MIRACLE OF BERN

24

SÖNKE WORTMANN, GERMANY, 2003

Das Wunder von Bern (*The Miracle of Bern*, 2003) unfolds around what is probably the most famous game in German football history: the 3-2 victory by the German national team against Hungary, in the final of the 1954 World Cup at Bern's Wankdorfstadion on 4 July. For many cultural historians, this event marked the end of the immediate postwar era and the beginning of the so-called *Wirtschaftswunder* ('economic miracle'). As director Sönke Wortmann quotes historian Joachim Fest on the commentary track to the DVD, the Federal Republic has three 'imaginary founding fathers': Konrad Adenauer, the first chancellor, as political father; Ludwig Erhard, the mastermind behind the swift economic recovery, as economic father; and Fritz Walter, the captain of the 1954 football team, as moral father. The film overlays and entangles the private and the public in three intersecting stories, which climax during that final. With three narratives, the film dramatises the (alleged) shift from a militarily and morally defeated nation at the end of World War II, to a (symbolically) reborn country, learning the values, pleasures and obligations of a democratic society. As will be shown, in its treatment of the historical past, the film self-reflectively brings to the fore its own place in media history.

The film, released on 16 October 2003, cost an estimated 7.5 million Euros, which was an unusually large budget for a German production. Nonetheless, it recouped its investment when it attracted more than 3.2 million spectators domestically. It had been a pet project of director Wortmann's since his film school days. An accomplished football player, Wortmann had given up a (potential) career in football for filmmaking. Two aspects of casting are particularly notable. Firstly, actors were cast for their football skills rather than their acting abilities. Whereas in most football films the on-pitch action is heavily edited, *The Miracle of Bern* takes into account that most spectators (at least in Germany) qualify as 'experts', through the intense media coverage of football, particularly on television. Secondly, actors were chosen who bore a similarity to the actual players of the 1954 team, some of whom (the Walter brothers, Helmut Rahn) are still recognised by many Germans.

Wortmann is a central figure of the commercial revival of German cinema in the 1990s, having directed comedies such as *Kleine Haie* (*Acting Out*, 1992), *Der bewegte Mann* (*Maybe*

... *Maybe Not*, 1994), *Das Superweib* (*The Super-Wife*, 1995) and *Der Campus* (*Campus*, 1997). As Michael Wedel pointed out, Wortmann's films were successful at the box office, but critically scolded: 'The mordant satirical potential of such subjects ... points towards Wortmann's commercial instincts, but his failure to live up to them also towards his limits as a director.' Either hailed as a supreme expression of popular cinema that addressed serious issues or criticised as a banal and superficial interweaving of the private and the public, *The Miracle of Bern* divided its audience as previous Wortmann films had.

The Miracle of Bern is unusually frank in announcing the cultural work it wants to undertake. Its tag line – 'Jedes Kind braucht einen Vater, jeder Mensch braucht einen Traum, jedes Land braucht eine Legende' – proposes the thematic fields of family relations ('every child needs a father'), of individual psychic fantasies ('every human being needs a dream') and of national identity ('every country needs a legend'). The formulation already hints at the fabricated nature of the basic and important categories that the film addresses. It is thus a triple lack that sets the film in motion and keeps it going throughout. The film does not represent a situation in which children have fathers, people have dreams and countries have legends – it wants to achieve this stability. The situation of the immediate postwar years in Germany is thus constructed as a situation in which fathers, personal dreams and national legends are largely absent. It is this 'need' the film works towards establishing and fulfilling at the same time.

The family is present in at least three different configurations in the film. Most obviously, the Lubanskis are a family that need to be reaffirmed after the long-term absence of the father, Richard (Peter Lohmeyer), who returns from a POW camp in Russia nine years after the end of World War II. He is caught up in a mentality of giving and receiving orders originating from his past life as soldier and prisoner; the film works toward his transformation to democratic behaviour, characterised by reasonable, free and equal discourse. Secondly, the national team is shown as an all-male family, in which the punishing father transforms into the benevolent father, as national coach Sepp Herberger's (Peter Franke) *éducation democratique* progresses. Herberger's transformation parallels Richard Lubanski's from authoritarian character to democratic leader. Thirdly, young sports journalist Paul Ackermann (Lucas Gregorowicz) and his newly-wed wife Annette (Katharina Wackernagel) stand in for a younger generation of Germans, not personally responsible for or involved in the guilt and traumas of World War II and the Holocaust. Their child, conceived during Germany's symbolic rebirth through the success at the World Cup, personifies the new beginning. All three 'families', individually as well as collectively, need to work through the past in order to be able to face the present and dream about the future. Yet, the past is only schematically alluded to in passing and never explicitly thematised at any length. In all three cases the 'fathers' have to change in order to live up to the new situation, which partner and children are much quicker to grasp.

The Lubanskis are shown as a functioning and harmonious, fatherless family at the beginning of the film. The three children help their mother Christa (Johanna Gastdorf) with running a pub, and they are shown at ease with each other at home. It is the unexpected letter announcing the return of father-husband Richard after eleven years as a Soviet POW that tips this precarious balance, creating a need that the film has not established before. The need is to help this ex-soldier, time-travelling from the Nazi war directly to the *Wirtschaftswunder* of the mid-1950s, reintegrate into society, to be reborn as a democratic subject. This strategy is confirmed in another scene, in which goalkeeper Toni Turek auctions a football signed by all members of the 1954 national team for the benefit of the so-called *Spätheimkehrer* ('late homecomers'). This is one of several instances in which the history of the national team intersects with that of the main characters of the film. The most important overlap of these two stories concerns the youngest son Matthias Lubanski (Louis Klamroth), who turns to left-winger Helmut Rahn (Sascha Göpel) as a surrogate father, carrying his bag and functioning as a lucky charm for the highly talented, yet slovenly genius. When his biological father comes home, the tensions between the real and the 'adopted' father mount. In a strange reversal of narrative and historical fact, the lack of fathers, which has famously been diagnosed in a 1963 study by psychoanalyst Alexander Mitscherlich, becomes an abundance of fathers.

The all-male family of the national team is first introduced via a TV report that the Lubanskis watch in their bar, while mounting their brand new television set. Every player is individually introduced, with mention of his home club, underscoring another important aspect of the film: *The Miracle of Bern* works extensively with the different dialects of the players, locating them regionally. Unlike today's professionals who travel globally, the film (somewhat nostalgically) evokes a time in which team members stood for specific local identities. Thus, the film reinforces the construction of a national imaginary: the rebirth of postwar Germany results from the victory of a troupe from different corners of the new Federal Republic. Conspicuously absent are players from the eastern part of Germany, but the mounting Cold War is alluded to and negotiated in comic asides aimed at Matthias's older brother Bruno (Mirko Lang), who runs away to East Berlin. Players from the Rhineland (Ottmar and Fritz Walter, Horst Eckel), the Ruhr valley (Helmut Rahn, Bernie Kloth), northern Germany (Jupp

Posipal), Franconia (Max Morlock), Bavaria, Hesse and other parts mix and mingle in the sworn group of the 'eleven friends', one of the many proverbial sayings by Herberger. The climactic nature of this unity from disparity is underscored by the final title before the end credits, stating that 'The team of Bern never played together again'.

The symbolic father, Herberger, who had been national coach since 1936, is at first portrayed as a character similar to Richard Lubanski, still caught up in the authoritarian mentality of the Nazi-era. Both learn the hard way that the times have changed – discipline and order are not the most important values anymore. Both Lubanski and Herberger learn to accept the different needs and wishes of the younger generation, thereby becoming role models for their family teams. It is the father who needs to be taught, because he has to adapt to the changing times. In a memorable scene, Herberger, still famous and widely-quoted in Germany for his aphoristic truisms about football – such as 'Der Ball ist rund' ('The ball is round'), 'Ein Spiel dauert neunzig Minuten' ('A game lasts ninety minutes'), 'Das nächste Spiel ist immer das schwerste' ('The next game is always the most difficult one') or 'Nach dem Spiel ist vor dem Spiel' ('After the game is before the game') – receives basic democratic education as well as these phrases from a Swiss cleaning woman, while musing late at night how to punish his 'favourite child' Helmut Rahn. (Interestingly, Tom Tykwer's *Lola rennt* [*Run, Lola, Run*, 1998] opens with a similar montage of Herberger quotes.)

Finally, the young sports journalist Ackermann and his wife Annette stand in for a new, democratic Germany, as well as providing some comic relief from the other two melodramatic family tales. In the beginning, Annette wants to travel to Egypt for their honeymoon, but must abandon the plan when her husband is assigned as a reporter to the world championship in Switzerland. Both receive their share of everyday wisdom: he learns to listen to his wife, who is the only one who can understand Herberger's tactics, while she learns to love football. Ultimately, their bet on the outcome of the final, with the right to name their first-born child as the stake, ties all three plot lines together. It is Annette's cheering 'Deutschland!' that helps captain Fritz Walter not to give up after being down 0-2 early on in the game, and Matthias's presence in the stadium that brings about the victory for Germany, when Rahn recognises his lucky charm amidst the spectators. The older generation, Richard Lubanski and Sepp Herberger, functions as an important catalyst, but in the decisive moment it is the younger generation that takes home the cup: Matthias, Annette and Helmut Rahn, the second-youngest member of the 1954 team. Neither Herberger on the sidelines nor Richard Lubanski outside the stadium is shown during the decisive phase of the match. Logically, Paul's and

Annette's child, conceived during the championship, signals Germany's new openness towards other cultures, as Annette's name 'Dante', possibly a nod to Italy as the most popular foreign destination for German tourists throughout the 1950s and 1960s, replaces Paul's restaurative proposals, 'Rüdiger' and 'Roswitha', typical German names of the 1950s.

Here, as in other instances, the film uses 1954 as a symbolic moment for postwar developments (economic recovery, late homecomers) as well as for the social configuration typically associated with 1968 (as a cultural shorthand): female emancipation, generational conflict and socialism. It is during the final that we also get a glimpse of Matthias's brother in front of a TV set in East Berlin, in a blue FDJ-shirt (*Freie Deutsche Jugend* – the youth organisation of the East German socialist party), cheering for the other, 'wrong' part of Germany. His attraction to American music, open resistance to his father and critical remarks about the Nazi past (he refuses a job because the boss is an old Nazi, he quips that 'the Russian' only kicked Germany's ass after he had been attacked, and he enthusiastically claims that in the socialist East everybody is free and equal) make him a character that is retrospectively often associated with the protest culture of the late 1960s. Similarly, the strong-willed and independent mother, not shying away from an open conflict with her husband, signifies a female self-assertiveness that found its social expression in the 1970s. Lastly, Helmut Rahn has often been seen as a countercultural icon and non-conformist character, who rose to prominence too early and would have fitted much better in the contemporary media-saturated sports arena. He embodies a prototype closer to Günther Netzer or Paul Gascoigne than to Fritz Walter or Toni Turek. Whereas Turek and Walter had already been (modest) football stars under the Nazis, Rahn was too young to have played an active role in fascism. Arguably, he anticipated later developments in professional football; Rahn frequently changed clubs (and even played abroad for a while, at SC Enschede in the Netherlands) at a time when Uwe Seeler was lauded for sticking with his team; Rahn's escapades are legion, and he behaved more like a rock or film star than a sportsman. Therefore, choosing Rahn as the centre of attention (rather than Fritz Walter) shows how the film prefigures and anticipates developments that are associated with today's media culture.

The film opens with children sitting in a tree and waiting for a carrier pigeon, which brings the result of a football game of their home team, *Rot-Weiß Essen*. In postwar and pre-*Wirtschaftswunder* Germany, this archaic 'media practice' is the only way they can learn the score. Rolf Niederer commented on the symbolic significance of this scene: 'The dove – certainly meant as a symbol – comes flying home to the Ruhr Valley, where the heart of

German football beats.' This instance inaugurates a series of scenes in which football games and results are communicated in different 'media formats', never duplicating one another. The first game of the world championship, Germany's 4-1 victory against Turkey, is represented by a newspaper headline; the 3-8 defeat against Hungary in the preliminary round is featured through a TV transmission on the newly acquired set in the Lubanski-pub; and the 7–2 success in the play-off against Turkey is brought to the attention of Matthias, confined to his room for trying to run away, by his friend Carola (Christine Linnemann), who holds up the result on a piece of cardboard opposite Matthias's window. The 2-0 quarter-final victory over Yugoslavia is presented through fragments of the German radio commentary, and the semi-final against Austria is represented by scenes replayed by the children on the playground, along with the Austrian radio commentary. It is only the final itself that is seen as 'unmediated' and thus 'real' within the film's fiction – that is, on the same level with the fictional story. Thus, the mythical status of the final, which eclipsed the rest of the tournament in Germany's public football memory, is underscored by the fact that the games before the final are only present indirectly, as media signs, historical artefacts and traces.

In this mediatisation of the past, *The Miracle of Bern* is a typical historical film of the early twenty-first century: history is seen neither as a Rankean 'wie es eigentlich gewesen ist' ('as it really was'), nor is it a completely fragmented and senseless universe. History is what happens in the media; or rather: history beyond the narrow confines of personal reminiscences cannot be separated from its representation in the media. When we remember an event, we remember the media representation of the event, as most historical sources relating to the twentieth century are 'media texts'. As Thomas Elsaesser points out, history in this sense is where the public (media) and the private ('Where was I when Germany became world champion?') intersect. In this sense, the radio commentary of Herbert Zimmermann, by which the final was mainly remembered in Germany (before Wortmann's film), has been compared to the Zapruder film of the Kennedy assassination: both illustrate a decisive historical break, which has congealed into a media artefact. Furthermore, since the radio commentary is routinely heard on TV with film images from the 'real' final, many people believe that Zimmermann's voice comes from a TV commentary – an irony illustrating the transformations that media images and sounds undergo when employed as public memories. Yet Wortmann's film, rather than critically investigating the highly mediatised nature of the 1954 tournament, celebrates the sheer diversity of formats. (*Good Bye, Lenin!*, 2003, released eight months prior to *The Miracle of Bern*, was both commercially and critically hugely successful, and offered a more profound analysis of the history/media nexus and turned the topic of the fabricated nature of history into its very subject.)

Yet in another sense *The Miracle of Bern* is interesting in the way it utilises and recycles the media past. The film evokes tropes and stereotypes well known from British working-class comedies of the 1990s, such as *The Full Monty* (1997), *Brassed Off* (1997) and *Billy Elliot* (2000), films that have been credited with changing the image of Britain's formerly industrial north. The region was de-industrialised in the wake of Margaret Thatcher's policies in the 1980s and attempted to recast itself as a service and media region in the 1990s, through tourism, modern service industries (including media) and film projects accompanied by attractive legislative measures such as tax breaks. A similar strategy is visible in the German policy of the regional film funding for Northrhine-Westphalia, a region including the most industrialised part of Germany, the Ruhr Valley, with its mining towns, steel and heavy industry – and also traditional football clubs such as Dortmund, Schalke, Bochum and Duisburg. The federal state of Northrhine-Westphalia is attempting to recast itself as a centre of the service industry, or to be more precise, of the media industry. The regional film funding board has the highest budget of all the German regional boards, and its successful director during the 1990s, Dieter Kosslick, became director of the Berlin Film Festival in 2002. *The Miracle of Bern* self-consciously models itself on England's (filmic) north, with its iconography of smoke stacks, soot-covered houses and honest hard-working proletarians, chatting and cursing in their local idiom.

The notion of a historical rebirth is not only played out *within* Wortman's film, it can also be found on an allegorical level, in its position within film history. Wortmann is routinely characterised as the figurehead of the commercial revival of German cinema since the early to mid-1990s. As Eric Rentschler and others have noted, the generation of Wortmann, Detlev Buck, Katja von Garnier, Thomas Jahn and Rainer Kaufmann has been regarded as rebelling in an oedipal fashion against the overt intellectualism, intricate formal artistry and social criticism of the New German Cinema of the 1960s and 1970s. By explicitly addressing the historical juncture of the 1954 World Cup, the film enters into an imaginary dialogue with a key film of the previous era, in which the Bern final played a similarly climactic role: *Die Ehe der Maria Braun* (*The Marriage of Maria Braun*, 1978). Rainer-Werner Fassbinder's account of Germany's shift from war and rubble through the immediate postwar years up to the beginning economic miracle is told through the focus of a female protagonist, played by Hanna Schygulla. Not like Christa Lubanski in *The Miracle of Bern*, Fassbinder's Maria Braun is a strong woman, who learns to stand on her own feet when her husband fails to return from a Soviet prisoner of war camp until many years after the end of World War II. Whereas in *The Miracle of Bern* the family is reunited, Maria's husband Hermann goes to jail taking the blame for the murder of Maria's GI lover, who was in fact killed by Maria. She subsequently enters into a relationship with a rich industrialist, after whose death she finds out that a deal between him and her husband had made her an object of trade between two men, rather than the autonomous woman she had imagined herself to be. While the famous commentary by Herbert Zimmermann is playing on the radio, Maria (accidentally?) kills both herself and her husband, by lighting a match after leaving on the gas of the kitchen stove.

In Fassbinder's version of subject formation, gender politics and national allegory, 'the miracle of Bern' is not a symbolic new beginning, but an overdetermined end (to two lives, to a story of emancipation, to an era, and to the film). As contested as the film's ultimate meaning may be, its outlook, for the protagonist as well as for the nation, to which Maria stands in an allegorical relation, remains doubtful and negative in any case. Quite the opposite can be said of *The Miracle of Bern*: in a long epilogue, the film dramatises the (historically accurate) triumphant tour of the football team across Germany. The final shot depicts their train vanish into a sunset over a bucolic landscape of farmers and peasants, waving to their heroes. Again, a triad of titles ties the personal and the collective, the private and the public, together: 'One year later the last POWs returned home. One year later the economic miracle began. The team of Bern never played together again.' The singularity of this historical event between postwar rubble and economic miracle, between military obedience and oedipal revolt, between lack and affluence is conceived as the moment in which Germany was symbolically reborn on 4 July 1954.

Malte Hagener

REFERENCES

Elsaesser, T. (1996) 'Subject Positions, Speaking Positions: From Holocaust, Our Hitler, and Heimat to Shoah and Schindler's List', in V. Sobchack (ed.) *The Persistence of History*. New York and London: Routledge, 145–83.

____ (2002 [1999]) '"One Train May Be Hiding Another": Private History, Memory and National Identity', in L. Belau and P. Ramadanovic (eds) *Topologies of Trauma: Essays on the Limit of Knowledge and Memory*. New York: Other Press, 61–72.

Mitscherlich, A. (1963) *Auf dem Weg zur vaterlosen Gesellschaft*. Munich: Piper.

Niederer, R. (2003) 'Review Das Wunder von Bern', *Neue Zürcher Zeitung*, 30 October.

Rentschler, E. (2000) 'From New German Cinema to the Post-Wall Cinema of Consensus', in M. Hjort and S. MacKenzie (eds) *Cinema and Nation*. London and New York: Routledge, 260–77.

Wedel, M. (1999) 'Sönke Wortmann', in T. Elsaesser with M. Wedel (eds) *The BFI Companion to German Cinema*. London: British Film Institute, 254–55.

DAS WUNDER VON BERN

FILMOGRAPHY

DES PFARRERS TÖCHTERLEIN 1913
Director: Adolf Gärtner
Production: Oskar Messter for Messter's Projection GmbH (Berlin)
Photography: Carl Froelich
Cast: Henny Porten (Klara), Rudolf Biebrach (the Pastor, Klara's father), Curt Bois (Heinz as a child), Lotte Müller (Klara as a child), Olga Engl, Frida Richard
Running time: 2 reels, 762m

DAS CABINET DES DR. CALIGARI THE CABINET OF DR. CALIGARI 1919
Director: Robert Wiene
Production: Erich Pommer and Rudolf Meinert for Decla-Film-Ges. Holz & Co. (Berlin)
Screenplay: Carl Mayer, Hans Janowitz
Photography: Willy Hameister
Special Effects: Ernst Kunstmann
Production Design: Hermann Warm, Walter Reimann, Walter Röhrig
Costumes: Walter Reimann
Cast: Werner Krauß (Dr Caligari), Conrad Veidt (Cesare), Friedrich Fehér (Francis), Lil Dagover (Jane), Hans Heinrich von Twardowski (Alan), Rudolf Lettinger (Dr Olsen), Ludwig Rex, Elsa Wagner, Henri Peters-Arnolds, Hans Lanser-Rudolff, Rudolf Klein-Rogge
Running time: 6 reels, 1780m

DER LETZTE MANN THE LAST LAUGH 1924
Director: F. W. Murnau
Production: Erich Pommer for Union-Film der Universum-Film AG (UFA) (Berlin)
Screenplay: Carl Mayer
Photography: Karl Freund
Special Effects: Ernst Kunstmann
Production Design: Robert Herlth, Walter Röhrig, Edgar G. Ulmer
Cast: Emil Jannings (hotel porter), Maly Delschaft (his niece), Max W. Hiller (her bridegroom), Emilie Kurz (bridegroom's aunt), Hans Unterkircher (hotel manager), Olaf Storm (young guest), Hermann Vallentin (guest with pot belly), Georg John (night watchman), Emmy Wyda (neighbour), Harald Madsen (musician at wedding), Carl Schenstrøm (musician at wedding), Neumann-Schüler, Erich Schönfelder, O. E. Hasse
Running time: 6 reels, 2315m

METROPOLIS 1926
Director: Fritz Lang
Production: Erich Pommer for Universum-Film AG (UFA) (Berlin)
Screenplay: Thea von Harbou, Fritz Lang (uncredited)
Story: Thea von Harbou
Photography: Günther Rittau, Karl Freund
Special Effects: Eugen Schüfftan, Ernst Kunstmann, Helmar Lerski, Konstantin Tschet

Editing: Fritz Lang

Production Design: Otto Hunte, Erich Kettelhut, Karl Vollbrecht

Costumes: Änne Willkomm

Cast: Brigitte Helm (Maria and the robot), Alfred Abel (Johann 'Joh' Fredersen), Gustav Fröhlich (Freder Fredersen, Johann's son), Rudolf Klein-Rogge (Rotwang, the inventor), Fritz Rasp (the thin man), Theodor Loos (Josaphat/Joseph), Erwin Biswanger (No. 11811), Heinrich George (Grot, the guardian of the Heart Machine), Olaf Storm (Jan), Hanns Leo Reich (Marinus), Heinrich Gotho (Master of Ceremonies), Margarete Lanner (lady in car/woman in Eternal Gardens), Max Dietze (working man), Georg John (working man), Walter Kurt Kühle (working man), Arthur Reinhardt (working man), Erwin Vater (working man), Grete Berger (working woman), Olly Boeheim (working woman), Ellen Frey (working woman), Lisa Gray (working woman), Rosa Liechtenstein (working woman), Helene Weigel (working woman), Beatrice Garga (woman in Eternal Gardens), Annie Hintze (woman in Eternal Gardens), Margarete Lanner (woman in Eternal Gardens), Helen von Münchhofen (woman in Eternal Gardens), Hilde Woitscheff (woman in Eternal Gardens), Fritz Alberti (creative human)

Running time: 12 reels, 4189m (1926), 9 reels, 3241m (1927)

BERLIN – DIE SINFONIE DER GROSSSTADT BERLIN – SYMPHONY OF A BIG CITY 1927

Director: Walther Ruttmann

Production: Deutsche Vereinsfilm AG (Berlin) on behalf of Fox-Europa-Produktion (Berlin)

Screenplay: Walther Ruttmann, Karl Freund, Carl Mayer

Photography: Reimar Kuntze, Robert Baberske, László Schäffer, Karl Freund, Erich Kettelhut, Reimar Kuntze

Editing: Walther Ruttmann

Running time: 5 reels, 1466m

DIE WEISSE HÖLLE VOM PIZ PALÜ THE WHITE HELL OF PITZ PALU 1929

Director: Arnold Fanck, G. W. Pabst

Production: Harry R. Sokal for H. R. Sokal-Film GmbH (Berlin)

Screenplay: Arnold Fanck, Ladislaus Vajda

Photography: Sepp Allgeier, Richard Angst, Hans Schneeberger

Editing: Arnold Fanck, Hermann Haller

Production Design: Ernö Metzner

Cast: Gustav Diessl (Dr. Johannes Krafft), Leni Riefenstahl (Maria Majoni), Ernst Petersen (Hans Brandt), Ernst Udet (as himself), Mizzi Götzel (Maria Krafft), Otto Spring (Christian Klucker), Kurt Gerron (guest at night club)

Running time: 7 reels, 3330m (1929)

DIE DREI VON DER TANKSTELLE THREE FROM THE FILLING STATION 1930

Director: Wilhelm Thiele

Production: Erich Pommer for Universum-Film AG (UFA) (Berlin)

Screenplay: Franz Schulz, Paul Frank

Photography: Franz Planer

Editing: Viktor Gertler

Production Design: Otto Hunte

Sound: Hermann Fritzsching

Music: Werner Richard Heymann

Lyrics: Robert Gilbert

Cast: Lilian Harvey (Lilian Coßmann), Willy Fritsch (Willy), Oskar Karlweis (Kurt), Heinz Rühmann (Hans), Fritz Kampers (Konsul Coßmann), Olga Tschechowa (Edith von Turoff), Kurt Gerron (Dr Kalmus), Gertrud Wolle (Dr Kalmus' secretary), Felix Bressart (Bailiff), Robert Biberti, Erwin Bootz, Erich A. Collin, Roman Cycowski, Harry Frommermann, Ari Leschnikoff (as Comedian Harmonists)

Running time: 2728m, 99 min

OLYMPIA – TEIL 1: FEST DER VÖLKER, TEIL 2: FEST DER SCHÖNHEIT OLYMPIA – PART 1: FESTIVAL OF THE NATIONS,
PART 2: FESTIVAL OF BEAUTY 1938
Director: Leni Riefenstahl
Production: Leni Riefenstahl for Olympia-Film GmbH (Berlin)
Screenplay: Leni Riefenstahl
Photography: Willy Zielke, Hans Ertl, Walter Frentz, Guzzi Lantschner, Kurt Neubert, Hans Scheib, Andor von
Barsy, Wilfried Basse, Josef Dietze, Edmund Epkens, Fritz von Friedl, Hans Karl Gottschalk, Richard Groschopp,
Willy Hameister, Wolf Hart, Hasso Hartnagel, Walter Hege, Eberhard von der Heyden, Albert Höcht, Paul Holzki,
Werner Hundhausen, Heinz von Jaworsky, Hugo von Kaweczynski, Herbert Kebelmann, Sepp Ketterer, Wolfgang
Kiepenheuer, Arthur Anwander, Ernst Kunstmann, Leo de Laforgue, Alexander von Lagorio, Eduardo Lamberti,
Otto Lantschner, Waldemar Lembke, Georg Lemki, C. A. Linke, Erich Nitzschmann, Albert Schattmann, Wilhelm
Schmidt, H. O. Schulze, Leo Schwedler, Alfred Siegert, Wilhelm Georg Siehm, Ernst Sorge, Helmuth von Stwolinski,
Karl Vass
Production Design: Robert Herlth
Editing: Leni Riefenstahl, Max Michel, Johannes Lüdke, Arnfried Heyne, Guzzi Lantschner
Sound: Siegfried Schulze, Hermann Storr
Music: Herbert Windt, Walter Gronostay (uncredited)
Narrators: Paul Laven, Rolf Wernicke, Henri Nannen, Johannes Pagels
Running time: [Part 1] 3429m, 126 min (1938), [Part 2] 2722m, 100 min (1938)

DIE GROSSE LIEBE THE GREAT LOVE 1942
Director: Rolf Hansen
Production: Walter Bolz for Universum-Film AG (UFA) (Berlin)
Screenplay: Peter Groll, Rolf Hansen
Photography: Franz Weihmayr
Editing: Anna Höllering
Production Design: Walter Haag
Sound: Werner Pohl
Music: Michael Jary
Lyrics: Bruno Balz
Cast: Zarah Leander (Hanna Holberg), Viktor Staal (Paul Wendlandt), Paul Hörbiger (Alexander Rudnitzky),
Grethe Weiser (Kaethe, Hanna's housekeeper), Hans Schwarz Jr. (Alfred Vanloo), Wolfgang Preiss (von Etzdorf),
Leopold von Ledebur (Herr Westphal), Julia Serda (Frau Westphal), Victor Janson (Mocelli), Agnes Windeck
(Hanna's mother), Wilhelm Althaus (Becker), Gothart Portloff, Jakob Tiedtke, Ilse Fürstenberg, Olga Engl, Grete
Reinwald, Armin Schweizer, Walter Lieck, Hugo Froelich, Walter Steinweg, Erna Sellmer, Karl Etlinger, Paul Bildt,
Ewald Wenck, Albert Florath, Henry Lorenzen, Erich Dunskus, Hermann Pfeiffer, Just Scheu
Running time: 2738m, 100 min (1942)

DER WEISSE TRAUM THE WHITE DREAM 1943
Director: Géza von Cziffra
Production: Erich von Neusser for Wien-Film GmbH (Wien)
Screenplay: Géza von Cziffra
Photography: Hans Schneeberger, Sepp Ketterer
Editing: Arnfried Heyne
Production Design: Eduard Stolba
Sound: Willy Radde
Music: Anton Profes
Cast: Olly Holzmann (Liesl Strolz), Wolf Albach-Retty (Ernst Eder), Oskar Sima (Josef Wildner), Lotte Lang (Lu
Panther), Hans Olden (Schmoller), Georg Lorenz (Franz), Hans Schott-Schöbinger (Theo Berg), Rudolf Carl (Toni

Muppinger), Petra Trautmann (Gertie Kramer), Fritz Imhoff (Bertram), Hans Kern (Bächlein), Richard Eybner (Scherzinger), Josef Menschik (Kugler), Polly Koß (Frau Wulitsch), Otto Hardtmann (Poldi), Karl Schäfer, Gisa Wurm
Running time: 93 min

DIE MÖRDER SIND UNTER UNS THE MURDERERS ARE AMONG US 1946
Director: Wolfgang Staudte
Production: Herbert Uhlich for Deutsche Film AG (East Berlin) (later DEFA)
Screenplay: Wolfgang Staudte
Photography: Friedl Behn-Grund, Eugen Klagemann
Editing: Hans Heinrich
Production Design: Otto Hunte, Bruno Monden, Alfred Schulz (uncredited)
Costumes: Gertrud Recke, Max Bransky, Anna Pfeifer
Sound: Klaus Jungk
Music: Ernst Roters
Cast: Wilhelm Borchert (Dr. Mertens), Hildegard Knef (Susanne Wallner), Erna Sellmer (Frau Brückner), Arno Paulsen (Ferdinand Brückner), Christian Blackwood (Otto, Brückner's son), Michael Günther (Herbert), Robert Forsch (Mondschein), Elly Burgmer, Marlise Ludwig (Sonja), Hildegard Adolphi (Daisy), Albert Johannes (Bartholomäus), Ursula Krieg (Carola Schulz), Wolfgang Dohnberg (Fritz Knochenhauer), Ernst Stahl-Nachbaur, Wanda Peters, Käte Jöken-König, Christiane Hanson
Running time: 2475m, 90 min (1946)

GRÜN IST DIE HEIDE THE HEATH IS GREEN 1951
Director: Hans Deppe
Production: Kurt Ulrich for Berolina-Filmproduktion GmbH (Berlin)
Screenplay: Bobby E. Lüthge
Photography: Kurt Schulz
Editing: Hermann Ludwig
Production Design: Gabriel Pellon, Peter Schlewski, Hans-Jürgen Kiebach
Costumes: Walter Kraatz
Sound: Hans Ebel, Hans Löhmer
Music: Alfred Strasser
Lyrics: Hermann Löns
Cast: Hans Stüwe (Lüder Lüdersen), Sonja Ziemann (Helga), Otto Gebühr (Gottfried Lüdersen), Margarete Haagen (Frau Lüdersen), Rudolf Prack (Walter Raine), Hans Richter (Hans), Kurt Reimann (Nachtigall), Ludwig Schmitz (Tünnes), Maria Holst (Nora von Buckwitz), Willy Fritsch (district judge), Josef Sieber (Oberförster), Oskar Sima (Circus Manager), Else Reval (Frau Zirkusdirektorin), Karl Finkenzeller (Pistek), Rolf Weih (Doctor), Kurt Pratsch-Kaufmann (Teacher), Ernst Waldow (Pharmacist), Franz-Otto Krüger, Franz Schafheitlin, Gerhard Gregor
Running time: 2482m, 91 min

DIE BRÜCKE THE BRIDGE 1959
Director: Bernhard Wicki
Production: Hermann Schwerin for Fono-Film GmbH (Berlin) in collaboration with Jochen Severin (München)
Screenplay: Michael Mansfeld, Heinz Pauck, Bernhard Wicki (uncredited)
Story: Manfred Gregor
Photography: Gerd von Bonin, Horst Fehlhaber
Editing: Carl Otto Bartning
Special effects: Erwin Lange (pyrotechnics), Karl Baumgartner (pyrotechnics), Oskar Sala (sound effects)
Production Design: Peter Scharff, Heinrich Graf Brühl
Costumes: Josef Wanke, Jutta Lürmann

Sound: Willi Schwadorf
Music: Hans-Martin Majewski
Cast: Folker Bohnet (Hans Scholten), Fritz Wepper (Albert Mutz), Michael Hinz (Walter Forst), Frank Glaubrecht (Jürgen Borchert), Karl Michael Balzer (Karl Horber), Volker Lechtenbrink (Klaus Hager), Günther Hoffmann (Sigi Bernhard), Cordula Trantow (Franziska), Wolfgang Stumpf (Stern), Günter Pfitzmann (Heilmann), Heinz Spitzner (Fröhlich), Siegfried Schürenberg (Bütov), Ruth Hausmeister (Frau Mutz), Eva Vaitl (Frau Borchert), Edith Schultze-Westrum (Frau Bernhard), Hans Elwenspoek (Herr Forst), Trude Breitschopf (Frau Forst), Klaus Hellmold (Herr Horber), Inge Benz (Frau Sigrun), Til Kiwe, Edeltraut Elsner (Barbara), Alexander Hunzinger, Johannes Buzalski, Vicco von Bülow (Queiser), Heini Göbel, Kurt Habernoll, Herma Hochwarter, Emil Josef Hunek, Georg Lehn, Hans Oettl, H. Struck, Alfons Teuber, H. Winninger, Hellmuth Bergmann, J. Herrmann
Running time: 2813m, 103 min

DER SCHATZ IM SILBERSEE THE TREASURE OF SILVER LAKE 1962
Director: Harald Reinl
Production: Horst Wendlandt and Leif Feilberg for Societé Nouvelle de Cinématographie (S.N.C.) (Paris), Rialto Film Preben Philipsen Filmproduktion and Filmvertrieb GmbH (Hamburg), Jadran Film (Zagreb)
Screenplay: Harald G. Petersson
Photography: Ernst W. Kalinke, Branko Ivatovic (second unit)
Special Effects: Erwin Lange
Production Design: Dusan Jericevic
Costumes: Irms Pauli
Editing: Hermann Haller
Sound: Erich Molnar
Music: Martin Böttcher
Cast: Lex Barker (Old Shatterhand), Pierre Brice (Winnetou), Götz George (Fred Engel), Herbert Lom (Colonel Brinkley), Karin Dor (Ellen Patterson), Eddi Arent (Lord Castlepool), Marianne Hoppe (Mrs Butler), Ralf Wolter (Sam Hawkens), Mirko Boman (Gunstick Uncle), Sima Janicijevic (Patterson), Jozo Kovacevic (Great Wolf), Slobodan Dimitrijevic (Rolling Thunder), Branko Spoljar Doc (Jefferson Hartley), Miliroj Stojanovic (Knox), Velimir Chytil (Woodward), Ilija Ivezic (Hilton), Antun Nalis (Bruns), Vladimir Medar (barkeeper)
Running time: 3027m, 111 min

DER GETEILTE HIMMEL THE DIVIDED HEAVEN 1964
Director: Konrad Wolf
Production: Hans-Joachim Funk for DEFA-Studio für Spielfilme (Potsdam-Babelsberg)
Screenplay: Christa Wolf, Gerhard Wolf, Konrad Wolf, Willi Brückner, Kurt Barthel
Story: Christa Wolf
Photography: Werner Bergmann
Editing: Helga Krause
Production Design: Alfred Hirschmeier
Costumes: Dorit Gründel
Sound: Konrad Walle
Music: Hans-Dieter Hosalla
Cast: Renate Blume (Rita Seidel), Eberhard Esche (Manfred Herrfurth), Hans Hardt-Hardtloff (Rolf Meternagel), Hilmar Thate (Wendland), Martin Flörchinger (Herr Herrfurth), Erika Pelikowsky (Frau Herrfurth), Günther Grabbert (Ernst Schwarzenbach), Horst Jonischkan (Martin Jung), Petra Kelling (Sigrid), Jürgen Kern (Hänschen), Horst Weinheimer (Ermisch), Hans-Joachim Hanisch (Kuhl), Frank Michaelis (Karßuweit), Paul Berndt (Melcher), Christoph Engel (Liebentrau), Uwe-Detlev Jessen (Mangold), Erik Veldre (Schwabe), Otto Lang (Professor), Lothar Bellag (Dr Seiffert), Siegfried Menzel (Dr Müller), Agnes Kraus (Frau Meternagel), Dorothea Volk (Rita's mother), Geseta von Etzel (Frau Professor), Hildegard Röder (Frau Seiffert), Waltraut Kramm (Frau Schwarzenbach), Angela

Brunner (Dr Müller's fiancée), Karin Seybert (Manfred's aunt), Peter Herden, Maria Sänger (Rita's aunt), Heinz Hellmich (doctor), Willy Jänsch, Fredy Barten, Rita Hempel, Arthur Gutschwager, Hilmar Baumann, Gerhard Hänsel, Michael Deyak, Gerd Müller, Carla Thomalla, Eva-Marie Fröhlich, Gerhard Büch, Uwe Germann, Sylvia Nechanitzky, Tinka Wolf, Willi Liebner, Herbert Krüger, Alfred Baier, Detlef Witte, Michael Dejak
Narrator: Lissy Tempelhof
Running time: 3103m, 113 min

DIE SÖHNE DER GROSSEN BÄRIN THE SONS OF GREAT BEAR 1965

Director: Josef Mach
Production: Hans Mahlich for DEFA-Studio für Spielfilme (Potsdam-Babelsberg)
Screenplay: Liselotte Welskopf-Henrich
Story Liselotte Welskopf-Henrich
Photography: Jaroslav Tuzar
Editing: Ilse Peters
Production Design: Paul Lehmann
Costumes: Günther Schmidt
Sound: Bernd Gerwien
Music: Wilhelm Neef
Cast: Gojko Mitic (Tokei-ihto), Jirí Vrstála (Red Fox), Rolf Römer (Tobias), Hans Hardt-Hardtloff (Major Smith), Gerhard Rachold (Lt Roach), Horst Jonischkan (Adams), Jozef Majercik (Tschetansapa), Jozef Adamovic (Tschopa), Milan Jablonsky (Thunder of the Mountains), Hannjo Hasse (Pitt), Helmut Schreiber (Ben), Rolf Ripperger (Joe), Brigitte Krause (Jenny), Karin Beewen (Cate), Ruth Kommerell (Tashina), Kati Székely (Uinonoah), Zofia Slaboszowska (Mongschongschah), Slabodanka Markovic (Sitopanaki), Hans Finohr (Hawandschita), Adolf Peter Hoffmann (Mattotaupa), Martin Tapák (Schonka), Horst Kube (Thomas), Walter E. Fuß (Theo), Sepp Klose (Taschunka-witko), Jozo Lepetic (Bill), Herbert Dirmoser (Alter Rabe), Willi Schrade (Tatokano), Günter Schubert (Feldger), Franz Bonnet (father of Tashunka-whitko), Dietmar Richter-Reinick (Leutnant Warner), Blanche Kommerell (Eenah), Helena Mach (Heladik), Brigitte Scholz (Sesoka), Johannes Wieke, Cordula Sonnabend (Lightning Cloud), Heiner Koch (Schaske), Henry Hübchen (Hapedah)
Voice actors: Karl Sturm (Gojko Mitic), Fred Düren (Jirí Vrstála), Ezard Haußmann (Jozef Majercik), Klaus Bergatt (Jozef Adamovic), Lothar Schellhorn (Milan Jablonsky), Horst Schön (Jozo Lepetic), Ursula Mundt (Zofia Slaboszowska), Gertrud Adam (Slabodanka Markovic), Horst Manz (Martin Tapák)
Running time: 2673m, 98 min

ABSCHIED VON GESTERN YESTERDAY GIRL 1967

Director: Alexander Kluge
Production: Alexander Kluge for Kairos Film (München), Independent Film GmbH (Berlin/West)
Screenplay: Alexander Kluge
Story: Alexander Kluge
Photography: Thomas Mauch, Edgar Reitz
Editing: Beate Mainka-Jellinghaus
Sound: Klaus Eckelt, Heinz Pusl, Hans-Jörg Wicha
Narrator: Alexander Kluge
Cast: Alexandra Kluge (Anita G.), Hans Korte (The Judge), Edith Kuntze-Peloggio (Parole Board Officer), Palma Falck (Frau Budek), Ado Riegler (Priest), Josef Kreindl (Record company's owner), Käthe Ebner (Record company's owner's wife), Peter Staimmer (The Young Man), Hans Brammer (The Professor), E. O. Fuhrmann (The Skydiver), Karl-Heinz Peters (A Man), Ursula Dirichs (Mother), Günther Mack (Pichota), Eva Maria Meineke (Frau Pichota), Fritz Werner (Furstore owner), Hedwig Wissing (Chambermaid), Nathan Gnath (Chief of the hotel), Maria Schäfer (Room renter), Harald Patzer (Professor), Alfred Edel (Assistant Professor), Gottfried Gerhard, Bowin-Schlegel (Commissionaire), Adam Delle (Dog trainer), Ingeborg Werneth (Room renter), Fritz Bauer (as himself, Attorney

General), Irma Kolmhuber (Jailhouse nurse), Erna Bepperling (Welfare worker in jail)
Running time: 2394m, 88 min

DIE LEGENDE VON PAUL UND PAULA THE LEGEND OF PAUL AND PAULA 1973
Director: Heiner Carow
Production: Erich Albrecht for DEFA-Studio für Spielfilme (Potsdam-Babelsberg)
Screenplay: Heiner Carow, Ulrich Plenzdorf
Story: Ulrich Plenzdorf
Photography: Jürgen Brauer
Editing: Evelyn Carow
Production Design: Harry Leupold
Costumes: Barbara Braumann
Sound: Georg Gutschmidt, Werner Blass
Music: Peter Gotthardt
Lyrics: Wolfgang Tilgner
Cast: Angelica Domröse (Paula), Winfried Glatzeder (Paul), Heidemarie Wenzel (Paul's wife), Fred Delmare (Tyre dealer 'Reifen-Saft'), Rolf Ludwig (Professor), Hans Hardt-Hardtloff (owner of a shooting gallery), Käthe Reichel (owner of the shooting gallery's wife), Frank Schenk (Schmidt), Dietmar Richter-Reinick, Eva-Maria Hagen, Jürgen Frohriep, Christian Steyer (Colly), Marga Legal, Peter Gotthardt, Willi Schrade, Frank Michaelis, Brigitte Beier, Elvira Schuster, Jessy Rameik, Wilfried Wolter, Victor Keune, Edgar Külow, Bodo Krämer, Bernd Manthey, Hans Merker, Detlef Willecke, Ruth Harter, Irina Süß, Manfred Rosenberg, David Wenzel-Veth, Robert Glatzeder, Robert Ströhl, Brigitte Kaukel, Constanze Engelhardt, Mike Zessin, Hertha Thiele
Running time: 2881m, 109 min

JEDER FÜR SICH UND GOTT GEGEN ALLE THE ENIGMA OF KASPAR HAUSER 1974
Director: Werner Herzog
Production: Werner Herzog for Werner Herzog Filmproduktion (München), Zweites Deutsches Fernsehen (ZDF) (Mainz)
Screenplay: Werner Herzog
Photography: Jörg Schmidt-Reitwein, Klaus Wyborny, Werner Herzog
Editing: Beate Mainka-Jellinghaus
Production Design: Henning von Gierke
Costumes: Gisela Storch, Ann Poppel
Sound: Haymo Henry Heyder
Music: Popul Vuh, Johann Pachelbel, Orlando di Lasso ('Requiem for Four Voices'), Tommaso Albinoni ('Adagio'), Wolfgang Amadeus Mozart (Tamino's aria from The Magic Flute)
Cast: Bruno S. (Kaspar), Walter Ladengast (Professor Daumer), Brigitte Mira (Servant Käthe), Hans Musäus (Unkown Man), Willy Semmelrogge (Circus director), Michael Kroecher (Lord Stanhope), Henry van Lyck (Cavalry Captain, Enno Patalas (Pastor Fuhrmann), Volker Elis Pilgrim (Pastor), Volker Prechtel (Hiltel the prison guard), Gloria Doer (Frau Hiltel), Helmut Döring (Little King), Kidlat Tahimik (Hombrecito), Andi Gottwald (Young Mozart), Herbert Achternbusch (Bavarian Chicken Hypnotizer), Wolfgang Bauer, Walter Steiner (Taunting Farmboy), Clemens Scheitz (Sribe), Johannes Buzalski, Willy Meyer-Fürst (Coroner), Alfred Edel (Professor), Florian Fricke (Florian), Franz Brumbach, Herbert Fritsch, Wilhelm Bayer, Peter Gebhart, Otto Heinzle, Dorothea Kraft, Dr. Walter Pflaum (Coroner), Dr. Heinz Niemöller (Coroner), Peter-Udo Schönborn, Markus Weller (Julius)
Running time: 2992m, 109 min

DEUTSCHLAND IM HERBST GERMANY IN AUTUMN 1978
Director: Alexander Kluge (prologue/episode 2, 8, 10, 11, 13), Volker Schlöndorff (prologue/episode 2, 12, 13), Alf Brustellin (episode 3, 4, 6), Bernhard Sinkel (episode 3, 4, 6), Rainer Werner Fassbinder (episode 1), Katja Rupé

(episode 5), Hans Peter Cloos (episode 5), Edgar Reitz (episode 7), Maximiliane Mainka (episode 9), Peter Schubert (episode 9), Hans Peter Kloos
Production: Theo Hinz and Eberhard Junkersdorf for Pro-ject Filmproduktion im Filmverlag der Autoren GmbH (München), Kairos Film (München), Hallelujah-Film GmbH (München), ABS-Filmproduktion (München), Tango-Film (München), Edgar Reitz Filmproduktion (München)
Screenplay: Alexander Kluge (prologue/episode 2, 8, 10, 11, 13), Volker Schlöndorff (prologue/episode 2, 12, 13), Alf Brustellin (episode 3, 4, 6), Bernhard Sinkel (episode 3, 4, 6), Rainer Werner Fassbinder (episode 1), Katja Rupé (episode 5), Hans Peter Cloos (episode 5), Peter F. Steinbach (episode 7), Edgar Reitz (episode 7), Maximiliane Mainka (episode 9), Peter Schubert (episode 9), Heinrich Böll (episode 12)
Photography: Rolf Gmöhling, Jürgen Jürges, Werner Lüring, Michael Ballhaus (episode 1), Dietrich Lohmann (episode 7), Colin Mounier (episode 12), Bodo Kessler (prologue/episode 2, 13), Jörg Schmidt-Reitwein (prologue/episode 2, 13), Günther Hörmann (episode 8, 10, 11)
Editing: Alexander Kluge, Beate Mainka-Jellinghaus, Heidi Genée, Ursula Goetz-Dickopp, Tanja Schmidbauer, Christina Warnck
Sound: Roland Henschke, Martin Müller, Günther Stadelmann
Production Design: Henning von Gierke, Toni Lüdi, Winfried Hennig (episode 7, 12)
Narrator: Alexander Kluge
Music: Joseph Haydn, Hoffmann von Fallersleben ('Deutschlandlied'), Peter Tchaikovsky ('Autumn Song', op. 37a), Ennio Morricone ('Here's to You'), Wolf Biermann ('Was wird bloß aus unseren Träumen')
Cast: Rainer Werner Fassbinder (as himself – episode 1), Liselotte Eder (as herself – episode 1), Armin Meier (as himself – episode 1), Wolf Biermann (as himself – episode 3), Horst Mahler (as himself – episode 4), Katja Rupé (Branka – episode 5), Hans Peter Cloos (Foreigner – episode 5), Vadim Glowna (Freiermuth – episode 7, 12), Petra Kiener (woman – episode 7), Hannelore Hoger (Gabi Teichert – episode 8, 11), Angela Winkler (Antigone – episode 12), Franziska Walser (Ismene – episode 12), Helmut Griem (Mahler's interviewer/Kreon – episode 12), Heinz Bennent (TV committee member – episode 12), Dieter Laser (TV committee member – episode 12), Enno Patalas (TV committee member – episode 12), Mario Adorf, Wolfgang Bächler, Joachim Bissmeier, Joey Buschmann, Caroline Chaniolleau, Otto Friebel, Hildegard Friese, Michael Gahr, Horatius Haeberle, Petra Kiener, Lisi Mangold, Eva Meier, Franz Priegel, Werner Passardt, Leon Rainer, Walter Schmidinger, Gerhard Schneider, Corinna Spies, Eric Vilgertshofer, Manfred Zapatka
Running time: 3378m, 123 min

DAS BOOT THE BOAT 1981
Director: Wolfgang Petersen
Production: Günter Rohrbach for Bavaria Atelier GmbH (München-Geiselgasteig), Radiant Film GmbH (München), Westdeutscher Rundfunk (WDR) (Köln), Süddeutscher Rundfunk (SDR) (Stuttgart) in collaboration with Neue Constantin Film GmbH & Co Verleih KG (München), British Broadcasting Corporation (BBC) (London), Österreichischer Rundfunk (ORF) (Wien), Radiotelevisione Italiana (RAI) (Rom)
Screenplay: Wolfgang Petersen
Story: Lothar-Günther Buchheim
Photography: Jost Vacano
Special Effects: Theodor Nischwitz, Ernst Wild, Jörg M. Kunsdorff, Rudolf Ruemmelt, Karl Baumgartner, Ludwig Kurz, Heinrich Bader
Editing: Johannes Nikel
Production Design: Rolf Zehetbauer
Costumes: Monika Bauert
Sound: Werner Böhm, Karsten Ullrich
Music: Klaus Doldinger
Cast: Jürgen Prochnow (Capt-Lt Henrich Lehmann-Willenbrock), Herbert Grönemeyer (Lt Werner Groney), Klaus Wennemann (Chief Engineer Fritz Grade), Hubertus Bengsch (1st Lieutenant), Martin Semmelrogge

(2nd Lieutenant), Bernd Tauber (Chief Quartermaster), Erwin Leder (Johann), Martin May (Ullmann), Heinz Hoenig (Hinrich), Uwe Ochsenknecht (Chief Bosun), Claude-Oliver Rudolph (Ario), Jan Fedder (Pilgrim), Ralf Richter (Frenssen), Joachim Bernhard (Preacher), Oliver Stritzel (Schwalle), Konrad Becker (Bockstiegel), Lutz Schnell (Dufte), Martin Hemme (Brückenwilli), Rita Cadillac (Monique), Otto Sander (Phillip Thomson), Günter Lamprecht (Captain of the 'Weser'), Jean-Claude Hoffmann (Benjamin), Helmut Neumeier (Schmutt), Wilhelm Pietsch (Franz), Günther Franke (1st Officier of the 'Weser'), Albert Kraml (Hagen), Sky Dumont (2nd Officier of the 'Weser'), Peter Pathenis, Dirk Salomon (Markus), Lothar Zajicek, Uli Kümpfel, Peter Musäus, Udo Suchan, Ulrich Günther, Dagobert Walter, Edwige Pierre (Nadine), Günther Geiermann, Gerhard Acktun, Norbert Gronwald, Maryline Moulard, Arno Kral, Christian Bendomir, Christian Seipolt, Roger Barth, Rolf Weber, Ferdinand Schaal, Thomas Boxhammer
Running time: 4069m, 149 min (1981 release version), 310 min (1985 TV version), 5705m, 208 min (1997 director's cut)

MÄNNER MEN 1985
Director: Doris Dörrie
Production: Elvira Senft, Helmut Rasp and Denyse Noever for Zweites Deutsches Fernsehen (ZDF) (Mainz), Olga-Film GmbH (München)
Screenplay: Doris Dörrie
Photography: Helge Weindler
Editing: Raimund Barthelmes
Production Design: Jörg Neumann
Costumes: Jörg Trees
Sound: Michael Etz
Music: Claus Bantzer
Cast: Heiner Lauterbach (Julius), Uwe Ochsenknecht (Stefan), Ulrike Kriener (Paula), Janna Marangosoff (Angelika), Dietmar Bär (Lothar), Marie-Charlott Schüler (Marita Strass), Edith Volkmann (Frau Lennert), Monika Schwarz, Lois Kelz (Florian), Sabine Wegener (Juliane Zorn), Cornelia Schneider (Caro), Gabriel Paklepppa, Roland Schreiber, Björn Banhardt, Werner Albert Püthe, Ulrich Günther, Astrid Pilling, Gerd Huber, Nasrin Khochsima, Jörg Neumann (Neumann)
Running time: 2703m, 99 min

LOLA RENNT RUN, LOLA, RUN 1998
Director: Tom Tykwer
Production: Stefan Arndt for X Filme Creative Pool GmbH (Berlin), Westdeutscher Rundfunk (WDR) (Köln), Arte G.E.I.E. (Straßburg)
Screenplay: Tom Tykwer
Photography: Frank Griebe
Special Effects: Gerhard Voll, Roland Tropp
Editing: Mathilde Bonnefoy
Production Design: Alexander Manasse
Costumes: Monika Jacobs
Narrator: Hans Paetsch
Sound: Dirk Jacob, Frank Behnke
Music: Tom Tykwer, Johnny Klimek, Reinhold Heil
Cast: Franka Potente (Lola), Moritz Bleibtreu (Manni), Herbert Knaup (Lola's father), Nina Petri (Frau Hansen), Joachim Król (Norbert von Au), Armin Rohde (Schuster), Heino Ferch (Ronnie), Suzanne von Borsody (Frau Jäger), Lars Rudolph (Kruse), Ludger Pistor (Herr Meier), Sebastian Schipper (Mike), Monica Bleibtreu, Ute Lubosch, Julia Lindig (Doris), Andreas Petri, Klaus Müller, Utz Krause, Beate Finckh, Volkhart Buff, Dora Raddy, Peter Pauli, Marc Bischoff
Running time: 2173 m, 79 min

GOOD BYE, LENIN! 2003

Director: Wolfgang Becker

Production: Stefan Arndt for X Filme Creative Pool GmbH (Berlin), X Filme Creativ Pool GmbH (Köln) in collaboration with Westdeutscher Rundfunk (WDR)/Arte (Köln)

Screenplay: Bernd Lichtenberg, Wolfgang Becker

Photography: Martin Kukula

Special Effects: Andreas Schellenberg

Editing: Peter R. Adam

Production Design: Lothar Holler

Costumes: Aenne Plaumann

Sound: Wolfgang Schukrafft

Music: Yann Tiersen

Cast: Daniel Brühl (Alex Kerner), Katrin Saß (Christiane, Alex's mother), Chulpan Khamatova (Lara), Maria Simon (Ariane Kerner), Florian Lukas (Denis), Alexander Beyer (Rainer), Burghart Klaußner (Robert, Alex's father), Michael Gwisdek (Klapprath), Christine Schorn (Frau Schäfer), Jürgen Holtz (Herr Ganske), Jochen Stern (Herr Mehlert), Stefan Walz (Sigmund Jähn), Eberhard Kirchberg (Dr Wagner), Hans-Uwe Bauer (Dr Mewes), Jelena Kratz, Nico Ledermueller, Ernst-Georg Schwill, Jürgen Vogel, Mennan Yapo, Svea Timander

Running time: 3322m, 121 min

DAS WUNDER VON BERN THE MIRACLE OF BERN 2003

Director: Sönke Wortmann

Production: Tom Spiess, Sönke Wortmann and Hanno Huth for Little Shark Entertainment GmbH (Köln) in collaboration with Senator Film Produktion GmbH (Berlin), Seven Pictures GmbH (Unterföhring) in collaboration with Sat.1 GmbH (Berlin), Traumwerk Filmproduktion GmbH (München), Das Werk GmbH (München and Frankfurt am Main)

Screenplay: Sönke Wortmann, Rochus Hahn

Photography: Tom Fährmann

Special Effects: Tom Fährmann, Andreas Korth, Daniela Schmidt, Ben Kötter

Editing: Ueli Christen

Production Design: Uli Hanisch

Costumes: Ursula Welter

Sound: Dirk Jacob

Music: Marcel Barsotti

Cast: Peter Lohmeyer (Richard Lubanski), Louis Klamroth (Matthias Lubanski), Lucas Gregorowicz (Paul Ackermann), Katharina Wackernagel (Annette Ackermann), Johanna Gastdorf (Christa Lubanski), Mirko Lang (Bruno Lubanski), Birthe Wolter (Ingrid Lubanski), Peter Franke (Sepp Herberger), Knut Hartwig (Fritz Walter), Sascha Göpel (Helmut Rahn), Holger Dexne (Horst Eckel), Martin Bretschneider (Hans Schäfer), Kai Schäfer (Werner Kohlmeyer), Jo Stock (Toni Turek), Andreas Barth (Werner Liebrich), Simon Verhoeven (Ottmar Walter), Sylvester Pezena (Jupp Posipal), Jan Holland (Karl Mai), Tobias Hartmann (Max Morlock), Joachim Kappl (Adi Dassler), Andreas 'Obel' Obering (Herbert Zimmermann), Stefan von Moers (Niersbach)

Running time: 3192m, 117 min

BIBLIOGRAPHY

NOTE: This bibliography contains only books (i.e., monographs and edited collections), mostly in English (e.g., translations of classic texts). It includes only books of general character, to expand upon the more specific citations actually referred to in each of the individual contributions to this volume. Thus the bibliography excludes essays in journals or edited volumes as well as books on specialist subjects of German cinema such as individual filmmakers.

Alter, N. M. (2002) *Projecting History: German Nonfiction Cinema, 1967–2000.* Ann Arbor, MI: University of Michigan Press.

Albrecht, G. (1969) *Nationalsozialistische Filmpolitik: Eine soziologische Untersuchung über die Spielfilme des Dritten Reichs.* Stuttgart: Enke.

_____ (ed.) (1985) *Die großen Filmerfolge: Vom Blauen Engel bis Otto, der Film.* Ebersberg: Edition Achteinhalb.

Allan, S. and J. Sandford (eds) (1999) *DEFA: East German Cinema, 1946–1992.* Oxford: Berghahn.

Barlow, J. D. (1982) *German Expressionist Film.* Boston, MA: Twayne.

Bergfelder, T. (2005) *International Adventures: German Popular Cinema and European Co-Productions in the 1960s.* New York and Oxford: Berghahn.

Bergfelder, T. and C. Cargnelli (2008) *Destination London: German-speaking Emigres and British Cinema, 1925–1950.* New York and Oxford: Berghahn.

Bergfelder, T., E. Carter and D. Göktürk (eds) (2002) *The German Cinema Book.* London: British Film Institute.

Berghahn, D. (2005) *Hollywood Behind the Wall: The Cinema of East Germany.* Manchester: Manchester University Press.

Berghaus, G. (1989) *Theatre and Film in Exile: German Artists in Britain, 1933–1945.* Oxford: Wolff.

Bock, H.-M. (ed.) (1984) *Cinegraph: Lexikon zum deutschsprachigen Film.* München: edition text + kritik.

Bock, H.-M. and A. Goodbody (eds) (2008) *The Concise Cinegraph: An Encyclopedia of German Cinema.* Oxford and New York: Berghahn.

Bock, H.-M. and M. Töteberg (eds) (1992) *Das UFA-Buch: Kunst und Krisen, Stars und Regisseure, Wirtschaft und Politik.* Frankfurt am Main: Zweitausendeins.

Brockmann, S. (2010) *A Critical History of German Film.* Rochester, NY: Camden House.

Calhoon, K. S. (ed.) (2001) *Peripheral Visions: The Hidden Stages of Weimar Cinema.* Detroit, IL: Wayne State University Press.

Cherchi Usai, P. and L. Codelli (eds) (1990) *Before Caligari: German Cinema, 1895–1920.* Pordenone: Edizioni Biblioteca dell'Immagine.

Clarke, D. (ed.) (2006) *German Cinema: Since Unification.* London: Contiunuum.

Coates, P. (1991) *The Gorgon's Gaze: German Cinema, Expressionism, and the Image of Horror.* Cambridge: Cambridge University Press.

Cooke, P. (2002) *German Expressionist Films.* Harpenden: Pocket Essentials.

Corrigan, T. (1983) *New German Film: The Displaced Image.* Austin, TX: University of Texas Press.

Costabile-Henning, C. A., R. J. Halverson and K. A. Foell (eds) (2001) *Textual Responses to German Unification: Processing Historical and Social Change in Literature and Film.* Berlin and New York: DeGruyter.

Davidson, J. E. (1999) *Deterritorializing the New German Cinema.* Minneapolis, MN: University of Minnesota Press.

Davidson, J. E. and S. Hake (eds) (2007) *Take Two: Fifties Cinema in Divided Germany.* Oxford and New York: Berghahn.

Drewniak, B.(1987) *Der Deutsche Film1938–1945: Ein Gesamtüberblick.* Düsseldorf: Droste.

Eisner, L. (1969 [1955]) *The Haunted Screen: Expressionism in the German Cinema and the Influence of Max Reinhardt.* Trans. R. Greaves. Berkeley, CA: University of California Press.

Elsaesser, T. (1989) *New German Cinema: A History.* London: British Film Institute.

____ (2000) *Weimar Cinema and After: Germany's Historical Imaginary.* New York: Routledge.

Elsaesser, T. and M. Wedel (eds) (1996) *A Second Life: German Cinema's First Decades.* Amsterdam: Amsterdam University Press.

____ (1999) *The BFI Companion to German Cinema.* London: British Film Institute.

Fehrenbach, H. (1995) *Cinema in Democratizing Germany: Reconstructing National Identity after Hitler.* Chapel Hill, CA: University of North California Press.

Feinstein, J. (2002) *The Triumph of the Ordinary: Depictions of Daily Life in East German Cinema 1949–1989.* Chapel Hill, CA: University of North Carolina Press.

Flinn, C. (2004) *The New German Cinema: Music, History, and the Matter of Style.* Berkeley, CA: University of California Press.

Fox, J. (2000) *Filming Women in the Third Reich.* Oxford and New York: Berg.

Franklin, J. (1986) *New German Cinema: From Oberhausen to Hamburg.* London: Columbus.

Frieden, S., V. R. Petersen and R. W. McCormick (eds) (1993) *Gender and German Cinema.* 2 vols. Providence: Berg.

Fuchs, A., M. Cosgrove and G. G. Grote (eds) (2006) *German Memory Contests: The Quest for Identity in Literature, Film, and Discourse Since 1990.* Rochester, NY: Camden.

Garncarz, J. (2010) *Maßlose Unterhaltung: Zur Etablierung des Films in Deutschland, 1896–1914.* Frankfurt: Stroemfeld.

Hake, S. (1993) *The Cinema's Third Machine: Writing on Film in Germany, 1908–1933.* Lincoln, NE: University of Nebraska Press.

____ (2001) *Popular Cinema of the Third Reich.* Austin, TX: University of Texas Press.

____ (2002) *German National Cinema.* London and New York: Routledge.

Halle, R. (2008) *German Film After Germany: Toward a Transnational Aesthetic.* Urbana, IL: University of Illinois Press.

Halle, R. and M. McCarthy (eds) (2003) *Light Motives: German Popular Film in Perspective.* Detroit, IL: Wayne State University Press.

Helt, R. C. and M. E. Helt (1992) *West German Cinema, 1985–1990: A Reference Handbook.* Metuchen, NJ: Scarecrow Press.

Hillman, R. (2005) *Unsettling Scores: German Film, Music, and Ideology.* Bloomington, IN: Indiana University Press.

Hoffmann, H. (1997) *The Triumph of Propaganda: Film and National Socialism, 1933–1945.* Trans. V. R. Berghahn and J. A. Broadwin. Oxford: Berghahn.

Hull, D. S. (1969) *Film in the Third Reich: A Study of the German Cinema, 1933–1945.* Berkeley, CA: University of California Press.

Jung, U. (ed.) (1993) *Der deutsche Film: Aspekte seiner Geschichte von den Anfängen bis zur Gegenwart.* Trier: WVT.

Jung, U. and W. Schatzberg (eds) (1992) *Filmkultur zur Zeit der Weimarer Republik.* München: Saur.

Kaes, A., M. Jay and E. Dimendberg (eds) (1994) *The Weimar Republic Sourcebook.* Berkeley, CA: University of California Press.

Knight, J. (1992) *Women and the New German Cinema.* London and New York: Verso.

____ (2004) *New German Cinema: Images of a Generation.* London: Wallflower Press.

Koepnick, L. (2002) *The Dark Mirror: German Cinema Between Hitler and Hollywood.* Berkeley, CA: University of California Press.

Kracauer, S. (2004 [1947]) *From Caligari to Hitler: A Psychological History of the German Film.* Princeton, NJ: Princeton University Press.

Kreimeier, K. (1996) *The UFA Story: A History of Germany's Greatest Film Company, 1918–1945.* Trans. R. and R. Kimber. New York: Hill and Wang.

Kuzniar, A. A. (2000) *The Queer German Cinema.* Stanford, CA: Stanford University Press.

Manvell, R. and H. Fraenkel (1971) *The German Cinema.* New York and Washington, D.C.: Praeger.

McCormick, R. W. and A. Guenther-Pal (eds) (2004) *German Essays on Film.* New York: Continuum.

Moltke, J. v. (2005) *No Place Like Home: Locations of Heimat in German Cinema*. Berkeley, CA: University of California Press.

Müller, C. (1994) *Frühe deutsche Kinematographie: Formale, wirtschaftliche und kulturelle Entwicklungen*. Stuttgart and Weimar: Metzler.

Murray, B. A. (1990) *Film and the German Left in the Weimar Republic: From Caligari to Kuhle Wampe*. Austin, TX: University of Texas Press.

Murray, B. A. and C. J. Wickham (eds) (1992) *Framing the Past: The Historiography of German Cinema and Television*. Carbondale, IL: Southern Illinois University Press.

Naughton, L. (2002) *That Was the Wild East: Film Culture, Unification and the 'New' Germany*. Ann Arbour, MI: University of Michigan Press.

O'Brien, M.-E. (2004) *Nazi Cinema as Enchantment: The Politics of Entertainment in the Third Reich*. Rochester, NY: Camden.

Petley, J. (1979) *Capital and Culture: German Cinema 1933–45*. London: British Film Institute.

Prawer, S. S. (2005) *Between Two Worlds: The Jewish Presence In German and Austrian Film, 1910–1933*. New York and Oxford: Berghahn.

Prinzler, H. H. (1995) *Chronik des deutschen Films 1895–1994*. Stuttgart: Metzler.

Reimer, R. C. (2000) *Cultural History through a National Socialist Lens: Essays on the Cinema of the Third Reich*. Rochester, NY and Woodbridge: Camden.

_____ (2008) *Historical Dictionary of German Cinema*. Lanham, MD: Scarecrow Press.

Reimer, R. C. and C. J. Reimer (1992) *Nazi-Retro Film: How German Narrative Cinema Remembers the Past*. New York: Twayne.

Reimer, R. C., R. Zachau and M. Sinka (2006) *German Culture Through Film: An Introduction to German Cinema*. Newburyport, MA: Focus.

Rentschler, E. (1988) *West German Filmmakers on Film: Visions and Voices*. New York: Holmes & Meier.

_____ (1996) *The Ministry of Illusion: Nazi Cinema and Its Afterlife*. Cambridge, MA and London: Harvard University Press.

Roberts, I. (2008) *German Expressionist Cinema: The World of Light and Shadow*. London: Wallflower Press.

Rogowski, C. (ed.) (2010) *The Many Faces of Weimar Cinema: Rediscovering Germany's Filmic Legacy*. Rochester, NY: Camden House.

Sandford, J. (1982) *The New German Cinema*. New York: Da Capo.

Saunders, T. J. (1994) *Hollywood in Berlin: American Cinema and Weimar Germany*. Berkeley, CA: University of California Press.

Scharf, I. (2008) *Nation and Identity in the New German Cinema: Homeless at Home*. New York: Routledge.

Scheunemann, D. (ed.) (2003) *Expressionist Film: New Perspectives*. Rochester, NY: Camden.

Schindler, S. K. and L. Koepnick (eds) (2007) *The Cosmopolitan Screen: German Cinema and the Global Imaginary, 1945 to the Present*. Ann Arbor, MI: University of Michigan Press.

Schoeps, K.-H. (2004) *Literature and Film in the Third Reich*. Rochester, NY: Camden.

Shandley, R. (2001) *Rubble Films: German Cinema in the Shadow of the Third Reich*. Philadelphia: Temple University Press.

Short, K. R. M. (ed.) (1996) *Catalogue of Forbidden German Feature and Short Film Productions*. Westport, CT: Greenwood Press.

Sigl, K., W. Schneider and I. Tornow (1986) *Jede Menge Kohle? Kunst und Kommerz auf dem deutschen Filmmarkt der Nachkriegszeit: Filmpreise und Kassenerfolge*. München: Filmland Presse.

Silberman, M. (1995) *German Cinema: Texts in Context*. Detroit, IL: Wayne State University Press.

Spieker, M. (1999) *Hollywood unterm Hakenkreuz: Der amerikanische Spielfilm im Dritten Reich*. Trier: Wissenschaftlicher Verlag Trier.

Thompson, K. (2006) *Herr Lubitsch Goes to Hollywood: German and American Film After World War I*. Amsterdam: Amsterdam University Press.

Welch, D. (2001) *Propaganda and the German Cinema, 1933–1945*. London and New York: Tauris.

Wilms, W. and W. Rasch (eds) (2008) *German Postwar Films: Life and Love in the Ruins.* New York: Palgrave Macmillan.

Winkel, R. V. and Welch, D. (eds) (2007) *Cinema and the Swastika: The International Expansion of the Third Reich Cinema.* New York: Palgrave Macmillan.

Wollenberg, H. H. (1948) *Fifty Years of German Film.* London: Falcon.

Zimmermann, P. (2005) *Geschichte des dokumentarischen Films in Deutschland.* 3 vols. Stuttgart: Reclam.

INDEX

A

Achternbusch, Herbert 140, 177
Adenauer, Konrad 142, 237
Adorf, Mario 191
Adorno, Theodor W. 125
Albers, Hans 3
Allgeier, Sepp 64
Anders, Georg 130
Ascheid, Antje 93
audience 1–5, 11, 13, 16, 20, 37,
    43, 65–8, 101, 149, 201–4,
    232, 243
Augstein, Rudolf 188

B

Baader, Andreas 187–8, 193
Baer, Volker 203
Baez, Joan 193–4
Barker, Lex 143–4
Bartel, Kurt 149
Barthel, Waldfried 7
Basinger, Jeanine 197
Bauer, Ina 105
Bäumler, Hans Jürgen 104
Becker, Ben 7
Becker, Wolfgang 227–34
Behn-Grund, Friedl 110, 113–14,
    117
Beindorf, Claudia 124
Bellour, Raymond 43
Benjamin, Walter 38, 40, 46, 164
Berger, Ludwig 4
Bergman, Ingmar 199
Bergmann, Werner 153–4
Biermann, Wolf 192, 194
Birr, Dieter 173
Bleibtreu, Moritz 218
Bloch, Ernst 141
Bohnet, Folker 130, 132
Böll, Heinrich 188
Boning, Wigald 69
Bonnefoy, Mathilde 218

Borchert, Wilhelm 110, 113
Bordwell, David 72, 197, 200, 218,
    222
Borzage, Frank 56
Boullée, Etienne-Louis 183
Brandt, Bill 58
Brauner, Artur 141, 143
Brecht, Bertolt 71, 163
Brice, Pierre 143–4
Brooks, Richard 134
Brückner, Willy 149
Brussig, Thomas 228–9
Brustellin, Alf 188
Buchheim, Lothar-Günther 197–
    200, 203
Budd, Michael 24
Burdon, Eric 214

C

Calvacanti, Alberto 54
Campe, Joachim Heinrich 183
Carow, Heiner 169–75
censorship 2, 13, 23, 51, 106, 109
Cloos, Hans Peter 188
Codelli, Lorenzo 19
Coleridge, Samuel Taylor 40
Collier, Jo Leslie 30, 34
comedies 5, 7, 76, 100, 197, 211,
    228, 237, 243
Cooper, James Fenimore 140
Cziffra, Géza von 99–107

D

Dadoun, Roger 44
Dagover, Lil 20
Delmare, Fred 169
Deppe, Hans 119
Diessl, Gustav 62
Dietrich, Marlene 24, 93
distribution 3, 7, 10, 23, 109, 159
Drewniak, Boguslaw 99–100, 105
Dupont, Ewald André 4

E

East Germany (German Democratic
    Republic, GDR) 6, 109, 139–
    41, 144–5, 149, 151, 156, 169
Ebert, Roger 217, 223
Eckel, Horst 239
Edel, Alfred 179
Edison, Thomas 43
Eggert, Martha 104
Eichinger, Bernd 7, 204
Eigel, Hanna 104
Einstein, Albert 141
Eisenstein, Sergei 52
Eisner, Lotte 23
Eliot, T. S. 220
Elsaesser, Thomas 15, 24, 100,
    225, 242
Erhard, Ludwig 237
Erhardt, Heinz 105
Ertl, Hans 82
expressionist film 5, 26

F

Falcon, Richard 220, 223
Fanck, Arnold 61–7
Fassbinder, Rainer Werner 187–8,
    190–2, 195, 243–4
Filbinger, Hans 189
Fischer, Robert 130
Flaherty, Robert 81
Fletcher, Angus 40, 42
Ford, John 56
Foth, Jörg 228
Fox, Jo 91
Franck, Paul 76
Franke, Peter 238
Fregonese, Hugo 143
Frentz, Walter 82
Freud, Sigmund 43, 121, 123
Freund, Karl 30, 54, 56–7
Friedrich, Evy 85
Frisch, Max 194

Fritsch, Willy   3, 69–70, 74–6, 121
Froelich, Carl   12

G
Gagarin, Yuri   150, 154
Garat, Henri   74–6
Garncarz, Joseph   7, 12, 86, 139, 143, 160
Garnier, Katja von   243
Gärtner, Adolf   9, 12
Gascoigne, Paul   241
Gastdorf, Johanna   239
George, Götz   143–4
Gerron, Kurt   63, 72, 76
Glass, Philip   38
Glatzeder, Winfried   169
Glaubrecht, Frank   131
Godard, Jean-Luc   222
Goebbels, Josef   42, 96
Goering, Hermann   111
Goethe, Johann Wolfgang von   174
Gottlob, Daniel   183
Gottschalk, Joachim   113
Gregor, Manfred   129
Gregorowicz, Lucas   238
Greiwe, Ulrich   199
Greverus, Ina-Maria   122
Griebe, Frank   222, 224
Griem, Helmut   192
Grierson, John   51, 53, 58
Griffith, David Wark   34
Grönemeyer, Herbert   210
Günther, Egon   228
Guevara, Che   213
Gutzkow, Karl   184

H
Haas, Willy   54
Haase, Christine   219–23
Habermas, Jürgen   162
Handke, Peter   184
Harbou, Thea von   40–8
Harlan, Veit   109–10
Harvey, Lilian   69–70, 74–5
Hawks, Howard   56
Haydn, Joseph   189
Heesters, Johannes   104
Herf, Jeffey   125
Herlth, Robert   29–30
Hertrampf, Dieter   173

Herzog, Werner   67, 159, 177–85
Heymann, Werner Richard   69, 76
Hickethier, Knut   185, 205
Hill, Terence   143
Hinz, Michael   130–1
Hinz, Theo   188
Hitler, Adolf   67, 79–84, 100, 113, 141
Hodgin, Nick   230
Hoff, Peter   151
Hoffmann, Günther   22, 130–1
Hoger, Hannelore   188, 194
Hölderlin, Friedrich   132, 136
Holst, Maria   120
Honecker, Erich   145, 175, 230

J
Jahn, Thomas   243
Jannings, Emil   30–1
Janowitz, Hans   20–5

K
Kael, Pauline   133
Kampers, Fritz   69
Karlweiss, Oskar   69, 74
Kassouf, Susan   211
Kast, Peter   111
Kaufman, Mikhail   58
Kaufmann, Rainer   243
Kessler, Frank   10
Kiesinger, Kurt Georg   189
Kilius, Marika   104
Kipping, Herwig   228
Kirsch, Sarah   174
Klamroth, Louis   239
Klemperer, Victor   80
Kloth, Bernie   239
Kluge, Alexander   6, 115, 130, 159, 161–5, 187–95
Knef, Hildegard   110, 113, 116–17
Koch, Gertrud   213
Kohl, Helmut   187
Korte, Helmut   74
Kosslick, Dieter   243
Kowa, Viktor de   116
Kracauer, Siegfried   19, 21, 24, 42, 46, 55, 57, 61, 74
Krauss, Werner   19
Kreimeier, Klaus   195
Kubaschewski, Ilse   7

Kubin, Alfred   23
Kubrick, Stanley   222
Kurtz, Rudolf   22

L
Lang, Fritz   4, 19, 24, 38–47, 55, 61, 70, 141
Lantschner, Guzzi   82
Laven, Paul   81
Leander, Zarah   3, 89–90, 93–5
Lechtenbrink, Volker   132
Ledoux, Claude-Nicolas   183
Lefèvre, René   74
Leuwerik, Ruth   3
Levinson, Barry   133
Lichtenberg, Bernd   229
Liebeneiner, Wolfgang   109
Ligensa, Annemone   7, 86, 147, 166, 195
Linnemann, Christine   242
Lohmeyer, Peter   238
Loiperdinger, Martin   16, 92, 96
Lorre, Peter   133
Lubitsch, Ernst   76, 207
Lutze, Peter C.   189

M
Madonna   38, 117
Maetzig, Kurt   113
Mahler, Horst   192, 194–5
Mainka, Maximiliane   193
Mainka-Jellinghaus, Beate   188–9
Mann, Heinrich   149
Mann, Klaus   141, 184
Marlitt, Eugenie   184
Maslin, Janet   218
May, Karl   140
Mayer, Carl   20–1, 23–5, 30–1, 54–5
Meier, Armin   190
Meinert, Rudolf   22
Meins, Holger   188
Meisel, Edmund   51, 53
Melodrama   38, 96, 113, 134
Messter, Oskar   9, 11–14
Mitic, Gojko   146
Mitscherlich, Alexander   115, 1239
Mitscherlich, Margarethe   115
Modernism   25, 42–3, 120, 125
Moltke, Johannes von   122–3

Morand, Paul 58
Morlock, Max 240
Moroder, Giorgio 38
Morricone, Ennio 189, 193
Morris, Glenn 84
mountain films 3, 67
Murnau, Friedrich Wilhelm 4, 29–37, 56
musical 38, 51, 53–5, 69, 71–2, 89, 95, 100–3, 125
Mutz, Albert 131–2

N
Nazi regime (Third Reich) 72, 79, 100, 106, 134, 141, 150, 192
Neeley, Richard 199
Netzer, Günther 241
Neubert, Kurt 82
New German Cinema 1, 5–6, 109, 116, 130, 159–62, 177, 187, 197, 208, 225, 243
Newman, Paul 198
Niederer, Rolf 241
Nielsen, Asta 10–12
Nothnagel, Klaus 183

O
Ondra, Anny 104
Owens, Jesse 83–5

P
Pabst, Georg Wilhelm 61, 64–5
Patalas, Enno 129, 177
Paulsen, Arno 110
Peckinpah, Sam 198
Petersen, Wolfgang 62, 197–205, 217
Peterson, Sebastian 228
Pilgrim, Elis 177
Plenzdorf, Ulrich 173–4
Pofes, Anton 104
Pommer, Erich 4, 22–3, 29–30, 70–1, 74–6
popular German films 3
Porten, Henny 3, 9–13
Posipal, Jupp 240
Potente, Franka 7, 69, 218
Powell, Eleanor 101–2
Prack, Rudolf 119–21
propaganda films 1–2, 160

Q
Quaresima, Leonardo 23–5

R
Rahn, Helmut 237, 239–41
Raspe, Jan Carl 187, 193
Redford, Robert 198
Reimann, Walter 24
Reitz, Edgar 115, 187–90
remake 26, 58, 69, 76, 100, 104–5
Renger-Patzsch, Albert 58
Resnais, Alain 152
Richter, Erika 151
Riefenstahl, Leni 1–2, 55, 62, 65–7, 79–86
Rilke, Rainer Maria 184
Ritzel, Fred 92
Robinson, David 24
Roehrig, Walter 24
Rohrbach, Günter 198–9
Rommel, Manfred 192–3
Roos, Hans-Dieter 129
Rossellini, Roberto 160
Rotha, Paul 54–5
Rousseau, Jean-Jacques 183
Rupé, Katja 191
Ruttmann, Walter 44, 51–6, 223

S
Sailer, Toni 105
Salomon, Erich 57
Sanders-Brahms, Helma 93
Santner, Eric L. 115
Schadt, Thomas 58
Scheel, Walter 192
Scheib, Hans 82
Schelsky, Helmut 7
Schifferle, Hans 222
Schleyer, Hanns-Martin 187–93
Schlöndorff, Volker 160, 187, 199, 225
Schlüpmann, Heide 93
Schmidt, Helmut 187, 193
Schneeberger, Hans 64
Schneider, Romy 3
Schönekas, Klaus 92
Schreber, Moritz 184
Schröder, Gerhard 130
Schubert, Franz 189
Schubert, Peter 188, 193

Schulz, Franz 76
Schweiger, Til 3, 7
Schygulla, Hanna 243
Seeler, Uwe 241
Sehr, Peter 184
Seidel, Hans-Dieter 150, 222
Sellmer, Erna 110
Sheeler, Charles 54
Siegel, Don 198
Silber, Rolf 211
Sinkel, Bernhard 188
Sirk, Douglas 93
stars 3, 5, 10, 30, 80, 84, 90, 104, 119, 139, 144, 150, 160, 198
Staudte, Wolfgang 109–17
Steel, Anthony 143
Steinbach, Peter 188
Steinbeck, Dietrich 103
Stemmle, Robert A. 184
Strand, Paul 52, 54
Straub, Laurens 130
Sturges, John 198
subsidies 6–7, 160
Syberberg, Hans Jürgen 115

T
Tchaikovsky, Pyotr Ilyich 189, 193
Theweleit, Klaus 194
Thiele, Jens 69, 74–6, 92
Timm, Peter 111, 228
Trantow, Cordula 132
Truffaut, François 160, 165, 185
Turek, Toni 239, 241
Twardowski, Heinrich von 20
Tykwer, Tom 217–18, 223–4, 240

U
Udet, Ernst 65
Ulbricht, Walter 149
Usai, Cherchi 19

V
Vajda, Fanckand Ladislaus 63
Veidt, Conrad 20
Ver, Moi 58
Vertov, Dziga 58
Vogel, Jürgen 7

W
Waalkes, Otto 207

Wackernagel, Christoph 188
Wackernagel, Katharina 238
Wakefield, Charles 143
Walser, Franziska 191
Warth, Angela 10
Wassermann, Jakob 184
Wedel, Michael 238
Weimar cinema 1, 23, 70–1, 74
Weimar Republic 54, 74
Weindler, Helge 209
Welskopf-Henrich, Liselotte 146
Wenders, Wim 140, 160, 223, 225
Wenzel, Heidemarie 169
Wepper, Fritz 130, 132

Werner, Ilse 104
Wernicke, Rolf 81
West Germany (Federal Republic
    of Germany) 3, 6, 115–16,
    122, 146–7, 149, 162, 192–3,
    197, 230
Whalen, Tom 219, 221
Wicki, Bernhard 129–36
Wiene, Robert 19–26
Wilder, Billy 76, 207, 231
Willinger, Laszlo 58
Wilson, Robert 38
Windt, Herbert 81
Winkler, Angela 191

Wolf, Christa 149
Wolf, Konrad 150–5
Wolff, Paul 57
Wortmann, Sönke 211, 237–43
Wyborny, Klaus 178

Z
Zehetbauer, Rolf 198
Zielke, Willy 82
Ziemann, Sonja 119–20
Zimmermann, Herbert 242, 244
Zinneman, Fred 141